Studies in English and American Literature, Linguistics, and Culture:
Literary Criticism in Perspective

Studies in English and American Literature, Linguistics, and Culture

Edited by
Benjamin Franklin V
(*South Carolina*)

Editorial Board

Literary Criticism in Perspective

James Hardin (*South Carolina*), General Editor

Eitel Timm (*British Columbia*), German Literature

Benjamin Franklin V (*South Carolina*), American and English Literature

Reingard M. Nischik (*Mainz*), Comparative Literature

* * *

About *Literary Criticism in Perspective*

Books in the series *Literary Criticism in Perspective*, a subseries of the series *Studies in German Literature, Linguistics, and Culture*, and *Studies in English and American Literature, Linguistics, and Culture*, trace literary scholarship and criticism on major and neglected writers alike, or on a single major work, a group of writers, a literary school or movement. In so doing the authors — authorities on the topic in question who are also well-versed in the principles and history of literary criticism — address a readership consisting of scholars, students of literature at the graduate and undergraduate level, and the general reader. One of the primary purposes of the series is to illuminate the nature of literary criticism itself, to gauge the influence of social and historic currents on aesthetic judgments once thought objective and normative.

Jeffrey A. Hammond

Edward Taylor:
Fifty Years of Scholarship and Criticism

CAMDEN HOUSE

Copyright © 1993 by
CAMDEN HOUSE, INC.

Published by Camden House, Inc.
Drawer 2025
Columbia, SC 29202 USA

Printed on acid-free paper.
Binding materials are chosen for strength and
durability.

All Rights Reserved
Printed in the United States of America
First Edition

ISBN:1-879751-76-3

Library of Congress Cataloging-in-Publication Data

Hammond, Jeffrey.
 Edward Taylor : fifty years of scholarship and criticism / Jeffrey A. Hammond.
 p. cm. -- (Studies in English and American literature, linguistics, and culture)
 Includes bibliographical references and index.
 ISBN 1-879751-76-3
 1. Taylor, Edward, 1642-1729--Criticism and interpretation--History--20th century. 2. Christian poetry, American--History and criticism--Theory, etc. I. Title. II. Series.
PS850.T2Z69 1993
811'.1--dc20   93-2228
                                                                    CIP

Acknowledgments

I INCURRED MANY debts while preparing this book. James Hardin and Benjamin Franklin V, editors of the "Literary Criticism in Perspective" Series, were unfailingly patient as I struggled against deadlines. Thomas M. Davis, who encouraged me to take on this project, provided valuable guidance and support. Raymond A. Craig generously offered his computer expertise in matters of layout and page design. I especially wish to thank Andrea Hammer of St. Mary's College of Maryland and Norma Tilden of Georgetown University; I have learned much from their perspectives on history, discourse, and gender, and although both reviewed portions of the manuscript and offered valuable criticisms, the flaws in this book most likely reflect the fact that I did not always follow their advice. Finally, my sense of the bibliographical essay as a genre has been shaped chiefly by William J. Scheick's insightful and entertaining reviews in *American Literary Scholarship*. Given my indebtedness to these models and my gratitude for his support and encouragement over the years, it is a pleasure to dedicate this book to him.

For Bill

Contents

Preface
ix

1: Discovery and Reaction — Before 1960
1

2: First Fruits — The 1960s
22

3: Maturation — The 1970s
55

4: Consolidation — The 1980s
94

5: Prospects — Since 1990
124

Bibliography
143

Index
163

Preface

KARL KELLER ONCE wryly noted what he called "The Problem of Edward Taylor: the criticism often looks better than the poet does" (1985:187). Like most good jokes, Keller's contained a measure of truth. Although Taylor has certainly proven a good enough poet to keep several generations of scholars busy, he has been particularly well served by those who have studied him. The rapid buildup of sophisticated critical commentary stemmed in part from his sudden arrival on the literary scene in the late 1930s. Edward Taylor's first readers were literary scholars who were immediately attracted not only by the quality of his verse, especially by critical standards prevalent at the time of his rediscovery, but by his obvious importance for American literary history. Second, Taylor benefited from the misperception, gradually corrected by what he taught us, that few other early American writers were worthy of serious literary analysis. For a while, enthusiasm for Taylor seemed to reinforce this belief: once the juggernaut got started it seemed that nearly every early Americanist was a Taylorian. Third, Taylor has always been fortunate in his editors, who presented his texts fully dressed — scrupulously edited, meticulously annotated, and meaningfully framed by introductory essays of permanent value. Taylor's editors — Thomas H. Johnson (1939), Donald E. Stanford (1960, 1962), Norman S. Grabo (1962, 1964), Francis Murphy (1962), Thomas M. and Virginia L. Davis (1981, 1983), and Charles W. Mignon (1989) — have made it easy to jump into the scholarly conversation. Finally, that conversation has always been easy to access in excellent secondary bibliographies by Constance J. Gefvert (1971), William J. Scheick and JoElla Doggett (1977), Catherine Rainwater and William J. Scheick (1980), and Norman S. Grabo and Jana Wainright (1984).

Since the last of these reviews of the criticism, however, the sheer quantity of work has become so extensive that it is once again difficult for beginning students to get their bearings. Moreover, the growing impact of theory on literary study has made possible a new perspective on the history of Taylor scholarship. Accordingly, this book has two primary goals. The first is to provide a comprehensive and reliable description of Taylor scholarship and criticism from its beginnings to the present. The second is to contextualize this work by placing it into broader frameworks of literary theory and critical practice that have shaped its direction. Scholarship, too, is a "story" that reflects the time and place of its telling. Anyone who explores *this* story will soon discover many Edward Taylors, some barely identifiable with others. In weaving these disparate strands into a single narrative, I have tried to describe the work as objectively as possible, although I realize that to describe is always to interpret. If any colleagues feel that their work has been insufficiently treated here, the usual reason has simply been the limitation of space. On matters of judgment, however, I can only plead that a bibliographer, like any writer, inevitably follows convictions that will seem mere blinders to someone else.

This review, chronological by decade and thematic within each decade, includes items I was able to see through late 1992. Unpublished dissertations, theses, and talks are excluded, as are book reviews except a few that have historical importance. Foreign scholarship is included, though more selectively than work in English. All items discussed in the text are keyed by year of publication and by page number, if quoted, to listings in the bibliography. The index will help the reader locate types of studies, discussions of specific Taylor texts, and the work of individual scholars. Throughout the text Taylor's *Preparatory Meditations* are identified by Series and poem number (Meditation 2.25 thus refers to Meditation 25 of the Second Series). In keeping with my emphasis on the historical development of Taylor studies, I have described the scholarship in the past tense. By so doing, I am in no way suggesting that studies from the past are somehow irrelevant for the present. On the contrary, this narrative has grown out of a belief that knowing how Taylor studies developed is indispensable not only for understanding the current state of the scholarship but for taking that scholarship into the future. This book describes a scholarly conversation that is still going on: I offer it as an invitation for readers not just to listen but to join in.

1: Discovery and Reaction — Before 1960

"IT APPEARS THAT the poems are of a nature unlike anything yet encountered in colonial American verse, and they warrant the belief that in Edward Taylor, Puritan America fostered unawares a poet of real, not merely historic, importance; one whose fertility in image-making, tenderness, rapture, and delicacy, as well as intense devotion, ally the staunch Puritan with the 'sacred poets' of the early seventeenth century" (1937:291). With these words, published in the summer of 1937, Thomas H. Johnson introduced the literary world to Edward Taylor, the obscure Puritan parson who revolutionized early American literary history.

In his own day Taylor was best known not as a poet but as the conservative pastor of Westfield in the Connecticut Valley, a rigid supporter of the New England way and an ally of the Mathers in their struggle against Solomon Stoddard's relaxed requirements for participation in the Lord's Supper. Michael Wigglesworth, some ten years Taylor's senior, was the most popular poet of the time; Taylor's first wife apparently memorized at least portions of his best-selling epic of the Judgment, *The Day of Doom*. Anne Bradstreet, who was first published in London soon after Taylor's birth in Leicestershire and whose posthumous *Several Poems* was in his library, was also famous as New England's "Tenth Muse." Roger Wolcott, whose classically-tinged poems were published when Taylor wrote the last of his *Preparatory Meditations*, was New England's most prominent poet at Taylor's death in 1729. As far as we know, the only portions of Taylor's verse published during his lifetime were two stanzas from one of his occasional poems, appended to a Cotton Mather sermon, and an elegy that appeared in a pamphlet commemorating David Dewey, deacon at Westfield. Still, Taylor probably enjoyed some reputation as a poet: such audience-centered poems as *Gods Determinations* and his funeral elegies suggest that he "published" periodically throughout his life, as did many other poets, by circulating his work in manuscript.

Although Taylor's poetic obscurity increased as years went by, it was never total. Just before the Civil War, Judge Henry Wyllys Taylor cited his great-grandfather's "poetical effusions through a period of about sixty-seven years, some of which may justly claim considerable merit." Thus came the first criticism of a poet who "appears to have had an abiding passion for writing poetry during his whole life" even though he lacked "a poetic genius of a very high order" (1857:180). Despite this passion, Taylor apparently never sought fame. Judge Taylor recalled a family tradition that the poet forbade his heirs from publishing "any of his writings." As we will see, this claim, repeated in John L. Sibley's *Biographical Sketches* of Harvard graduates (1881), would play a crucial role in early assessments of the poetry. A few scraps of Taylor's writings surfaced during the nineteenth century, most notably his diary in the 1880 *Proceedings* of the Massachusetts Historical Society; in addition, a brief biography by descendant John Taylor Terry appeared in 1892. In the 1920s John Hoyt Lockwood reprinted some of Taylor's prose (1922), while Thomas Goddard Wright noted that Taylor "filled a notebook with verse, none of which has ever been published, as the writer forbade publication" (1920:162). When Johnson came upon the description of Taylor's verse in Sibley and examined the "Poetical Works" quarto at Yale, he immediately recognized that the poems were unlike any previously known specimens of Puritan verse (1939b).

The full impact of Johnson's discovery can be appreciated only in light of how Puritan poetry was then viewed. Six decades earlier Moses Coit Tyler had concluded that a few of Bradstreet's lyrics were the only genuine poems produced in colonial New England, chiefly because of an "unappeasable" Puritan "feud between religion and art" (1878:228). Early in this century William B. Cairns similarly lamented Bradstreet's "tendency to sacrifice everything to rather profitless moralizing" (1910:146), while F. O. Matthiessen characterized Wigglesworth as "a hard intellect" whose poetic "fire" was "walled in" by theology (1928:500). Kenneth B. Murdock conceded in the 1920s that the "breath of that rare spirit which indefinably marks poetry for most of us is all too sadly lacking" (1927:lxiii). Two decades later Murdock reaffirmed that Puritanism was "unfriendly" to successful poetry (1949:140). Even Johnson, then collaborating with Perry Miller on the first anthology to suggest the richness and depth of Puritan writing, maintained that Puritan poets "remained curiously indifferent to the quintessential breath and finer spirit of the poetic idiom" (1938:547, 552). The key phrases here — "fire," "rare spirit," "quintessential breath" — were intended to describe literary qualities that Puritanism had supposedly suppressed. But the feud between religion and art was really a conflict between Puritan religion and the postromantic art that critics were seeking. Stanley Fish has summarized these modernist aesthetic expectations by citing "the assumption that what distinguishes literary from ordinary language is its invulnerability to paraphrase; the assumption that a poem should not mean, but be; the assumption that the more complex a work is, the more propositions it holds in tension and equilibrium, the better it is" (1980:354). Little wonder that critics found Puritan verse so disappointing. Harold S. Jantz, writing shortly after Taylor was rediscovered, complained of such anachronistic approaches to the Puritan poem, noting a "misapplication of eighteenth-century smoothness and nineteenth-century romantic lyricism to seventeenth-century Baroque verse which had no interest in being either smooth or romantic" (1944:6-7).

Not only was Taylor unlike other Puritan poets, but he was unlike them in ways that had special appeal in the 1930s and 1940s, when critics were still caught up in the revival of seventeenth-century English devotional poets like John Donne, George Herbert, and Richard Crashaw. A mere sixteen years before Taylor's rediscovery, T. S. Eliot had spearheaded this renewed interest in the metaphysicals, whose texts provided important support for the development of the New Criticism in England and America. Eliot's classic essay on the metaphysical poets, which praised their juxtaposition of spiritual intensity and concrete imagery, proposed their artful blend of deep matter and sensory manner as a universal criterion for true poetry — a criterion that the newfound poet seemed to satisfy. As Matthiessen confirmed a little over a decade after Johnson's announcement, Taylor's poetry "gives a deeper American taproot" to the metaphysical revival "in our own day" (1950:xv). Matthiessen's comment also suggests a second reason for Taylor's impact: the poet arrived on the scene when American literature was becoming a viable object of literary study. In this light it is important to remember that the journal *American Literature* was only eight years old when the first specimens of his verse appeared. As the title of Matthiessen's classic 1941 *American Renaissance* revealed, however, seventeenth- and eighteenth-century American writing had not yet benefited from this revival despite pioneering work by Wright, Murdock, Vernon Louis Parrington, and Samuel Eliot Morison. Miller, whose studies were beginning to make the field intellectually respectable, had been advised at the start of his career to seek a more promising field in which to apply his talents. A sensational reception was thus virtually assured for this "American Traherne," as Richard Altick later called him, whose sudden appearance recalled Traherne's publication with similar fanfare in 1903 (1950). Initially perceived as a newfound link between English metaphysical verse and American romantic symbolism, both of which were enjoying great popularity among critics, Taylor could scarcely have come along at a better time.

In the initial publication of this American "sacred" poet, Johnson mostly let the poems themselves demonstrate Taylor's importance (1937). Beginning with "Huswifery," Taylor's most Donne-like and perhaps least representative meditative poem, Johnson reprinted "Upon Wedlock, & Death of Children," the piece later known as "When Let by Rain," nine lyrics, in whole or part, from *Gods Determinations*, and nine "Sacramental Meditations," named after a title in the "Poetical Works" manuscript later determined to have been supplied by Taylor's grandson, Yale president Ezra Stiles. Johnson also printed the "Prologue," which he assigned to *Gods Determinations* rather than to the Meditations. Johnson's tastes — and those of his era — were clearly reflected in these selections. Praising *Gods Determinations* for its "metaphoric brilliance and unity of design," Johnson cited "Taylor's artistry in stating orthodox covenant theology in terms of sensuous imagery" (301), qualities fully consistent with metaphysical poetry and the developing New Critical agenda. As a poet who appeared "to love poetry for its own sake" (322), Taylor seemed almost to foreshadow Oscar Wilde's *ars gratia artis*. For Johnson, the *Preparatory Meditations*, which demonstrated Taylor's metaphysical sensibility even more clearly, embodied a "poetic imagination" and "inventive fancy" close to George Herbert's (317). Johnson also found echoes of Herbert's metrical sophistication in *Gods Determinations*, a claim that would diminish when critical emphasis later shifted to the prosodically monotonous Meditations. Taylor's rhetoric intensified the dramatic situation of the verse, and his "seraphic exaltation" seemed to approach that of Catholic convert Richard Crashaw, whose verse, Johnson conceded, Taylor probably did not read (318). Other parallels included Sir John Davies's philosophical poem *Nosce Teipsum* (London: 1599) and Francis Quarles's *Emblemes* (London: 1635), which may have supplied the model for the Meditations. But while Taylor's similarities to these poets justified his importance, such comparisons forced Johnson to admit that his verse was marked with "occasional bad rimes or strained figures" suggestive of "a piety that perhaps lacked wings" (317). In his wide-ranging diction, for instance, Taylor sometimes sacrificed literary polish for spiritual intensity — a view that later critics would develop into an image of the poet as an independent American primitive (320). Johnson conceded, however, that the details of Taylor's biography did not seem to square with his poetic gifts. Indeed, the mundanity of his life and the report that he suppressed his work suggested a poet with something to hide, even though Johnson insisted that the injunction merely reflected strong "modesty" and a Calvinist "sense of human unworthiness" (321). While Johnson took pains to assert Taylor's orthodoxy, he opened the door to other possibilities. Citing the rarity of a "sacramental *cultus*" among Puritans, Johnson found it "little short of extraordinary" that this New England pastor could write like Donne and the "Anglo-Catholic conceitists" (322).

Two years later, in the first selected edition of the poetry, Johnson again presented a poet at artistic odds with his contemporaries even as he walked in perfect social step with them (1939a). Whatever the poetry suggested, Taylor was an orthodox Puritan minister who forged lifelong friendships with such prominent New Englanders as Increase Mather, mintmaster John Hull, Harvard president Charles Chauncy, and Judge Samuel Sewall. Clearly, Taylor was not a man who would willingly offend the sensibilities of his contemporaries through his writing. As in his initial article, Johnson highlighted those features that set the poetry apart from other New England Puritan verse, particularly the inventive language and eclectic diction that would remain central to subsequent appreciations. Commenting less fully than before on Taylor's artistic flaws, Johnson now argued that Taylor's development of unifying figures helped him avoid the random and contradictory structures that marred lesser religious poets. Invoking the imperfect parallels to metaphysical verse, especially Herbert's, Johnson argued that Taylor "struck out for himself" (17) with an artistic independence intensified by his isolation in provincial Westfield. This tension between tradition and innovation — or between skill and ineptitude, depending on the critic's point of view — would mark Taylor studies from this time forward. So would the related issue of Taylor's theological orientation. Johnson now more emphatically declared in favor of his orthodoxy, insisting that his "spiritual fervor" required no recourse to Anglican or Catholic devotional modes (17). Nor did his intense focus on the Lord's Supper. On the contrary, Taylor showed that "Puritan doctrine can at times take on a radiant sweetness" (19). Supporting this reading by citing a source that would not be developed for another thirty years, biblical typology, Johnson provided a theological glossary intended to strengthen the connections between the verse and covenant theology, although the list, as Constance Gefvert later observed (1971:xxviii), may not have sufficiently distinguished Taylor's beliefs from Christian beliefs generally. Further evidence of Taylor's orthodox status came from his library inventory, a collection that any Puritan pastor and physician could be expected to own.

Although Miller had recently rehabilitated the "New England mind," the time was not right for the radical rethinking of the New England heart implicit in Johnson's comments. As Johnson well knew, many "unwary" readers would question Taylor's orthodoxy based on the emotional pitch and sensuality of the verse (24). In addition, the "metaphysical" autonomy of the poems would soon encourage scholars to isolate the poet from his Puritan milieu as a means of accounting for his artistry and establishing his importance for subsequent American literature. Surely, many readers would assume, Taylor suppressed the verse because he knew how shocking it would be to his fellow New Englanders. But Taylor *had* been published, as Johnson soon discovered when he found that Cotton Mather had reprinted stanzas five and seven from "Upon Wedlock, & Death of Children" and excerpts from a Taylor letter at the end of a sermon on grief entitled *Right Thoughts in Sad Hours* (London: 1689) (1941). While Mather's excerpting was hardly evidence of a negative contemporary response to Taylor's work, Johnson did not yet have this small but important clue when he introduced the *Poetical Works*. Moreover, he unintentionally aided the opposition by describing Taylor's more conventional poems as verse exercises "not stamped with the image of his personality" (1939a:18). The lure of a secret poet proved irresistible, reinforced as it was by Taylor's seeming isolation from his literary culture. It was indeed "curious," Johnson noted, that his library contained only one volume of English verse, by Anne Bradstreet (202), and even her influence seemed minimal. It was a private, idiosyncratic poet that Johnson presented to the world, and it was as this kind of poet that Taylor would be approached nearly exclusively for the next half century.

Further refutation of an anomalous Taylor might have come from Johnson's decision to present *Gods Determinations* — later recognized as a decidedly public poem — in first position and in its entirety, followed by five occasional poems, seventeen Meditations from the First Series and fourteen from the much longer Second Series. As Johnson's commentary suggested, his esteem for *Gods Determinations* reflected the New Critical validation of poetic closure and psychological struggle that Eliot had praised in the metaphysicals. Johnson also implicitly fostered formalist approaches to Taylor in his heavy emphasis on the earlier Meditations, which, like the occasional poems, echoed Herbert and Donne more closely than did the later Meditations, which were less volatile in tone and more explicitly biblical in content. Five years later Johnson reiterated his view that the poems written after 1700 were "metrical exercises, repetitious in thought, image, and even in phrasing" (1944:681). Still, his complete listing of the Meditations, with dates of composition and scriptural headnotes, enabled readers to sense the overall thrust of both Series and thus be less dependent, at least conceptually, on his selections.

Although Donald Stanford would find significant textual errors in the *Poetical Works* while preparing his 1960 edition, Johnson's achievement was second only to his painstaking editing of that other secretive New Englander, Emily Dickinson. He had ushered a major figure into the canon and started a nearly complete rewriting of early American literary history. As he rightly observed a quarter of a century later, the modern "reassessment of Puritanism, especially in those aspects which reveal the Puritan's feeling for beauty in his hungry search for Heaven, has been given impetus by the appearance of Taylor's poetry" (1966:8). Johnson soon supplemented his edition with a selection of Taylor's topical verses (1942), for which he made few critical claims except that they shed light on the poet's life and confirmed his skill with the acrostic form. The following year he published more "gleanings": "Upon a Wasp Child with Cold," "Upon the Sweeping Flood," a second version of "Huswifery," and eight additional Meditations (1943). Stating that the remaining unpublished poems would do little to "advance either the cause of letters or Taylor's reputation as a craftsman or seer" (280), Johnson believed that the case for the poet had been adequately made. Except for a sketch written for the first supplement to the *Dictionary of American Biography* (1944), his involvement with Taylor was over.

Once on the literary scene, Taylor immediately provoked a battle that pitted tradition, polish, and England against innovation, roughness, and America. Placed against his New England contemporaries, he seemed like a poetic brother to Parrington's Roger Williams, another individualist who fled the strictures of Puritanism. Foster Damon, for example, favorably contrasted Taylor's more "humane" sensibility with Wigglesworth's gloom, praising him as a poet who transcended the aesthetic constraints of Puritan culture even as he remained a full participant in that culture (1939:779). Speculating that Taylor recognized his artistic shortcomings in an era that was beginning to favor "polish and Pope" (780), Damon saw Taylor as a poet too brave — or too stubborn — to follow such English fashions. It is not difficult to find a strain of literary nationalism in Damon's conclusion that the "nation should be glad that Edward Taylor loved his rhymes too well to destroy them." This pioneer American poet, however, lost some of his luster when judged by the established English canon. Howard Blake complained that "too much belated homage" was being given to a poet who was, after all, "no American Donne" (1940:167). In Blake's view, a close formalist reading merely revealed "all the provincial inadequacies" of colonial American writing, especially a "frontier exaggeration" mercifully absent from Donne and Herbert. These two reviews illustrate Taylor's role in a larger critical struggle for American literary independence. Although his metaphysical affinities made him interesting to Anglo-centered scholars, he inevitably came up short whenever such affinities were pursued in detail. Damon, however, anticipated a solution by which artistic flaws could be turned into nationalistic virtues: Taylor could be defended precisely because he did *not* write as smoothly as those Englishmen of his parents' generation. That is, he could be defended as an independent American poet. Hadn't Henry Wyllys Taylor confirmed that his great-grandfather was "an ardent republican in principle" with a healthy "aversion to the aristocracy of England, alike in Church and State" (1857: 177)?

While these issues were simmering, Taylor quickly became a standard entry in anthologies and reference works. Even before the *Poetical Works* appeared, Johnson had rushed him into the massive collection of Puritan writing that he and Miller were then preparing, though he figured only briefly in Johnson's discussion of Puritan verse as "one authentic indication that the indigenous Puritan muse, even when tied down to the fashions of an earlier style, soared with metaphoric brilliance" (1938:552). But the first real steps in Taylor's popularizing came with his inclusion in William Rose Benét and Norman Holmes Pearson's *Oxford Anthology of American Literature* (1938) and his description in James D. Hart's *Oxford Companion to American Literature* as a metaphysical poet who requested the suppression of his verse (1941:748). Norman Foerster's *American Poetry and Prose* similarly placed him, though "no imitator," in the school of Donne and the Anglo-Catholic poets (1947). Ironically, Taylor's rapid acceptance into the anthologies predated a full scholarly case for his inclusion. Only four substantial discussions had appeared by 1948, when Oscar Williams devoted seven pages to Taylor in *A Little Treasury of American Poetry* (1948). The following year Robert Spiller and Harold Blodgett included five poems from *Gods Determinations*, five Meditations, and five occasional poems in their anthology of American writing before 1830 (1949). And the year after that Matthiessen's *Oxford Book of*

American Verse devoted nearly twenty pages to Taylor, almost twice as many as to Bradstreet (1950). In 1952 Taylor officially entered the canon when he was assigned space in *Major American Writers*, edited by Howard Mumford Jones and others, as the last great writer "to be discovered, largely because he forbade his heirs to publish his work" (1952:20). Four years later Miller's *The American Puritans: Their Prose and Poetry* included selections from this poet who wrote in secret, yielding "to the temptation to create forms of his own" (1956:309). In the early 1960s canonical status was reconferred by Austin Warren in Miller's *Major Writers of American Literature*, where Taylor joined the select company of Bradford, Edwards, and Franklin as the sole representatives of colonial America (1962). The following year Taylor's popularity came full circle, when Miller and Johnson reissued their 1938 anthology as a two-volume paperback. The thin selections in the original edition so clearly needed augmenting that the Taylor section required fourteen supplementary pages, numbered 656a through 656n so that the rest of the book would not have to be reset (1963). Taylor came full circle in another sense as well, when he was reunited with the writers of his home culture by Alexander Witherspoon and Frank Warnke in the second edition of their anthology of seventeenth-century English literature (1963).

Taylor soon began to make his way into general and thematic studies. Miller mentioned him in the first volume of *The New England Mind* as someone who "gave ingenious poetic expression" to Ramist and Puritan rhetoric and an advocate of a "plain style, even in poetry" (1939:326, 361). In Miller's second volume Taylor emerged as a defender of New England's mission in "secretive lyrics," expressing his "anxiety in a verse technique that Puritans considered suitable only to the sensualities of the Church of England" (1953:31, 155). Morison, bringing Taylor into the revision of his 1936 *Puritan Pronaos*, insisted that there was "nothing unusual" in Taylor's devotional fervor even though its expression was decidedly "uncommon" (1956:240). Although Morison mistakenly thought that Taylor had come to New England with his father, he astutely asked — as few did — why the poet failed to destroy these supposedly subversive poems (236). The same year, in a study of musical influences on American poetry, Charmenz S. Lenhart defended the appropriateness of Taylor's musical imagery as evidence of his "tremendous physical responsiveness to spiritual experience" (1956:51). Two years later Walter J. Ong took issue with Miller by arguing from the dramatic quality of the verse that Taylor managed to escape the more restrictive effects of Ramist logic and Puritanism generally (1958:287).

Predictably, Taylor had the greatest impact on early American literary history. In a 1943 survey of early New England poetry, reprinted the following year as a monograph, Harold S. Jantz was the first to incorporate Taylor into a substantial discussion of American Puritan verse (1944). Jantz maintained that despite his links with the English poets, Taylor's relation to other poets of early New England provided the most important context for the verse. Jantz argued that distorted assessments would inevitably result if critics placed among the metaphysicals this poet who wrote in a "typically late Baroque manner: lavishly but purposefully and consequently, in an ordered, well-disposed intricacy" (82). Kenneth B. Murdock had greater difficulty fitting the new poet into New England literary culture. In a series of lectures delivered for the Lowell Institute in 1944 and published five years later as *Literature and Theology in Colonial New England*, Murdock's description of Puritan literary attitudes almost encompassed Taylor's poetry, even though he stressed the poet's artistic exceptionalism (1949). Finding precedent in the Puritan sermon for Taylor's affective style, Murdock argued that Puritans had few problems with such flourishes so long as they clarified or enhanced the doctrine at hand. English preacher Richard Baxter, for instance, defended pulpit appeals to the senses, and realistic imagery figured prominently in the so-called plain style. Still, Murdock argued that Taylor went well beyond his contemporaries in using language with "the most direct sensuous appeal" (167). Although Murdock considered Taylor to be an orthodox Puritan, he suggested that the poet suppressed his work because he knew that "his passionate expression, his delight in color and fragrance, and his sometimes erotically suggestive imagery would offend his graver colleagues" (167). In the influential *Literary History of the United States*, Murdock reiterated this somewhat ambiguous judgment (1948). Although Taylor's verse offered an especially vivid illustration of Puritan poetic practice, his "emotions may have been too strong for the tightest bonds of Puritan theory" (67). By 1951 Murdock saw Taylor not as a breaker of Puritan artistic rules but as a gifted poet who "showed what admirable use a genuine artist could make of the Puritan literary code" (1951:57).

While Murdock called Taylor "the greatest poet of New England before the nineteenth century" (1948:65), Jantz cautioned against prematurely accepting his "superiority" over his contemporaries: too much depended on the findings of future scholarship (1944:85). Such caution became outright reaction in

Stanley T. Williams, who issued one of the few discouraging words of the era by objecting to what he saw as an Edward Taylor craze (1951). Williams insisted that despite all the excitement about Taylor, "No major poet" and "no single great poem appeared in Puritan New England" because of "the bleakness of the poetic climate" (13). Conceding Taylor's superiority to other American Puritan poets, "at least for the moment" (32), Williams argued that the poetry was marred by repetition and extravagant diction despite its sensuous and metaphoric quality. Unusually conscious of the vagaries of critical reputation, Williams remarked that Taylor's popularity was due to traits "not altogether different from similar qualities in twentieth century poetry" (14). If Bradstreet's discovery had been similarly belated, he claimed, "she might have inspired a similar cult" (32). Another reaction came from Sidney E. Lind, who agreed that if Taylor had been published during his lifetime he "would finally have come to a peaceful rest" in Tyler's *History of American Literature* (1948:518). Lind saw in the Taylor ballyhoo a general failure to admit the extent to which Puritanism harmed the poetry. Casting a wet blanket on the whole enterprise, Lind insisted that Taylor was "doomed" as a Puritan and a provincial to poetic mediocrity (519).

If a Taylor cult existed, it was because he seemed so mysteriously un-Puritan. And when critics tried to define what, in literary terms, he actually *was*, their attempts to classify him became entangled in debates over quality of his work. That Taylor's defenders tended to see him as a metaphysical was no surprise in an era that valued English devotional poetry so highly. Critics whose praise was more reserved tended to classify his work as baroque, then largely regarded as an aesthetic based on looser structures and subject to lapses in taste. Those who were least impressed, like Lind and Williams, saw Taylor as simply another Puritan poet hampered by the artistic restrictions described by Tyler, Miller, and the earlier Murdock. At the heart of the matter lay an issue that would not be explicitly addressed for another thirty years, when literary theory began to reshape the practice of literary history: the inevitable interpenetration of history and aesthetics, of attempted objectivity and unavoidable taste. This theme first played itself out in the debate over which seventeenth-century sacred poets were Taylor's closest models. On one side was Austin Warren, who had advised Johnson during the editing of the *Poetical Works*. Fresh from a book on Crashaw, Warren argued that Taylor manifested a baroque sensibility rather than a truly metaphysical one. Opposing Warren was Wallace Cable Brown, who sided with Johnson by aligning

Taylor with the metaphysicals. "Metaphysical," as Warren pointed out, had become a vague term of "eulogy" (1941:355). In his view, a better characterization for pre-neoclassic verse that stressed "false wit" was "baroque," a "Christian and supernaturalist and incarnational" mode that grew out of the Counter-Reformation (356). Although the great poets linked the baroque sensibility either to cosmology, like Du Bartas, or to psychology, like Donne, Taylor's "minor ingenuities" and homely conceits fell short of either mode (360). Even though he wrote with a "primitive vigor" (366), images like Sharon's Rose in "The Reflexion" both encouraged and frustrated visualization in a manner that revealed his unschooled tastes. Taylor, Warren concluded, was "sometimes a neat little artisan but more often an unsteady enthusiast, a naive original" and "intermittently inspired Primitive" (370) not unlike another "uneven village poet," Emily Dickinson (371). In his rebuttal Brown insisted that Taylor overcame baroque limitations to become "a full-fledged, if minor metaphysical poet" (1944:186). Defining metaphysical wit in terms of Samuel Johnson's *discordia concors* and Eliot's "sensuous apprehension of thought," Brown declared that Taylor was a genuine metaphysical in his ability to cast abstract ideas into colloquial images and thus to merge thought and feeling into a "tight logical structure" (193). For Brown, the presence of unifying structures in the verse justified Taylor's stature not just relative to his contemporaries but as "the best American poet before Freneau and the first (and perhaps only) American Metaphysical" (197).

Each side soon gained adherents. Among the early defenders of a metaphysical Taylor was William B. Goodman, who argued that the courtship letter and pictorial poem that Taylor sent to his first wife Elizabeth Fitch matched the metaphysical mode of the Meditations (1954). The baroque side was taken up, as we have seen, by Jantz, who argued that Taylor wrote in a "typically late Baroque manner" (1944:82). In the mid-1950s Biancamaria Tedeschini Lalli agreed, arguing that Taylor's spiritual goals virtually forced him into verbal excesses normally associated with the baroque as the only means by which he could express his love for God (1956). But Jantz did not accept the standard equation of the baroque with artistic excess. As he observed three decades later, a critical bias against the baroque that prevailed when Taylor rose to prominence reinforced the widespread assumption that he somehow lagged behind English writers (1985:270). Gradually, however, this bias faded, and both terms became less judgmental. For Goodman, Taylor's metaphysical affinities were less a matter of literary classification than of thought patterns natural to a poet for whom the production of polished literature was not the primary issue. Lalli was similarly less concerned with the baroque as a formal rubric than as a verbal embodiment of spiritual intensity. This transformation of terminology would be complete by 1970, when Walter Reinsdorf argued that the essentially metaphysical Taylor sometimes employed a baroque style in which the image "transforms, takes fire, and melts under the pressure of an extreme intensity of religious feeling" (1970:36). In retrospect it seems clear that whether Taylor was a metaphysical or baroque poet depended not only on critical predilections but on the affective level of the poem at hand. Still, the debate was by no means fruitless. While the baroque Taylor arose chiefly because the verse seemed not to hold up to exacting New Critical standards for explication, the emotional underpinnings of the baroque encouraged a shift from purely formal analysis to a focus on the religious and artistic processes informing the texts. Louis Martz and Norman Grabo would soon describe Taylor in contemplative terms that rendered traditional belletristic categories like metaphysical and baroque far less relevant than they had seemed to Taylor's earliest critics.

Meanwhile, other frameworks as broad as the baroque-metaphysical polarity was narrow were soon proposed as keys to Taylor's place in literary history. Perhaps his real roots lay deeper than seventeenth-century England, in the echoes of medieval folk traditions that continued to hold sway in the country hamlets of Leicestershire, where he grew up. Nathalia Wright invoked these traditions by arguing that *Gods Determinations* resembled a morality play in its frankly allegorical characters, rough prosody, homely language, and doctrinal themes (1946). Taylor had been born near Coventry, where a Corpus Christi procession was still being performed; moreover, poets like Spenser, the Fletchers, Quarles, Joshua Sylvester, Milton, and Marvell could have served as intermediate sources. For Wright, the characters of Mercy, Satan, and other such personified abstractions suggested that Taylor had "a mind more responsive to medieval than to Renaissance influence" (17). Wright's Taylor, who embodied Miller's characterization of the Puritans as the last of the medievals, dwelt in an Augustinian cosmos constructed from dogma and Scripture. While Wright suggested that Taylor's indebtedness to the moralities accounted for the absence of Renaissance classicism in his work, Willie T. Weathers came to the opposite conclusion (1946). Pointing out that Taylor's library contained six volumes of classical poetry, Weathers argued that classical echoes in the verse, especially in *Gods Determinations*, explained Taylor's deviations from the morality tradition. The debate between Justice and Mercy, for instance, recalled pastoral song contests in Theocritus; Homer was echoed in the martial attacks on Taylor's soul-hero; "Christs Reply" recalled Aphrodite's consoling of the young Eros; the raging Satan suggested the Nemean lion of the Hercules story. Concluding that the "main tenor" of *Gods Determinations* was "Hellenistic" (19), a characterization that she also briefly applied to a few occasional poems and Meditations, Weathers argued that Taylor suppressed his work because he feared that its classical content would offend his scripturally-bound contemporaries (26). Eight years later Weathers proposed a specific seventeenth-century source for Taylor's "non-Puritan exaltation": the Cambridge revival of Platonic interpretations of Christian doctrine (1954:2). The Cambridge Platonists, chiefly Henry More and Ralph Cudworth, had developed a more optimistic view of human reason than that espoused by strict Calvinism, along with a greater acceptance of erotic metaphor and symbolism — all traits that Weathers identified as central to Taylor's verse. In *Gods Determinations*, for example, Taylor combined Calvinism with Platonic "natural theology" as a means of identifying "Calvinistic Law with Platonic Love" (13). Weathers maintained that as a result of the Cambridge influence Taylor rejected Calvinist notions of election and predestination. Arguing that the poem treated "the salvation of *all* mankind" (13), she assumed that this "good New England Puritan" — despite his universalist beliefs — owed his artistic successes to an influence foreign to his faith (31).

It was quickly becoming obvious that this metaphysical-baroque-Hellenist writer of moralities could be all things to all people. As Lind complained, Taylor studies were becoming a "critical parlor-game" leading "only into a semantic maze" (1948:521). The many-faceted Taylor of the 1940s and the 1950s indeed suggests that critics were putting literary labels before the poems themselves. Clearly, a great deal of careful work was needed before such definitive explanations could be proposed, especially detailed investigations of Taylor's sources, both literary and theological. Although permanently valuable source work would not come until biblical and exegetical structures central to the Puritan imagination were better understood, modest contributions during the first two decades of Taylor scholarship began the necessary spadework. The search for the origins of specific images began in 1948, when G. Giovannini linked the "Artificial Angels" found in "The Glory of and Grace in the Church Set Out" from *Gods Determinations* with the formal gardens and topiary art of baroque Europe (1948). In the late 1950s Robert R.

Hodges traced the allusion in Meditation 2.56 to the "Artificiall man Aquinas slew" to the legend of Albertus Magnus, who built an automaton — either a talking head or a mechanical woman — that was destroyed by his pupil Aquinas because it interfered with his studies (1959). Specific work on Taylor's archaisms began when Sister M. Laurentia proposed that the "crickling" of Meditation 1.42 was a cricket, not a pork crackling as Johnson had suggested (1949). Critics also began to pursue source-informed explications of individual poems, usually following Brown in confirming a metaphysical *discordia concors* and a consequent unity of theme and structure. Anne Marie McNamara, for example, argued for such unity in Meditation 1.6 by connecting the lily of the valleys in the preceding poem's headnote with Taylor's image of the "Angell" coin (1958). But at this early stage in the scholarship, even small stones could make large waves. McNamara's reading prompted Norman S. Grabo to deny such a close connection between the biblical headnotes and the poems, arguing instead that Taylor based the Meditations on the doctrine preached in the accompanying sermon rather than on the Bible verse at hand (1960d).

In the early rush to validate Taylor's standing in terms of the English canon, contexts provided by the Bible, Puritan theology and rhetoric, and other Puritan poets remained largely undeveloped. Lind offered a sobering corrective to this by pointing out that Taylor's verse had been "snatched up" and "inflated unrecognizably" by critics who ignored the simple fact that he was a New England Puritan poet (1948:520). But like the critics he refuted, Lind was seduced by a predefined label — in his case, "Puritan." Arguing that the Puritan poem was designed to edify and thus had to be clearly written, Lind found plainness in Taylor where others found sensuality. What critics were praising as "homely imagery," for example, did not reflect an innovative escape from the dictates of Puritan art but merely fulfilled the poet's adherence to a thoroughly Puritan "principle of intelligibility" (525). For Lind, Taylor's apparent originality resulted from what a Puritan could not help doing: his imagery was "conditioned and shaped at the source of his imagination by the Puritan theories of rhetoric and psychology" (527). Although Lind conceded that the five occasional poems included in the *Poetical Works* hinted at what Taylor might have achieved if his "poetic genius" had "rested on a basis broader than the theological compulsions of his community," Taylor the poet only occasionally transcended Taylor the orthodox minister (528). Reprising Tyler's conflict between religion and art in the Puritan sensibility, Lind implicitly applied modern poetic standards not just to Taylor but to the poet's entire culture when he insisted that the "primacy of doctrine over poetic expression" is what "spells the difference between mediocrity and greatness" (527). Although Taylor tried to write acceptable Puritan poetry, he "did not, unfortunately for the modern reader, fail in his appointed task often enough" (530).

While some critics overpraised Taylor because he did not write like a Puritan, Lind devalued him because he did. Still, Lind was the first to answer Johnson's call to read Taylor within his Puritan milieu. Roy Harvey Pearce soon agreed that for all the baroque or metaphysical influences on the verse, what really mattered was "its matrix in Taylor's Puritan culture" (1950:31). Citing Ramist invention as a search for divine order in the world, Pearce described a Puritan "poetics of discovery" rather than sentiment, creativity, or personal expression (42). If Taylor failed to invoke human drama with a sensitivity equal to Herbert's, it was because he was more concerned with "God and God's order" than with the "human experience" of that order (31). For Pearce, Taylor was the antithesis of a confessional poet. "What is primary in the poems is not the poet's experience — the poet as man speaking to men — but rather the meaning and understanding — the discovery — which is the end of that experience" (33). *Gods Determinations* thus had little dramatic appeal for modern readers because Taylor's deeper interest lay not in personal experience for its own sake but in its revelation of the redemptive scheme. Justice and Mercy were flat characters because they existed only to clarify abstract arguments and not to invoke "any interpersonal dramatic quality" (36). Similarly, Taylor did not develop paradoxes as fully or consistently as Donne because of his overriding belief in the divine resolution of all such enigmas. Finally, Pearce argued that if Taylor seemed to pursue simplistic parallels between the mundane and the spiritual, it was because his Puritan faith made him repeatedly seek "an earthly counterpart — however poor and dim — of that which is ineffably holy" (32).

Although Pearce tried to assess Taylor on the poet's own terms, his implicit definition of good verse doomed even the best Puritan poem to failure. His confirmation that "reading Taylor's poetry, we read his Puritanism" (46) seemed to present the Puritan poem not as art but as theological compulsion. In this he ended up not far from Lind. Puritan culture, Pearce argued, was "inadequate for major poetry" because it "allowed for little play of the individual will — in the last analysis, for little real human drama" (43). Ultimately, Pearce's validation of the "individual will" colored his assessment of Taylor. For him, as for other readers less sensitive than he to historical context, good poetry demanded the more individualistic ethos of a later America that was not so "reactionary, orthodox, and static" (40) — an America of Whitman and Dickinson, for whom Taylor and his contemporaries would serve as primitive antecedents in *The Continuity of American Poetry*, which Pearce published eleven years later. Pearce's comment that "technique is little or nothing" for Taylor (45) was not a neutral observation but an expression of disappointed modernist aesthetic expectations. There even seemed to be a hint of Wallace Stevens's "poem of the mind in the act of finding / What will suffice" in Pearce's statement that for Taylor, "the end of the poem inhibits the act of composition, and ultimately the act of the poem itself" (43).

Despite this encroachment of post-romantic definitions of good verse, Pearce's stress on Puritan aesthetics played a pioneering role in the scholarship. Equally important, and for similar reasons, was Mindele Black's assertion that Taylor's spiritual intensity was almost — though not quite — fully Puritan (1956). Black argued that Taylor blended the intellective matter of Calvinist theology with a "baroque manner" consistent with Catholic devotional tradition (171). Uncomfortable with the sensuous images derived from this tradition, however, Puritans compensated with a "copious allegorization" (170) that produced an unconscious "aesthetic schizophrenia" embodied in Taylor's split between rigid doctrinal content and baroque verbal expression (180). The tension between Taylor's Calvinist orthodoxy and his evocative treatments of the Bridegroom and the Supper indicated two strains whose "incompatibility" was "itself inherent in the Puritan devotional tradition." This split, which accounted for Taylor's characteristic juxtaposition of homely with theological diction, explained how an orthodox preacher could write poems suggestive of high Anglican and Catholic devotional modes. Black nevertheless argued that the poet's similarity to Herbert was "established at some cost to Taylor's orthodoxy" (174). Citing sermon 15 from the *Christographia* manuscript as "typical of the Puritan's attraction to themes which he subsequently tries to explain away" (170), Black finally depicted Taylor less as a Puritan poet than as a harbinger of an "increasing humanization" in Anglo-American religious life and expression (181).

While Pearce saw Taylor as a Puritan whose beliefs partly diminished his poetry, Black saw him as a poet whose emotions partly compromised his

Puritanism. Herbert Blau pushed the latter approach to an extreme, thereby bringing the simmering question of Taylor's orthodoxy to a boil (1953). Although Blau, like Pearce and Black, focused on the artistic implications of Puritan theology, he ended up joining Weathers in depicting a decidedly un-Puritan Taylor. For Blau, it was a Calvinistic paradox in which the doctrine of predestination contradicted any possibility of repentance that prompted the compassionate poet to stray from Puritan orthodoxy. Taylor, he maintained, felt far more rapture at the Lord's Supper than his faith allowed; unlike Anglicans and Catholics, he had "no excuse" for his "intense feeling for the ritual as ritual" (338). Moreover, Taylor took the humanistic side in the question of free will versus determinism, especially in *Gods Determinations*, where his stress on repentance showed his refusal to accept man's predestined inability to repent. Taylor thus adopted a theological fiction in order to make art equal to Donne's and Crashaw's by accepting "the illusion of good works (no illusion for Herbert, but definitely one for a sound Puritan)" (340). Although Blau overlooked Taylor's call to do good works "As if you should be sav'd for doing so" (*Poems* 444) and thereby labeled as unorthodox the central message of virtually all Puritan texts, he was instrumental in shifting the critical focus from *Gods Determinations* to the *Preparatory Meditations* as the sequence "better suited to Taylor's genius" (343), a shift that stimulated a focus on inner processes by which the meditating Puritan could finally be joined to the gifted poet. Most early critics had agreed with Jantz that *Gods Determinations* was Taylor's "greatest work" (1944:82), though its predominance in early studies was due in part to the fact that Johnson's edition reprinted it entire. Although Blau praised its metrical variety as evidence of Herbert's influence, he criticized its "slight" characterization and unsustained "action" (342). Yet he avoided overstating the poem's flaws, a feature common in most comparisons with Herbert. Blau concluded that although Taylor was capable of imagistic "brilliance" in such poems as "The Reflexion" (346), he often failed "the demands of poetic decorum" because of a gulf between divine tenor and homely vehicle that was intrinsic to the sharp separation of heaven and earth mandated by Puritan theology (359).

Blau prompted timely inquiry not so much into what kind of poet Taylor was, but what kind of Puritan he was. Two years after Blau's essay, Donald E. Stanford began to lay the un-Puritan Taylor to rest by demonstrating that the allegedly unorthodox Meditations articulated a thoroughly orthodox view of the Supper (1955). In contrast to Blau's view that Taylor's sacramentality was unusual, Stanford confirmed at least some degree of mystical experience in Puritan sacramental and devotional life. As he pointed out, Calvin had "asserted the real spiritual presence of Christ at the Lord's Supper and the union of Christ with the believer" (173), and even Cotton Mather, the very embodiment of New England orthodoxy, experienced "ecstasy upon contemplating the Eucharist" (175). Taylor's view that such ecstasy was reserved for the converted was clear from his participation in theological controversy. When Solomon Stoddard, influential pastor of neighboring Northampton, proposed that the Supper be opened to all believers, whether converted or not, Taylor's vehement opposition hardly revealed a shaky or reluctant orthodoxy. The following year Stanford reinforced his case with specific reference to Taylor's anti-Stoddard Meditations (2.104-109 and 2.111), which he published for the first time (1956). Adhering to the conclusion of the 1662 Half-Way Synod that the Supper was not a converting ordinance, Taylor sided with Increase and Cotton Mather against his Connecticut Valley neighbor and thus took a position that was conservative even for his time. In Taylor's view, the Synod, the Westminster Shorter Catechism of 1648, and Calvin's *Institutes* had settled the issue: the Supper was properly a "seal" of a spiritual betrothal already made, not a sacrament open to all. Stanford conceded, however, that Taylor's orthodoxy did not make him a better poet, as evidenced by his "homely, colloquial diction, the extravagant tropes, and the all-too-frequent awkwardnesses of phrasing and rhythm" (62). Four years later Stanford cited Taylor's prose to refute Weathers's charge that the poet was a universalist and not a predestinarian (1960b). In his analysis of sermon 10 of the *Christographia*, Stanford confirmed that Taylor's "rigid Calvinism" inspired "his most powerful writing in poetry and prose" (10). Earlier Stanford had conceded that Taylor's Puritanism did not make him a good poet; here he maintained that Taylor's religious beliefs did not automatically keep him from being one either. Regardless of whether particular texts struck modern readers as successful or not, Taylor's faith was the motivating force behind all of the verse, and not simply an obstacle that the poet had to overcome in order to write.

Stanford was soon joined in the defense of Taylor's orthodoxy by Norman Grabo, who found further support in documents related to the Stoddardean controversy. The first of these was the sermon Taylor preached in 1679 at the founding of the Westfield church (1960b). As Taylor's title suggested, "God's House" was a "particular church" charged with screening out those who were unworthy of the sacrament. Reaffirming Taylor's role as an orthodox minister,

Grabo also argued that the Meditations were direct responses to the doctrines featured in the sacrament-day sermons. In contrast to the figure torn between belief and art depicted in much of the early criticism, Grabo's Taylor was a man for whom intellective doctrine and emotional response were inseparable. In the engagingly titled "The Poet to the Pope," Grabo published Taylor's cordial but firm letter of February 13, 1687/8 to Stoddard, the "Pope of the Connecticut Valley," along with Stoddard's brief reply (1960c). Written nearly ten years after the "Foundation Day" sermon, Taylor's letter was prophetic of New England's growing attraction to what Grabo called Stoddard's "easier" religion (201). In a third essay Grabo took a broader focus. Although he concurred with Stanford regarding Taylor's orthodoxy, he expanded the definition of what such orthodoxy entailed (1960a). Asserting the existence of mystical and Catholic elements in Puritan devotional life, Grabo argued that such experience was fully articulated by the Mathers and Samuel Willard. Extending Black's stress on the richness of Puritan spiritual life (1956), Grabo maintained that anti-Catholic sentiments did not keep Puritans from drawing on a venerable tradition of Catholic devotion, often filtered through English advocates of meditation like Richard Baxter. Unlike Black, however, he posited no Puritan discomfort in appropriating this tradition. Citing Protestant guides to meditation, Grabo insisted that devotional intensity like Taylor's was perfectly acceptable among devout New Englanders.

After 1960, with the settling of Taylor's Puritan credentials, the debate over what it actually meant to *be* a Puritan would intensify. The eventual result was a more pluralistic view of Puritan inner experience than earlier critics had been willing to embrace, one in which Wigglesworth's stern thunderings, Bradstreet's conflicted musings, and Taylor's emotional volatility all found a place. Significantly, the question of Taylor's orthodoxy was resolved first in his prose and only later in the poetry. Moreover, the question had been raised in part because critics had been limited to the selections in the *Poetical Works*, the "topical" poems and "gleanings" that Johnson published in the 1940s, and twenty-six additional Meditations published in the 1950s by Morris Neufeld (1951) and Barbara Simison (1954). As Stanford noted when he published nineteen more Meditations, if more of the poetry had been available Taylor would not have seemed so much like a "modified Anglican or a neo-Platonist rather than the Calvinist he actually was" (1957:18). By publishing a much broader selection of the writings, Stanford and Grabo would soon reveal a more representative Edward Taylor, whose connections with the religion and art of early New England could be explored in depth. As a result, critics would return to Johnson's view that Taylor was not so unusual for his milieu as the poems suggested. As Grabo observed, the poet "had no more to hide" than such pillars of the New England Way as the Mathers (1960a:402). And as Grabo would confirm early in the new decade (1962c), Taylor was helping to lift a "veil" from the perceptions of early Americanists by which the old feud between Puritanism and poetry could finally come to an end.

2: First Fruits — The 1960s

BY 1960 TAYLOR'S IMPORTANCE was established, and as a result, the rush to classify him as metaphysical, baroque, medieval, classical, and even Puritan became less urgent. The question of his doctrinal orthodoxy was nearly settled, though a fuller demonstration would soon come with the publication of two sermon sequences. Taylor's place among his New England contemporaries would also become clearer as experiential and expressive possibilities available within Puritan culture were better understood. Although this development had begun with the early work of Donald Stanford and Norman Grabo, they soon disagreed on whether Taylor or any other Puritan could be called a mystic. This debate served an important function in moving the criticism beyond formalist criteria for assessing Taylor's work. The defensive or dismissive extremes of some of the early commentary soon gave way to more balanced attempts simply to understand how the poetry worked in light of the spiritual life that it recorded.

In 1960 solid ground for this understanding arrived with Stanford's edition of *The Poems of Edward Taylor*, which made the complete *Preparatory Meditations* available for the first time. Stanford, introduced to Taylor in a graduate course taught by Yvor Winters and intrigued, as he later wrote, by "the metaphysical characteristics of Taylor's style" (1990:3), submitted a critical edition of the poems in 1953 to Stanford University as his doctoral dissertation. As he labored over Taylor's crabbed hand in the "Poetical Works" manuscript, he found numerous errors in Johnson's texts, a list of which can be found in the dissertation. Responding to the still common view that Taylor "had secret leanings toward Anglicanism, perhaps even towards Rome" (4), Stanford was convinced that a multi-volume edition of the complete verse and the *Christographia* sermons would settle the orthodoxy issue once and for all. After several publishers rejected the expensive project, Yale University Press agreed to publish it. Meanwhile, Grabo, then a graduate student at U.C.L.A., received Stanford's permission to edit the sermons. Yale soon decided on a one-volume edition of the poetry, requesting that Stanford condense his introduction and replace most of his annotations with a glossary. As he later observed, the decision to present a smaller selection "probably did more for Taylor's immediate reputation and popularity than a multi-volume edition would have done" (7). Despite its abbreviated form, *The Poems of Edward Taylor* presented the poet in textual and critical dress befitting a major figure. In first position were the complete Meditations, including 128 previously unpublished poems, now called "Preparatory" rather than "Sacramental," a title that had derived from Taylor's grandson, Ezra Stiles. The "Prologue" was now assigned to the Meditations because, as Louis Martz pointed out, it matched them metrically and thematically and because *Gods Determinations* already had a "Preface." Next came a fresh text of *Gods Determinations*, followed by a selection of "Miscellaneous Poems" chosen for their "literary value" (1960a:lxi). Finally, Stanford included the "Funerall Poem" for Elizabeth Taylor, "A Fig for Thee, Oh! Death," the elegy on Samuel Hooker, and brief selections from the *Metrical History of Christianity*. In addition to Martz's foreword and Stanford's biographical, critical, and textual introduction, the edition included a bibliography of previous publications of Taylor's work, a full description of the manuscripts, and a glossary of archaisms and theological terms. After more than thirty years, the Yale *Poems* remains a model of scholarly editing.

The first position of the complete *Preparatory Meditations*, a decision urged by Martz and Norman Holmes Pearson, hastened the shift in critical focus away from *Gods Determinations* as Taylor's masterwork. Although Johnson praised the edition, he believed that it "unwarrantably" downgraded *Gods Determinations* (1960:24). Most critics, however, came to agree with Martz that the poem was "a labor of versified doctrine" that only occasionally approached the quality of the Meditations (1960:xiii). Grabo, who thought that too many poems were omitted, anticipated the critical thrust of the new decade by commenting that the *Poems* would force a reexamination of basic and longstanding "assumptions about American Puritanism" (1961b:142). By showcasing the Meditations, composed in unvarying meter and rhyme over a period of some forty years, the Yale edition encouraged critics to stop judging the poetry in formalist terms and to start considering the religio-aesthetic processes that informed it. In his review Austin Warren confirmed that Taylor was best appreciated not in single poems but for the "goodness of the brain-work and heart-work" that went into the poetry as a whole (1960:18). Seen as ongoing, repeatable expressions of Taylor's inner life, the Meditations began to seem less like well-wrought urns than Whitman's barbaric yawp. Stanford, Martz, and Grabo established solid precedent for this approach, all three confirming that Taylor's was a Calvinist yawp fully consistent with his calling as an orthodox Puritan minister.

In his introduction Stanford tenaciously gleaned the available documents to portray a man who, though by no means a progressive thinker, was fully engaged with the issues of his time (1960a). In his principled and even stubborn pursuit of his pastoral responsibilities, Taylor's external life was entirely consistent with his orthodox and even conservative beliefs. Drawing on the sermons and theological writings, Stanford reconfirmed Taylor's support of the Westminster Confession, stressing — as it was still necessary to do in 1960 — that his life was "unmarked, as far as we know, by any deviations on his part from orthodox theology or church polity" (xlix). For Stanford, Taylor's "dramatic intensity" and lapses in taste were attributable to a theology that stressed thorough self-castigation (l). The poet's meditative ecstasies were similarly inseparable from a thoroughly orthodox belief in divine mercy, an affirmative dimension of the faith in which some Puritans "were often moved to ecstasies which might be called mystical" (liv). Citing Calvin and Cotton Mather, Stanford affirmed that Taylor's records of such experience compromised neither his clear distinction between the two covenants nor his vehement rejection of Catholic transubstantiation and Lutheran consubstantiation. Like other Puritans, Taylor saw the Supper as a sacramental sign "in which Christ is present in a real spiritual sense and in which the participant enjoys a real spiritual and mystical union with the Lord" (lii). Developing Johnson's suggestion of the importance of biblical typology (1939a:18), Stanford argued that the Bible and biblical exegesis profoundly affected Taylor's poetic method, not just in the typological poems but in the Meditations based on the allegorical Song of Songs. Like Johnson, Stanford reinforced these biblical and theological contexts by appending a glossary, which included some thirty concepts defined by extracts from Taylor's own prose. The longest entries, on "Election and the Elect" and the "Old and New Covenant," ensured that no one would again mistake Taylor for a covert believer in universal salvation.

Martz, approaching the poetry from the standpoint of literary history and aesthetics, argued that the deeper structures informing the Meditations were not so much literary as spiritual: terms like "metaphysical" and "baroque" were too limited to describe poetry written to intensify the poet's experience of his faith (1960). Although he conceded Taylor's indebtedness to Herbert, Martz suggested that to dismiss him as "a burlap version of Herbert" or "a quaint primitive" (viii) would be to devalue one poet for not writing like another — a common fault, as we have seen, in the metaphysical-baroque debate. The real key to Taylor's poetry, Martz argued, was a bold "quest for truth" (xviii) in which the poet often invoked "deliberate roughness" as he struggled for spontaneous expression rather than careful artifice (xix). Arguing that Taylor's poetic flaws were less significant that "the whole poem" and the deeper process that it manifested (xxi), Martz espoused a big-picture reading in which the individual image was less important than the poem, the individual poem less important than the poetry, and the poetry less important than the process that generated it. Accordingly, he stressed the consecutive and interlocked themes of the Meditations as evidence of Taylor's tenacious search for larger structures in which to write. The First Series, for example, formed a unit perhaps based on the square of seven, a number signifying perfection. Martz also identified smaller units based on biblical texts as well as the longer sequences dealing with typology (Meds. 2.1-30), Christology (2.31-56, including the *Christographia* poems), the Lord's Supper (2.102-111), and the Canticles allegory (2.115-153). For Martz, the process embodied in these sequences was Puritan meditation, which included not just the self-convicting variety represented by Thomas Hooker's *The Application of Redemption* (London: 1657) but the contemplation of heavenly joys recommended in Richard Baxter's *The Saints Everlasting Rest* (London: 1650). Unlike Grabo, who saw this tradition as a continuation of older Catholic devotional modes (1960a), Martz argued that heavenly contemplation was a newer Puritan movement that emerged as a counterbalance to the "fearsome rigor of the older generation" (xxiv). Baxter's call to root doctrine in the believer's heart lay behind Taylor's poetic attempts to arouse his affections for the Supper. In his earlier study of *The Poetry of Meditation*, Martz had included Taylor in a list of poets, ranging from Donne to Eliot, whose meditative style embodied, in Hopkins's phrase, "current language heightened" (1954:324). Summarizing the traditions surveyed in that study, Martz defined a three-part method, developed by Ignatius of Loyola and adapted by Protestants from Catholic devotional guides, that corresponded to the traditional division of the faculties into the memory, the understanding, and the will. Applying this structure mainly to the First Series, Martz reinforced the orthodoxy of a poet who was participating in a widespread religious movement of the day. Not only did Baxter's defense of sensory imagery account for Taylor's "bold and often unseemly" figures (1960:xxix), but the poet's search for spiritual experience and not fine writing explained his imagistic leaps and his tendency to strain an image to "excessive ingenuity" (xxx). For Martz, the meditative method provided an underlying structure for the poems that accounted for many of their alleged flaws (xxxi). Writing in relative isolation in frontier Westfield, the meditating Taylor created poetry of "rugged and original integrity" that helped "mark the beginning of an American language, an American literature" (xxxvii).

The Yale *Poems* prompted a second wave of interest in Taylor, but not before provoking a final outburst against the Taylor cult that had annoyed Stanley Williams and Sidney Lind a decade earlier. European critics were especially harsh toward this American poetic pioneer. In a review appearing in the *Times Literary Supplement*, Douglas Grant complained that Taylor was "unable to view the world except through the transforming medium of the Bible," a medium that worked "to the impoverishment of his poetry" (1961:72). If Taylor had stayed in England, his taste would have matured and he would have avoided becoming "fossilized, unmodified and entire." It was his American identity, Grant argued, that accounted for his enthusiastic reception. A. J. Smith was equally unimpressed, finding the Meditations "tediously uniform" in their failure to excite the imagination (1962). Invoking the smoother metaphysicals, Smith called Taylor an "incorrigible flaunter of obsolete fashion." A German scholar, Johannes Hedberg, agreed that Taylor had been "overpraised by eager American scholars" caught up in the current "vogue for baroque poetry" (1960:268, 267). These charges hurt — but not much, as Hayes Jacobs suggested when he humorously urged critics to stop "picking" on Taylor (1960:72). Jacobs's "Save Taylor" project notwithstanding, attacks on his poetic quality and literary importance were largely at an end. In their place came the first fruits of serious scholarship, which pursued five basic lines of inquiry in the 1960s and 1970s. The first was a search for additional manuscripts and biographical information. The second was a more specific reconstruction of Taylor's meditative and poetic processes. The third was the explication of individual poems in light of those processes. The fourth was a closer study of his sources. Finally, there were new attempts to situate the poet at the beginning of an American tradition of visionary and symbolic writing.

The Yale edition whetted critical appetites for additional biographical information and publication of more of the material listed in Stanford's manuscript census. Stanford soon added to the biographical record by reporting that Taylor's father, William Taylor or Tealer of Sketchley, died in 1658, and that the poet's mother had probably died earlier (1961a). The oldest of five brothers, Richard, died in 1689. Taylor's family, Stanford learned, consisted of relatively well-to-do farmers who probably could not write (they "marked" their wills). But writing and reading were separate skills in the seventeenth century, and perhaps Richard and more probably his wife could read; a Bible and some religious books, including Thomas Doolittle's 1665 and 1682 treatises on the Lord's Supper, were listed in Richard's estate. Alexander Medlicott found new information regarding the other end of Taylor's life in entries from the diaries of Stephen Williams, minister at nearby Longmeadow, whose ordination the aging poet attended and who was present at Taylor's funeral (1962). Williams's account of an old minister who was "too sharp" in his opposition to Stoddardeanism accorded well with the uncompromising figure who was emerging from Taylor's own writings (271).

Stanford soon incorporated his findings into his introduction to an abridged edition of the *Poems* (1963). He also included fuller discussions of Puritan sacramentality and Taylor's use of the Bible and typology, and cited new sources, including Lorenzo Scupoli's *The Spiritual Conflict* and the case divinity of William Ames. Perhaps in response to Johnson's and Grabo's reviews, Stanford included a more detailed treatment of *Gods Determinations* in his overview of the poetry, though he reiterated his belief that Taylor's "eventual reputation will rest" on the Meditations (xxxv). Two years later, in the fullest presentation yet of the poet's life, Stanford countered the romantic notion of a secretive poet by depicting a man who was "already well versed in the matter of earning a living from the soil" when he settled at Westfield in late 1671 (1965:8). As Stanford pointed out, Taylor could have derived his images of crafts and technology from village life in Sketchley and nearby Hinckley, where he may even have worked in the developing weaving industry. Taylor apparently taught school briefly in Bagworth until the 1662 Act of Uniformity made it impossible for him to teach or to attend one of the universities. Once in Westfield, he became fully engaged with worldly duties as pastor, physician, husband, father, and leading citizen. Stanford's Taylor was conservative and even stubborn in his determination to lead Westfield into the millennium, refusing to abandon the town during King Philip's War, holding his ground in at least three serious divisions within his congregation, and refusing to occupy a new meetinghouse that had been built, against his wishes, on higher ground.

For Stanford, the poetry reflected the major influences of Taylor's time and place: Calvinist theology, Protestant meditation, biblical typology and allegory, and the metaphysical poets, especially Herbert. *Gods Determinations* was influenced, Stanford argued, by verse satires common among pamphleteers of the day. Agreeing with Nathalia Wright (1946) that the young Taylor may have seen the Corpus Christi procession that was still being held near Coventry, Stanford cited more immediate sources in Wigglesworth's *The Day of Doom*, Scupoli's *The Spiritual Conflict*, and Bunyan's *The Holy War*. The martial imagery of *Gods Determinations*, which echoed Edward Johnson's *Wonder-Working Providence*, reflected a Puritan "obsession" with the "battle between the chosen people of God and the Devil" (1965:29). Other influences included Joshua Sylvester's translation of Guillaume Du Bartas's *Divine Weeks and Works*, Abraham Cowley's *Davideis*, Thomas Shepard's *The Sincere Convert*, and Samuel Lee's *Eleothriambos*. Most pervasive, however, was the Calvinism lined out in the *Institutes* and the theological works in Taylor's library. A historically grounded poet also emerged from Stanford's comments on the sermons, which exhibited the conventional division into doctrine, reasons, and uses, as well as a plain style well-suited to Taylor's Westfield audience despite occasional "flights of rhetorical eloquence" suggestive of his poetic gifts (43). Comparing the Meditations with the work of the English metaphysicals, Stanford reconfirmed that theological and doctrinal consistency did not necessarily produce great poetry by traditional standards. "There are too many lapses in taste, there is too much repetition of theme and phrase, too much dependence on Biblical language, and not enough classical and humanistic refinement in the verse of the Puritan parson to claim equal rank with the British metaphysical school" (44). Despite these defects, however, Stanford confirmed Taylor's considerable artistic achievement, maintaining that a few of the poems would "remain permanent contributions to our American heritage of devotional poetry" (44).

The 1960s saw the description and publication of a great deal of material that Stanford had been forced to cut from the Yale edition. The year before the *Poems* came out, Francis Murphy described Taylor's 500-page transcription of Origen's *Contra Celsus* and *De Principiis*, located in the Westfield Athenaeum (1959). Also in 1959 Stanford published Taylor's poem on the "Giant Bones" discovered in 1705 in upstate New York, which revealed the poet's interest in natural science (1959). In 1960 Stanford published Taylor's earliest poems, written before he left England and discovered in the "Diary" manuscript in the Redwood Athenaeum in Newport (1960c). Something of Taylor's poetic development could now be traced, along with the first articulations of his theological and political concerns. Of greater importance, if only in sheer bulk, was Taylor's *Metrical History of Christianity*, which Stanford published in a microform edition in 1962. The massive *History,* so different from the meditative verse, was as puzzling as it was disappointing, especially in its blunt expression of "the seamy side of the Puritan character" (1961b). How could a poet so capable of expressing "the sweetness of God's grace," Stanford asked, have written such a distasteful poem (294)? But one could just as easily blame Taylor's sources as his invention, since he had consulted such standard histories as John Foxe's *Acts and Monuments* and Matthias Flaccius's Latin *Magdeburg Centuries*. As Stanford observed, Taylor's disregard for "belles-lettres and literary standards" in favor of "the propagation of the gospel and the state of his own soul" informed all of his poetry, "his best and his worst" (292). While much was added to the Taylor corpus in the 1960s, a bit was taken away by Leo M. Kaiser and Stanford, who pointed out that two Latin elegies found in the "Poetical Works" manuscript were not by Taylor but by President Chauncy of Harvard, himself the subject of a Taylor elegy in English (1965).

The 1960s also saw the first publication of Taylor's prose. Convinced that Taylor's orthodoxy would be obvious once critics had access to the sermons, Stanford published a portion of sermon 10 from the *Christographia* to illustrate the poet-preacher's doctrinal agreement with the Westminster Confession (1960b). Arguing that Johnson's glossary in the *Poetical Works* gave a misleading view of Taylor as a universalist, Stanford refuted Weathers (1954) by demonstrating the poet's predestinarian beliefs. Two years later Grabo reinforced the poet's orthodoxy by publishing "The Appeale Tried," Taylor's answer to Solomon Stoddard's *Appeal to the Learned* (Boston:1709); the document refuted Miller's charge that Taylor contributed nothing to the Lord's Supper debate (1953:240) and confirmed the poet's active involvement with "the intellectual and social problems of his day" (1962a:400). That Taylor had a thoroughly Calvinist sense of sin was underscored by Stanford's publication of the "Spiritual Relation" that he gave at the founding of the Westfield church (1964). In his study of early American autobiography, Daniel Shea saw this brief narrative as the record of "a textbook conversion which allows only a fleeting glimpse of the rich meditative life regularly encountered in his poetry" (1968:92). Shea argued that the conventional nature of Taylor's relation stemmed from its occasion and from his pastoral duty to provide an "instructive and exemplary" narrative (93) designed to make his inner experience "rationally available to his audience" (97). In 1964 Francis Murphy re-edited Taylor's short diary, which had first seen light in the 1880 *Proceedings* of the Massachusetts Historical Society. The diary, as Murphy noted in his introduction, revealed an intensely curious and energetic man whose considerable pride may have been wounded by his vocation in frontier Westfield (1964:9). The widespread hope that additional manuscripts might turn up was voiced by Charles W. Mignon, who reprinted Ezra Stiles's 1767 "Memoir" of his grandfather and noted that Taylor manuscripts tended to remain in the family (1965). The following year Mignon described the "Manuscript Notebook" of theological headings with Latin glosses that had been given to Yale by a Taylor descendant (1966b). Mignon was prophetic in observing that genealogy and manuscript provenance tended to correlate: some ten years later a previously unknown sequence of sermons on the types — again owned by a Taylor descendant — turned up in Lincoln, Nebraska, where Mignon was teaching.

With Grabo's publication of the fourteen *Christographia* sermons and the eight sermons comprising the *Treatise Concerning the Lord's Supper*, scholars gained a wealth of material for probing broader contexts for the content and language of the poems. In addition, the sermons gave the final lie to charges that Taylor flamed privately in the Meditations because he could not to do so in public. While Stanford's work focused primarily on establishing Taylor's orthodoxy, Grabo's chief interest was exploring the aesthetic implications of that orthodoxy. Intrigued by an "uneasy sense," as he later wrote, that the criticism was failing to account for "the source and power" of Taylor's poetry (1990:13), Grabo was convinced that a full edition of Taylor's sermons on Christology, preached in 1701 and 1702, would force critics to stop reading the poetry in a vacuum and would, in addition, demonstrate a fundamental unity of the poetry and prose. Although Grabo confirmed the conventional nature of Taylor's covenant theology in the sermons, he argued that Taylor's Christology invested humanity with particular dignity. Taylor, obsessed with the human-divine mutuality of the spiritual marriage, was more "humanistic" than Increase Mather and less morbid than Wigglesworth (1962b:xxviii). Building on Martz's emphasis on Taylor's contemplative processes, Grabo united the poetry and the prose within traditions of formal meditation set forth by Catholic as well as Puritan writers. The sermons and the poems, Grabo argued, reflected two basic stages in traditional meditation: while the sermons took up a primarily intellective consideration of doctrine, the poems stressed the believer's affective response. The implications of Grabo's view that the Meditations were not self-contained texts but half of a poem-sermon continuum were considerable. Critics attacking Taylor's alleged poetic flaws from the standpoint of New Critical explication were failing to realize that the poems were not meant to stand alone; rather, they were responses to the doctrine preached in their corresponding sermons, written after the sermons to intensify Taylor's spiritual appetite for the Supper. Grabo's poem-sermon connection ended Taylor's days as a schizophrenic figure whose private poetry conflicted with his public profession. By stressing this point, Grabo hastened the shift in Taylor studies from formalist readings of the poems as self-contained verbal artifacts to processual readings that referenced the poet's inner life.

Four years later Grabo published *Edward Taylor's Treatise Concerning the Lord's Supper* (1966). Discouraged by a rejection from Kenneth Murdock at Harvard, Grabo decided that the *Treatise* would reach print sooner in modernized form than in an exact transcription (1990). Given that the prose was of interest chiefly as a commentary on the poetry, this decision did not impair the edition's usefulness. Although Taylor's transcriptions from his sources, entered on ruled half-pages in the manuscript, were omitted from the final edition, Grabo's extensive annotations gave full demonstration of the poet-preacher's impressive learning. In his introduction Grabo argued that the poems generally presented a "distillation" of information and themes initially worked out in the sermons (1966:ix). Warning against "technical" readings based on the assumption that individual poems could be isolated for analysis (xi), Grabo used the famous "Huswifery" to demonstrate the prose contexts of the poetry by linking its weaving imagery with the doctrines implicit in the "wedding garment" of Matthew 22:1-14. "Huswifery," too, was "preparatory" in that it witnessed Taylor's intense self-examination prior to participating in the Supper (xiii). Grabo also defended Taylor's skills as a theologian and polemicist, arguing that his refutations of Stoddard in the *Treatise* and elsewhere were more cogent than those offered by the Mathers, and that the poet's concern with the signs of election provided a bridge between Thomas Shepard and Jonathan Edwards in the history of American Puritan soteriology. While Edwards was more philosophical and Taylor more experiential, both shared what Taylor called a "festival frame of spirit" that made a joyous necessity of writing divine praise (xliii). Arguing that Taylor's views on redemptive psychology and metaphoric language challenged modern expectations of a metaphysical decorum in the poetry, Grabo made a persuasive case for reading the poems in the context of the poet's world rather than the modern reader's.

Stanford and Grabo established the Taylor corpus as it would stand for the next two decades. Enough material now existed to permit a reconstruction of the "whole" Taylor from his own words. Such comprehensive treatment came with the 1961 publication of the first critical monograph devoted to the poet, Grabo's *Edward Taylor*. Written while the *Christographia* sermons were in press, the book brought Taylor's poetry and prose, his inner and outer lives, and his meditative exuberance and doctrinal sobriety into a single, coherent picture. Grabo's central aim was to establish the seamless blending of life and art in a poet who, though "undoubtedly a rare bird," was "a very conventional and perfectly orthodox — indeed, conservative to the point of reactionary — Calvinist of the New England school" (1961a:19). Invoking a traditionally Catholic distinction, Grabo surveyed the "Active Life" of a bookish Puritan whose orthodoxy was so complete that he felt that his accord with the Westminster catechism and the Cambridge Platform of 1647 made a separate profession of faith unnecessary at the founding of the Westfield church. As Grabo confirmed, "Nothing Taylor wrote in the following fifty years indicates the slightest modification of these doctrines" (29). Enacting an "imitation of Christ" both as believer and as poet, Taylor unified his concerns around the sanctity of the Supper (31). Grabo reviewed the controversy with Stoddard not only as evidence of Taylor's conservatism but as the chief inspiration for the poetry. When, in the *Treatise*, Taylor urged his congregation to meditate on the benefits of the sacrament, he urged them toward a devotional response central to his own private contemplations. And when, in the last year of his life, the Westfield congregation voted to make a conversion narrative optional for participating in the Supper, they "undid," as Grabo affirmed, "the work of Taylor's entire ministry" (39).

For Grabo, Taylor's "Contemplative Life" was enlivened by what could only be called a "mystical" dimension. While this thesis will be taken up separately a bit later, suffice it to say at this point that Grabo argued for Taylor's devotional intensity as well as its fully Puritan nature. Although Taylor's sermons, typical of those produced in early New England, disproved his alleged attraction to high Anglican or Catholic worship, the poetry itself offered the clearest revelation of the inner life of a solidly Congregational minister whose "theory of poetry was derived from his mysticism" (87). Grabo maintained that for Taylor, flawed thoughts and words could be rectified only by God's grace; although Grabo agreed with Roy Harvey Pearce (1950) that the Ramist demotion of poetry and rhetoric kept Puritans from developing "a serious art and philosophy of poetry" (98), he found a more sophisticated aesthetic at work in Taylor's verse than Puritan statements about art suggested. The key to this aesthetic, Grabo insisted, was not poetic "philosophy" but a "symbolic theory" that assumed the inherently symbolic nature of language and the sensory manifestations of God in the world (99). Christ's very nature as divinity revealed in human form, for example, justified Taylor's "reducing of the most noble and magnificent metaphysical facts to kitchen images." Through such verbal activity, the poet could imitate Christ, through whom the divine was rendered at least partly comprehensible to human understanding. For Taylor, such imitation was inseparable from both faith and art: writing sacred poetry was a "religious act" and a sacrificial "duty" to be performed to the limits of his ability (102). For this reason Grabo did not see Taylor's poetic "roughness" as intentional; on the contrary, the poet constantly begged to be made "fit to sing heroics in praise of the Lord" (107).

In his survey of Taylor's poetic development, Grabo argued that the rich aesthetic of the Meditations was a long time coming. The early poems revealed a poet caught up in the religious polemics, conventional forms, and superficial wit that he abandoned once King Philip's War, ministerial responsibilities, and family tragedy provoked a deeper "personal involvement" in his art (124). For Grabo, Taylor's non-meditative poems were of value chiefly as "a kind of sketchbook" for the Meditations (135), whose composition may have been prompted by the 1682 publication of Increase Mather's *Practical Truths Tending to Promote the Power of Godliness* and the reissue that same year of Philip Pain's *Daily Meditations*. Identifying within Taylor's poems a three-fold meditative structure consisting of a question or statement of the subject, the development of the subject, and an application of the subject to the poet's "own condition" (139), Grabo disagreed with Martz's view that the larger sequences of poems were deliberate, instead arguing that these poetic units were merely "an accident of the sermon sequence" (141). Maintaining that Taylor's rhyme, meter, repetition, and choppiness gave flexibility to "what would ordinarily be a rigid form" (145), Grabo found precedent for the "inharmonious harmony" of Taylor's images (149) in the common meditative practice of yoking sublime referents to natural objects in order to illustrate moral themes. For Grabo, Taylor's consistent translation of the created world into biblical and domestic metaphors produced five recurring classes of images: those derived from writing, warfare, technology and crafts, gardens, and feasts — the latter two predominating in the verse and especially popular in devotional writing. Grabo underscored the conventional nature of most of Taylor's figures in light of meditative traditions based on Jesuit devotional manuals. Taylor's handling of imagery also owed much to the emblem books popular in late sixteenth- and early seventeenth-century England. Although the emblematic mode contributed to the seemingly illogical development of his imagery, Taylor deviated from the emblem tradition by focusing on "ideas rather than images" (158). This doctrinal focus prompted his frequent shifts from image to image as he developed his themes. While the poetry had strong sensory appeal, its "unnatural" perspective stemmed from Taylor's especially bold juxtaposition of the domestic and the infinite (159).

Grabo treated *Gods Determinations* as a multi-layered text best read as a "literary meditation of the Ignatian kind, an expanded version" of the *Preparatory Meditations* (159). Suggesting that Taylor conceived of the poem as an inner meditative drama whose final lyrics comprised a "statement of moved affections" (166), Grabo conceded that the poem revealed Taylor's difficulty with longer forms. The poet's achievement in this sustained work paled in comparison with the more spontaneous Meditations as expressions of Puritan inner life. While it was true, as Grabo noted, that the modern regard for these poems was linked to an esteem for English devotional poetry, Taylor's more insistent concern with vision made it impossible to dismiss him as "only an American metaphysical" (171). So did his use of emblematic and allegorical modes, which linked him with such later poets as Dickinson and Hopkins. Grabo insisted, however, that Taylor's "American experience" was solidly grounded in Congregational polity and covenant theology specific to his time and place (172). Taylor did not repudiate Puritan New England but transformed its concerns through "mystical introversion" into "intellectual, aesthetic, and spiritual universals" as he sang God's praise in "the suburbs of glory in America" (173).

As the work of Grabo, Stanford, and Martz began to take hold, the widespread assumption of secrecy behind Taylor's alleged injunction against publication could not stand. The issue came to a head the year after Grabo's book appeared, when Austin Warren argued that Taylor suppressed his poems because they were "his private dialogues with God" (1962:51) and Emmy Shepherd, who reminded critics that Taylor allegedly suppressed all of his writings and not just his poetry, proposed that his reticence reflected "simple, genuine humility" and "self-respect and pride in his work" (1962:513). Francis Murphy finally questioned whether the injunction had any real basis in historical fact (1962). Pointing out that Taylor's alleged wishes derived solely from Henry Wyllys Taylor's brief sketch, Murphy asserted that there was no real authority for what could only be called a family tradition. Indeed, when Murphy checked with the Probate Office of Hampshire County, Massachusetts, he discovered that the poet had died intestate. This news, together with Stanford's and Grabo's arguments for the integrity of private poem and public sermon, finally laid to rest the image of a clandestine poet whose sensual or unorthodox proclivities had driven him underground. Grabo's reaffirmation of the privacy of the Meditations revealed the simplest answer of all: Taylor never published them because they had been written purely for his own spiritual arousal.

The central question now was not whether Taylor was a Puritan, but whether he was a mystic — and if so, whether he was unusual in being one. Grabo's views regarding this dimension of the poetry comprised the most controversial part of his book. Attacking the persistent tendency to paint Puritan inner life "in blacks and grays," Grabo underscored "a gloriously bright side" of Puritan devotion that the Meditations perfectly illustrated (1961a:40, 41). He described Taylor's devotions in terms of a mystical progression from an "awakening" to sin to the "illumination" afforded by divine grace (44). Once grace awakened the entire soul — understanding, will, and affections — the saint experienced the heartfelt disgust regarding sin confessed so dramatically in Taylor's purification images. The verse thus served as a vehicle for the poet's repeated verbal "self-flagellation" and spiritual purgation (58). Citing the *Christographia* sermons as evidence of a Puritan *imitatio Christi* that provided an effective release from self-loathing, Grabo related Taylor's moods to contemplative states described by such writers as Frances de Sales and Ignatius of Loyola, whose *Spiritual Exercises* had entered Protestant culture largely through the efforts of Richard Baxter, who in turn influenced devotional practices endorsed by the Mathers and Samuel Willard. Grabo argued that the affective response to doctrine articulated in Taylor's poetry especially embodied Loyola's final stage of formal meditation, the "colloquy with the Lord" (66). Grabo admitted, however, that terms like "mystical" and "vision" were highly ambiguous (41), and this ambiguity made its way into his discussion of Taylor's verse. What Taylor repeatedly sought, Grabo argued, was "vision, not perhaps for his eyes, but for the eye of the soul that is the mirror or image of God in him" — vision conveyed in the Meditations through "highly conventional mystical language" (67). Although Grabo maintained that Taylor "experienced heavenly visions quite often," he conceded that "he seems to claim actual visions on very few occasions" (68). Moreover, Taylor's illuminations seemed "less actual than imaginary," a characterization that did not diminish their power and reality for the poet (69). Suggesting that Taylor occasionally assumed representative stature as the generic elect soul, Grabo maintained that the rapture the poet sought "both as mystic and communicant" was nothing less than "a complete loss of identity in God, union with his Maker" (69). In his quest for this union, his spiritual exercises sometimes produced "visions," or at least an "active use of the imagination that finds expression in his poetry" (82). Taylor "passes beyond these, finally, to a state of complete mystical union with Christ — he is elevated above all things, nearly deified" (82). The following year Grabo argued for a similar degree of emotional intensity in Puritan devotional life generally (1962c). Developing his earlier assertion of "a Puritan literature within a Catholic tradition" (1960a: 396), he identified a considerable level of unconscious aesthetic sophistication in Puritan artistic practice that was accessible through "the symbolism of artistic form" (1962c:499). Affirming that the deepest wellspring of true poetry — symbolic thought — was central to the culture of early New England, Grabo argued that Puritan aesthetic theory, as articulated in such statements as the preface to the Bay Psalm Book and Cotton Mather's recommendation in his *Manuductio ad Ministerium* of "a little Recreation of poetry," was not consistent with Puritan artistic practice (500). Similarly, general denunciations of spiritual enthusiasm did not square with Puritan inner experience as it was actually recorded. Mather, for instance, attested to enthusiasms hardly typical of Miller's intellective Puritans, and Taylor "reeled and staggered at least as frequently as Mather" (505). The widespread assumption that Puritan writing was unemotional and dry, Grabo concluded, had more to do with modern blinders — with a critical and perceptual "veil" — than with what seemed to be evidenced by the writing itself (510).

Seeds of Grabo's argument had been planted here and there by earlier scholars. In a review of Johnson's *Poetical Works*, Percy Hutchison had called Taylor "only a little less a poet than his brother mystics, whether Protestant or Catholic, in England," and had identified "mystic exaltation" in the Meditations and *Gods Determinations* (1940:3). In addition, Harold Jantz had suggested a common source for *Gods Determinations* and the German pietists in "the mystical literature of the later Middle Ages" (1944:82). And as we have seen, Stanford had confirmed a mystical element in Puritan sacramentality (1960a:lii). But concerning the more extreme parts of Grabo's thesis, Stanford was unconvinced, stating that "the great bulk of Taylor's poetry is not mystical, and Mr. Grabo exaggerates this aspect of the poet's writing" (1962:412). While Stanford acknowledged a "feeling of assurance and exaltation" in some of the poems, he reiterated a solidly Protestant context for such moods (1965:15). Much of Taylor's most affective language was "in the common Protestant tradition of the mystical marriage of Christ and the elect" derived from the Song of Songs; the wedding garment and banquet that he invoked were also "stereotypes of sacramental writing" (16). Stanford carefully distinguished between Taylor's "ecstatic joy" at the benefits of grace from the Catholic emphasis on the "sufferings of Christ," and although he agreed with Grabo and Martz that Catholic traditions existed as the ultimate source for Puritan meditation, he believed that this was true only in the broad sense that Protestant thinkers generally either extended or repudiated earlier Catholic formulations (17). In contrast to Grabo's stress on mystical self-transcendence, Stanford emphasized "logical order" in the poetry, though he conceded that Taylor manifested such order less successfully than Donne or Herbert (18). For Stanford, Taylor's two chief sources remained the metaphysical poets and the Bible as filtered through Protestant exegesis.

Although Ola Winslow praised Grabo's attempt to address "an area of New England Puritanism far too scantily understood" (1962:612), Stanford's more conservative accounting of Taylor's spirituality won more adherents. Stephen Fender, for instance, connected the spiritual paradigm dramatized in *Gods Determinations* with Thomas Hooker's solidly Puritan *Application of Redemption* (London: 1656); it was Hooker's influence, Fender argued, that probably accounted for Taylor's juxtaposing of "homely with exalted" images (1964:334). Thomas E. Johnston, Jr., similarly placed Taylor not among Ignatian contemplatives but among the solidly Puritan voices of Bradstreet, Philip Pain, and Roger Williams (1968). Still, Grabo's thesis provoked valuable reflection on the devotional dynamic that generated the poetry. While Stanford cited the metaphysicals in his critique of Taylor's insistent biblicism, lack of "humanistic" breadth, and "lapses in taste" (1965:44), Grabo helped redefine the basis of evaluation from formal criteria to a religio-aesthetic process that needed to be understood "before we can judge its fruits, his poetry" (1961a:82). Grabo also helped broaden Martz's meditative framework, an important modification since not every poem manifested the three-part structure of a formal Ignatian meditation. Finally, Grabo complicated the expectation that a simple linear structure could be imposed on the *Preparatory Meditations* as a whole: "Taylor's expression of the [mystical] process must, therefore, be repetitious and unending, and all the stages of it must be uttered throughout his entire life" (83). Grabo would come to modify his views, conceding a decade later that his emphasis on mysticism "proved the most objectionable and least tenable part" of *Edward Taylor* (1971:351). And in his 1988 revision of the book he would state that "Taylor could operate within a mystical literary tradition without himself being a mystic" (1988:xi). In the later study he placed Taylor's spirituality within a more conscious and deliberate framework by claiming that the poet recognized "the parallel character of mysticism with the ordinary pattern of redemptive experience," and thus "used the contemplative way to intensify more ordinary Protestant religious experiences" (51). But by the late 1980s, as we shall see, the deeper implications of Grabo's original reading would seem less novel. Edmund S. Morgan's *Visible Saints* (1963) and Norman Pettit's *The Heart Prepared* (1966) had paved the way for studies of the Puritan psyche that confirmed something of the rich devotional life that Grabo found in Taylor.

While Stanford connected Taylor's interiority with his historical situation and Grabo linked it with broader patterns of Christian devotion, Martz combined both approaches by seeing Taylor as a Puritan contemplative who worked within historically specific structures. All three, however, agreed on his orthodoxy, and all three stimulated attempts in the 1960s to examine the poems in light of that orthodoxy in order to describe a unified and integrated poet whose inner life and verbal art did not conflict. Although Austin Warren conceded that Taylor was a poor prosodist compared to Herbert, Quarles, and Bradstreet, he confirmed that reading him in terms of Puritan devotional processes put him in a far better light. Retreating from his earlier insistence on Taylor's "baroque" aesthetic (1941), Warren now argued that "good metaphysical poetry" like Taylor's exhibited "a thinking *through* images" (1962:60). Citing a shared seventeenth- and twentieth-century assumption that "there is nothing a poet can't use," Warren defended Taylor's extremes of diction on the basis of a poetics of "transformation" (60). Commenting on Taylor's generally straightforward preaching style in the *Christographia*, Warren argued that the closing exhortations nevertheless revealed the "apostrophic intensity" of a genuine poet (56). Stressing Taylor's covenant theology and his indebtedness to the Psalms and to meditative models adapted by Baxter from Catholic writers, Warren underscored the new emphasis on process by arguing that Taylor was difficult to appreciate in a few brief selections because his ambitious religio-aesthetic aims produced "uneven" results (59). Freed by the private situation of his verse to apply language with Elizabethan vigor, Taylor balanced his confessions of unworth with a deeply affirmative "sense of wonder at Infinite God's bothering with finite man" (59).

Readings in the 1960s tended to support this assumption that the poems were fully consistent with rather than opposed to Taylor's Puritanism. The most specific form that this broad issue took was the relation of the poems to the sermons. As we have seen, Grabo maintained that the two were linked by the "doctrine preached": each poem was written after its corresponding sermon as an affective response to the doctrine at hand (1961a:141). This view was challenged by Robert M. Benton, who proposed a stronger connection between the poems and their scriptural headnotes (1967). Arguing that Taylor developed the Meditations and the sermons from the scriptural texts on which both were based, Benton moved the Bible closer to the center of Taylor's poetic practice by maintaining that the poems frequently incorporated specific biblical themes, images, phrases, and narrative contexts in a manner consistent with a preacher's explication and application of the Word. The next year E. F. Carlisle sided with Grabo, arguing that what differentiated the poems from the sermons was their relation to Taylor's meditative faculties. Comparing Meditation 2.46 with its corresponding sermon, Carlisle maintained that the sermons developed the "reasoning of the Puritan minister" while the Meditations dramatized "the response of the *whole* Puritan man" (1968:159). Donald Junkins soon took a position between Grabo and Benton: although the poems were indeed based on the doctrines of the sermons, the Bible headnotes provided important keys to Taylor's affective application of his doctrinal themes (1969/70). Arguing for an underlying unity of poem and sermon that underscored the interdependence of Taylor's professions as poet and preacher, Junkins insisted that Taylor's poetic process was "religio-aesthetic and can only be understood in that context" (67). This statement summarizes a central trend in the scholarship of the 1960s. Once the unity of Taylor's thought and art was firmly established, the goal of classifying and assessing his poetry became secondary to defining more precisely how the verse functioned as an expression of his faith. Although Pearce insisted early in the decade that Taylor's images were not coherently developed and that his syntax was "confused and confusing," he set the tone for subsequent criticism by insisting that the poetry be read within the context of Taylor's experience of Puritanism (1961:53). Pearce maintained that because Puritanism forced the poet "to put Art below Nature, and both below God," Taylor created from theological necessity "an 'artless' art, one which in the hands of a master like him is art indeed" (54). Unlike Pearce, however, most critics joined Martz, Grabo, and Junkins in arguing that the poet was enabled and not restricted by his beliefs. Grabo applied this assumption to "Huswifery" by relating its central conceit to the weaving industry of Taylor's boyhood Leicestershire, his use of the image in other writings, and the theological import of the "wedding garment" imagery so prominent in the sermons. "Huswifery," less the record of an isolated occasion than another poem "preparatory" to the Supper, exemplified the sacramental core of Taylor's artistic practice (1964:560). Evan Prosser agreed that Taylor's poetry could not be divorced from its "theological framework" (1967:375). Although he echoed Pearce by arguing that Taylor subordinated artistic invention to the discovery of divine truth, Prosser maintained that Christ's dual nature unified Taylor's cosmos and stimulated a duality in his own voice, as saint and sinner, that produced the poetic drama and tension characteristic of his best work. Finding a human-divine intimacy in Taylor's images of containment and flow, Prosser argued that Taylor found his voice of praise by speaking in the saintly mode.

Junkins soon argued that what struck modern readers as "didactic" in Taylor was actually "the exploratory mystic-religious consciousness at work" (1968:116). For Junkins, an anachronistic separation of the spiritual from the aesthetic effected by modern critics distorted the poetry and held Taylor to artistic standards not his own. His self-castigation, for instance, was an essential expression of his Calvinist humility and a necessary prelude to his meditative themes. Junkins also argued that Taylor equated artistic with spiritual success: while episodes of "spiritual depression" resulted in flat verse (104), an effective poem conveyed the successful result of "a miniature worship service" (107). Identifying artistic creativity with meditative intensity, Taylor achieved a "religious wholeness" (115) that defined the organic unity of his aesthetic. Carlisle confirmed similar unity, answering Grabo's call for an aesthetic reading of the verse by arguing that Taylor's work presented "a poetry of human experience and emotion" (1968:147). Invoking R. P. Blackmur's definition of "deep form" as "the form in which the author apprehends the condition of life," Carlisle claimed that traditional meditative structures were only "the most obvious *conscious* forming principle in Taylor's poetry" (148). A grasp of the deep form of Taylor's work, he argued, freed the poems from sermonic logic and doctrinal rigidity. The most basic of these structures, the gap between humanity and divinity, gave rise to Taylor's characteristic forms of contrast, ascent, interrogation, and metaphoric association necessitated by the ineffability of the divine. Arguing that the "Puritan minister, man, and poet" achieved unity within this deep structure, Carlisle mildly critiqued Pearce by affirming that "When one reads Taylor's best poetry, he does read his Puritanism, but he reads his *poetry*, too" (163). Carlisle's claim that virtually every feature of the verse reflected "the Puritan way of viewing experience" was echoed by Bert C. Bach, who argued that Taylor's self-deprecation served a specific theological and artistic function as a necessary contrast to his images of the divine, a dichotomy reinforced by images of darkness and light as the poet moved from a sense of unworth to a "realization of grace" (1966:51). Charles W. Mignon soon offered a more detailed examination of the sin/grace dichotomy at the heart of Taylor's poetic (1968). With particular reference to the "Prologue" and "The Reflexion," Mignon argued that Taylor's emphasis on Calvinist depravity offered not only his clearest point of difference from the metaphysical poets but the key to the relation of form to function in his poetry. For Taylor, effective praise was impossible without grace, and grace was impossible without a vivid sense of unworth. Taylor thus pursued a "fallen poetic decorum" perfectly suited to his meditative aims, one based not on the making of polished poems but on an assumption of "imperfection" and his consequent internalizing of a thoroughly Calvinist view of himself "both as a man and as an artist" (1425). Relating this process to categories of formal rhetoric, Mignon argued that Taylor's two basic techniques consisted of meiosis, or dispraise of the self and mankind generally, and amplification in praise of God. Since he could not hope to perfect the latter technique, he wrote in the ongoing recognition of his need for "Grace and true poetry" as "God's free gift" (1428).

This work acknowledged that Taylor wrote by his own rules, not those of the metaphysical poets. As Mignon confirmed, "if we are to see Taylor for what he is we *must* distinguish him from such a poet as Herbert" (1968: 1428). Mignon underscored this point with the term "decorum," a word that New Critics of the 1940s and 1950s would scarcely have used to describe

Taylor's work. Junkins added to this growing view of an artistically accomplished poet by demonstrating the care and effectiveness with which Taylor revised his poems (1965). Examining early and final versions of several poems, Junkins countered Pearce's indifferent craftsman, for whom "technique is little or nothing" (1950:45, 1961:53), with a deliberate artist who was fully capable of revising for "smoother lines, sharper images, simpler syntax, and more dramatic expression" (136). Taylor's roughness, Junkins concluded, was not accidental but a deliberate trait central to his meditative goals. Peter Thorpe also defended Taylor's artistry, arguing for the thematic and rhetorical function of a number of features often cited as evidence of the poet's poor taste (1966). Thorpe's defense ranged widely, from the harsh diction and metrical choppiness to the inverted syntax and often confusing imagery and structure. Taylor's unusual coinages, for instance, often gave his language more power, and his seemingly inconsistent images were appropriate for a poet "groping his way toward the light" through a "middle feeling of uncertainty" regarding his election and his ability to handle such sublime themes (369). When Taylor "found evil" within, Thorpe concluded, he was able to "make some fine poetry out of it" (372).

In addition to these general studies, critics in the 1960s began to answer John Clendenning's call for "a deepened understanding of particular poems" (1964:203). Not surprisingly, single-poem explications tended to confirm thematic and formal unity consistent with the growing respect for Taylor's skill as a poet. Clendenning, demonstrating such unity in "The Reflexion," argued for Taylor's skillful control of ambiguity in his handling of the image of the rose. Raymond J. Jordan found a consistent progression to renewed faith in "The Ebb and Flow," a movement appropriately conveyed by the images of the tinder and censer (1962). Robert Secor identified similar coherence in "Upon a Spider Catching a Fly," citing Taylor's movement from an exemplum taken from nature to an allegorical interpretation of the exemplum in the final four stanzas. For Secor, the earlier stanzas illustrated Taylor's ability to address a natural event on "its own amoral terms" before shifting to its theological significance (1968). Suggesting a biblical source for many of Taylor's images, Gene Russell defended the imagistic consistency of "Upon Wedlock, & Death of Children," in which Taylor's merging of the images of marriage and the branch invoked his hoped-for union with Christ through a blend of personal grief and doctrinal lessons (1969). Explications of individual Meditations during the 1960s also correlated artistic form with theological content. Applying the *Christographia* to a reading of Meditation 1.1, Allen R. Penner argued for the imagistic coherence of Taylor's celebration of Christ's mediation and the love between God and the elect (1967). Taylor's artistry, Penner argued, could be appreciated only through a careful re-creation of "the intensity and the significance of the theology" that inspired him (199). Grabo discussed Meditation 1.6 as a consistent expression of Taylor's theological themes (1960d), while William K. Bottorff called this Meditation a "flawless poem" built on the conceit of Taylor's soul as Christ's gold coin (1968:20). George Montiero demonstrated the imagistic coherence of Meditation 1.8, arguing that the bird depicted in the opening stanza unified the entire poem in its invocation of Taylor's soul caged in the flesh (1969). Gerhard T. Alexis untangled the difficult syntax of this poem's opening lines by suggesting that "Divine" be read as a verb, not an adjective (1966). Johannes Hedberg's discussion of Meditation 1.29 stressed the poem's "baroque" unifying of diverse elements into an intentionally open-ended structure (1960). In a discussion of Meditation 1.42 Erdmute Lang defended Taylor's success in finding rhetorical equivalents for his religious response (1967). Japanese scholar Ken Akiyama related the types of Joseph and Jonah in Meditations 2.7 and 2.30 to Matthew 12 and William Perkins's *Art of Prophesying* (1968); Akiyama also explicated Meditation 2.91 by means of a full glossary that similarly underscored the biblical sources of the poem (1963). Edward M. Griffin demonstrated the poet's use in Meditation 2.112 of question-and-answer syllogisms to counter the harsh images of death, though he argued that the poem's rational structures failed to "support the emotional weight" of those images (1968/69:207).

Voicing an increasingly common assumption during the 1960s, Griffin observed that "the non-Calvinist can enter the world" of Taylor's poetry "only by a conscious suspension of disbelief" (1968/69:207-08). Most critics began to enter Taylor's world as a means of illuminating specific aspects of his poetic practice. Clark Griffith, for example, argued that since metaphor provided the poet's only access to the divine realm, the imagistic extremes of the verse were inseparable from his artistic purposes (1966). Metaphor effected this meditative ascent in two ways. Through allegory, Taylor the penitent tried to glimpse as much of the divine as possible; through the conceit, Taylor the poet used language to diminish his distance from God. Once invoked, Taylor's metaphors took on a "momentum" that pushed him toward "increasingly bold" comparisons designed to intensify his faith (459). Through the act of writing,

Taylor's "speaker-as-penitent" could become the "speaker-as-creator," an "outright competitor of heaven" capable of addressing a simultaneously majestic and intimate God (458). A more specific defense of Taylor's imagery came from Robert D. Arner, who demonstrated the purpose and coherence of the elaborate gaming images and sexual puns in Meditation 1.40 (1969). Citing precedent in Dryden and Charles Cotton, among others, Arner argued that this language, however surprising it seemed in the verse of a Puritan parson, was admirably suited to Taylor's aims; the pun on "ware," for instance, enabled the poet to compress "several sins into one word" and thus sharpen his portrayal of sin as a foil to grace (40). Taylor's difficult textual surface increasingly came to be seen in terms of rhetorical or religious purpose. Hedberg, for example, argued that Taylor's seeming off-rhymes reflected his probable pronunciation (1960:261). William R. Manierre II, examining the rhetoric of *Gods Determinations*, agreed with Grabo (1961a:147) that ploce (concentrated repetition) and polyptoton (repeated inflections of a root) were Taylor's most frequent and important devices, not as mere ornament but as expressions of a Puritan-metaphysical epistemology based on "words" rather than "things" (1962:299). Cándido Pérez Gallego argued for Taylor's ingenious and varied use of the word "sweet" in the poetry (1966). Joseph M. Garrison, Jr., analyzing portions of Meditations 1.30 and 2.26, defended Taylor's stanza form as an appropriate vehicle for casting his "commitment and hope" into a verbal "Worship-mould" that reflected an ongoing tension between uncertainty and assurance (1968:130). Fritz Schulze similarly defended Taylor's stanzas, rhymes, and sound patterns (1969). Charles Mignon made the fullest study in the 1960s of Taylor's diction, including dialect words, archaisms, localisms, foreign words, and scientific and technological terms (1966a). Arguing that Taylor's language would have been difficult even for his contemporaries, Mignon stressed the connection in Taylor's mind between art and grace; the poet's difficult vocabulary, however "dangerously obscure in contrast to his orthodoxly comprehensible contemporaries," was justifiable in light of the private nature and function of the poetry (253).

Gods Determinations received little attention after the appearance of Stanford's *Poems*, especially relative to its earlier prominence. We have seen that Manierre cited the poem to illustrate Taylor's rhetoric (1962) and Fender related its redemptive structures to those set forth by Thomas Hooker (1964). At mid-decade Jean L. Thomas examined the poem's dramatic aspect, a focus that Nathalia Wright had taken nearly twenty years earlier (1946). Finding a blend of doctrine and drama in which the former superseded the latter, Thomas traced the poem's chief source not to the moralities, as Wright had argued, but to an older and broader tradition of homiletic writing and pulpit literature that contained "scattered vestiges of the medieval imagination" (1965:454). Although this tradition allowed Taylor to create structures consistent with covenant theology, it diminished the poem's dramatic effectiveness. Because religious and didactic goals took precedent over any interest in drama for its own sake, Thomas concluded that Taylor neglected the human dimensions of belief (462). A nearly antithetical view soon came from Michael Colacurcio, who found in *Gods Determinations* evidence of Taylor's skill in addressing the needs of a specific audience of "half-way" members of his congregation who yearned for conversion and full church membership (1967). In contrast to Thomas's charge that the poem lacked human appeal, Colacurcio argued that Taylor showed a "keen and sympathetic sense of audience" by casting the religious doubts of his readers in a consolatory light and thereby coaxing them toward a renewed hope of conversion (299). From its opening emphasis on cosmic and personal sin to its concluding celebration of church membership, the poem served as a comforting guide to salvation for readers whose tender consciences kept them from claiming their election. For Colacurcio, the closing lyrics especially articulated the final stage of conversion as Taylor exposed the reader's self-doubts as fruitless "despair" and "presumption" (303). At the decade's end John F. Lynen discussed the depiction of time in *Gods Determinations*, arguing that Taylor balanced an episodic, human sense of time with the "fixed pattern" of the divine plan (1969:62).

Despite the developing picture of a conscious artist, not everyone was convinced that Taylor's poetic flaws were intentional. Most critics who faulted the verse continued to invoke aesthetic limitations in Taylor's mental and geographical world. Precedent for this view had come in the early 1950s from Charles Feidelson, whose influential *Symbolism and American Literature* argued that even though "the symbolizing *process* was constantly at work" in the Puritan mind, Ramist logical structures stunted the development of true symbolism in a culture for whom "the truth of Scripture was not aesthetic but propositional" (1953:78, 84). As we have seen, Stanley Williams (1951), Sidney Lind (1948), and Roy Harvey Pearce (1950; 1961) found imaginative strictures in Puritanism that accounted for Taylor's shortcomings. This view recurred in Thomas's argument that *Gods Determinations* suffered as a play because of its doctrinal agenda (1965) and in Lynen's statement that the

Puritan distinction between "present" time and God's eternity kept Taylor from developing his metaphors into true symbols (1969:68). Lynen claimed that because Taylor's "way of seeing" precluded the ability to "unite the sensible object and the universal meaning" (50), his conceits remained analogic rather than fully symbolic. Taylor's separation from a sophisticated literary community emerged as another explanation for such shortcomings. Although Warren (1941:368) and Stanford (1965:44) connected Taylor's lack of polish with his isolation, the strongest statement of this view came from Grant, who asserted that if Taylor had stayed in England his taste would have been refined, probably in the direction of the verse of Isaac Watts (1961). At the end of the decade M. G. Krishnamurthi similarly argued that Taylor's removal from the established literary culture of England limited his imagery to local references and "personal relationships," and thus impeded his full development of a metaphysical decorum, especially in his diction (1969:39). But Taylor's isolation could be seen as a blessing if the critic valued the deliberately "primitive" as a signature of American writing. Thomas H. Johnson had set the precedent for transforming Taylor's flaws as a polished poet into the virtues of a proto-American primitive who "struck out for himself" (1939a:17). Martz agreed that Taylor's isolation from English literary society contributed to the vigor and honesty of his language. "Out of his very deficiencies," Martz commented, Taylor created "a work of rugged and original integrity" that anticipated an American language and literature (1960:xxxvii). Grabo, who argued that Taylor's inner life may have been intensified by his relative isolation in "the suburbs of glory in America" (1961a:173), later suggested that devotional intensity like that voiced in Taylor's work provided a meaningful link between seventeenth- and nineteenth-century American writing (1969). Arguing that "the art of Puritan meditation was basically a method for channeling emotion into verbal structures — a poetic method" (21), Grabo replaced literary form with visionary intensity as the defining characteristic of an American tradition of writing.

Remarking that it is "a nice theoretical question whether Taylor is an 'American' poet," Warren concluded that "it is his isolation," if anything, "that makes him so," especially in the Meditations as "the fruits of his aloneness" (1962:61). Some critics, however, were less ambivalent about Taylor's "American" identity. National pride in this genuine colonial poet moved many to reject the assumption that he failed at something that his English forebears did better. In their view, he succeeded in doing something new in anticipation of subsequent American writing. The metrical choppiness, the quirky syntax, the idiosyncratic diction, the seeming disregard of normal poetic standards — all could be seen as the beginning of an American tendency to push language to its limits as a means of breaking through the mask and achieving a warmer sense of the divine. This approach, a particularized application of Perry Miller's influential 1940 argument for a literary progression "From Edwards to Emerson," from Puritan spirituality to Transcendental vision, had also been foreshadowed by Randall Stewart, who argued for a seventeenth-century Puritan humanism that extended, "with modifications," into the nineteenth-century American Renaissance (1946:341). A. W. Plumstead reaffirmed the role of Puritanism in fostering subsequent American literary traits, especially a propensity toward symbolism, a sense of national destiny, a conflict between rationality and emotion, and the relation of the individual to society (1963).

With the Puritans positioned as forerunners of a later America, the search for Taylor's literary heirs became nearly as urgent as the search for his predecessors had been in earlier decades. In the mid-1960s Jared Curtis compared Taylor to an obvious descendant, Emily Dickinson (1964). Curtis found a particular analog in a double vision that encompassed dichotomies of outer and inner self, matter and spirit, time and eternity, and finitude and infinity. Curtis concluded that Dickinson was even more isolated than Taylor: for once, it was another poet's "range of experience" and expression that was "not so wide or so rich." Martha Ballinger united Taylor and Bradstreet with such later poets as Dickinson and Elinor Wylie in their shared invocation of a "metaphysical heredity" stemming back to Taylor (1965:80). Betty E. Chmaj compared metaphors of resurrection and transcendence in Puritan verse, including Taylor's, with American Finnish Lutheran hymns, confirming the eschatological thrust of both and their sources in Isaiah, Canticles, and Revelation (1964). At the end of the decade Lynen identified in Taylor's Puritan thought the germ of an American notion of an eternal present holding an analogous relation to an eternal reality (1969). Lynen found a parallel to Whitman and Eliot in Taylor's tendency in *Gods Determinations* to repeat the "whole pattern in small in each phase of the poem's development," thereby creating an episodic structure central to subsequent American writing (66). The following year saw the English translation of Ursula Brumm's 1963 study, which connected Puritan typology as practiced by Taylor, the Mathers, and Edwards, with symbolic perception and expression in nineteenth-century America (1970). Brumm's Taylor, whose biblical sources will be discussed below, represented a crucial stage in the gradual liberation of the American imagination from its initial obsession with biblical and doctrinal revelation toward a truly symbolic reading of nature.

Hyatt Waggoner also depicted Taylor as a proto-American, finding in Puritan verse an awareness of evil that foreshadowed a "dark strain" in American literature (1964:292). For Waggoner, however, Taylor's proto-American beliefs did not result in coherent poems. Arguing that the "Preface" to *Gods Determinations* contained images that were not true symbols but merely "signs" without "implicit meaning," Waggoner maintained that Taylor was doomed by his theological preoccupations to write "minor poetry" (305). Waggoner developed these views four years later in his study of American poetry to Whitman (1968). Although Taylor's Puritan "bigotry" pushed him toward extremes of dogmatism and bad taste, his use of the senses in search of the divine made him a forerunner of the American romantics; for Waggoner, Taylor was a visionary who manifested "perhaps equal parts of Puritan eschatology and Transcendental seeking" (16). Waggoner also identified American precedents in Taylor's preoccupation with human nature and his insistent stress on visionary matter over literary manner. Citing "Upon a Spider Catching a Fly" as an example of these pre-Emersonian tendencies, Waggoner judged Taylor to be a poet able to "bend language to his purposes" if it furthered the vision that he sought (24). As Waggoner noted, whether Taylor was seen in a British or an American context made a profound difference in assessing his achievement. Echoing Martz's warning against seeing Taylor as a "burlap version of Herbert" (1960:xviii), Waggoner commented that comparison with Herbert made him seem "hardly worth reading" (24). But as the growing interest in Taylor as a Transcendental precursor suggested, the status of burlap had risen considerably in the 1960s: reading Taylor in the context of Emerson and later American symbolists made him seem like a "poetic pioneer."

Reading Taylor without reducing him to a cruder Herbert also demanded a closer look at the intellectual and cultural materials that he turned into poetry. Most source studies in the 1960s countered the image of an American primitive, instead revealing a learned, even bookish figure whose intellectual curiosity was clear from the remarkable range and depth of his reading. Sister M. Theresa Clare affirmed the competence of Westfield's poet-physician by showing that the medicinal plants cited in Meditation 2.62 were not simply appropriate thematically but were actual sources of therapeutic substances

(1960). Calvin Israel found precedent in Sidney and Suckling for Taylor's reference to "barleybreaks," a popular game mentioned in Meditation 1.40 (1966); as we have seen, Robert Arner focused more generally on the sources and functions of gaming images in this poem (1969). Extending the work of Robert D. Hodges (1959), Robert H. Woodward suggested several sources, including Sir Thomas Browne's *Religio Medici* and Bishop John Wilkins's *Mathematical Magick* (London: 1680), for allusions to Albertus Magnus's talking head and the "Fly of Steele" in Meditation 2.56 (1963). A more specifically literary source, first suggested by Johnson (1937:319) and Grabo (1961a:154-59), was pursued by Thomas E. Johnston, Jr., who argued that Taylor was a deliberate emblematist, participating in a tradition popularized by such writers as George Wither, Francis Quarles, Herbert, and Bunyan (1968/69). Johnston argued that Taylor explicitly referred to emblems and other pictorial devices, invoked emblem-like religious symbols, used his biblical headnotes like an emblem writer's *sententia*, and framed moral interpretations of the images that he invoked. For Johnston, emblem books shaped Taylor's conception of his role as God's poet, though he modified the tradition in Puritan ways by basing his emblems exclusively on the Bible. Maintaining that Taylor created emblems more skillfully as the Meditations progressed, Johnston stressed the poet's desire to be made into God's "emblem" as an elect soul (195). Allan I. Ludwig also noted Taylor's relation to iconography in his study of New England gravestone art, citing Taylor's "love-drenched poetry" as evidence of a rich Puritan devotional life (1966:5). Ludwig found numerous parallels between tombstone carvings and such Taylor images as death's arrows, the tree of life, the breasts of the Bride-Church, the eucharistic wine, and the spherical orb of the saved soul.

Emblematists and tombstone carvers, of course, shared a common source that the Puritan Taylor could hardly have escaped. While nearly everyone acknowledged his extensive reliance on the Bible, it was not until the 1960s that detailed work on his indebtedness to Scripture and scriptural exegesis began. Earlier critics like Lind (1948) and Pearce (1950) tended to see the Bible as an impediment to the development of his poetic imagination, and even as sympathetic a critic as Stanford, for whom Taylor's best work had even greater power than Herbert's, conceded that the poetry was harmed by "too much dependence on Biblical language, and not enough classical and humanistic refinement" (1965). Increasingly, however, the Bible came to be seen as an enabling influence on the poems. Karen E. Rowe advanced this newer view by arguing that reading the poetry in light of its biblical contexts could "illuminate" Taylor's art considerably (1968). Rowe demonstrated this point in a discussion of Meditation 2.27 in terms of its proper text — the descriptions of leprosy in Leviticus 13:45-46 and 14:1-32, and not Exodus 29:20 as Stanford (1957) had maintained. Clendenning similarly defended the importance of biblical contexts in his reading of "The Reflexion," stressing Taylor's unusual inversion of the Bride/Bridegroom roles in the Canticles allegory (1964:210). The growing scrutiny of biblical sources in the 1960s was reflected in the fact that the decade saw no fewer than four treatments of a single Bible image, the Tree of Life. Hedberg's analysis of Meditation 1.29, more a series of lists than a unified discussion, briefly cited the role played by the Tree in concretizing Taylor's "homely mysticism" (1960:265). Cecelia Halbert Tichi, tracing the image to the flower and "knot" motifs of "Upon Wedlock," argued that in Meditation 1.29 Taylor's hope to be grafted into the "all-encompassing tree of God-universe-celestial hierarchy" reflected a more personal application of the image than could be found in the poetry of Quarles and Marvell (1966:26). Thomas Werge and Ursula Brumm soon accused Tichi of neglecting the biblical and theological sources of the image. In an article originally published in German in 1967, Brumm traced the grafting images to Romans in support of her view that Taylor's poetic was "theological" rather than metaphysical (1968:73). Arguing that the Tree's exegetical status as a type of Christ helped Taylor give concrete form to his doctrinal themes, Brumm cited Meditations 1.29 and 2.113 to connect the Genesis Tree with the Tree of Jesse, a popular medieval representation of Christ's spiritual ancestry. For Brumm, these biblical underpinnings suggested that Taylor did not see his verses as "poetry in the secular sense," but as theological clarifications and acts of praise (82). Werge similarly argued that Taylor's figures were as "not narrowly poetic but theological, not simply aesthetic fancies but fundamental Puritan ideas" (1968/69:199). Citing the medieval use of the Tree as a representation of the Fall and redemption, Werge suggested Tertullian, Augustine, and Calvin as Taylor's sources for the image, which he also found in Wigglesworth and Thomas Shepard. Widespread theological tradition, and not specific poems by Marvell and Quarles, provided the source for grafting imagery that illustrated a "dialectic" of sin and grace central to Taylor's verse as well as to Puritan thought (202).

Owing in part to an interest in biblical and critical hermeneutics in European universities, Brumm and fellow German Peter Nicolaisen offered the fullest discussions in the 1960s of Taylor and the Bible. Although Brumm's work appeared first, its full impact on Taylor studies was not felt until seven years later, when its English translation appeared. Nicolaisen's study, revised from his dissertation at the University of Kiel, never received the recognition it deserved because it was never translated (the book did, however, include a five-page summary in English). Nicolaisen stressed the Bible as Taylor's nearly exclusive source for images appropriate to his meditative aims (1966). Taylor's images were neither local nor naturalistic representations, but theological vehicles by which he contrasted the sinful nature of man with the glory of Christ, the real and unchanging subject of the Meditations. Maintaining that the Word-centered dimension of Puritanism pushed Taylor to rely more heavily than the metaphysicals on the Bible for his themes and images, Nicolaisen argued that Taylor saw earthly images as useful only for depicting human sin and underscoring the ultimate impossibility of bridging the gap between the human and the divine with language. Exploiting biblical images to intensify his response to Christ and the Supper in a manner consistent with methods advanced by such meditative writers as Richard Baxter, Taylor sharpened the contrast between personal unworth and Christic glory through a rhetorical *amplificatio* that exaggerated both extremes. The more restrained Herbert and the other metaphysicals, by contrast, relied chiefly on *illustratio*, which generally resulted in more coherent and stable images. In contrast to Johnston's stress on the visual quality of the poetry (1968/69), Nicolaisen argued that Taylor's images consistently resisted clear visualization; the poet's often-noted leaps from one image to another served to amplify but not concretize the ineffable. In *Gods Determinations*, Nicolaisen argued, Taylor's aims were more directly illustrative; as a result, the imagery was more sensory and tangible. Agreeing with Grabo (1961a:86) that *Gods Determinations* was best seen as an extended meditation leading from intellectual understanding to emotional arousal, Nicolaisen argued that its earlier sections, which contained more images derived from everyday life, contrasted with the final lyrics, which invoked the eternal and biblical mode of the Meditations. Taylor's occasional poems aligned themselves with the earlier sections of *Gods Determinations* in their acknowledgment of the physical world. In the more otherworldly Meditations, typology provided a major source of imagery, particularly at the beginning of the Second Series. Relating the typological matching of Old Testament prefiguration and New Testament fulfillment to Taylor's covenant theology, Nicolaisen argued that typology helped Taylor clarify his themes without descending to the created world and thereby sullying the picture. In the later Meditations Taylor turned to the ahistorical allegory of the Song of Songs for the same purpose: to ground his contemplations in biblically-sanctioned pointers to the divine.

Brumm, narrowing her focus to typology but applying it more broadly, placed Taylor in a sequence in American writing that led from historically bound and theologically rigid Puritan typology to the looser, more sophisticated, and partially secularized symbolism practiced by the classic writers of the American Renaissance (1970). Like Nicolaisen, Brumm argued that critics had ignored the biblical structures from which Taylor's imagery derived much of its theological coherence and significance. Maintaining that Puritans avoided Catholic mysticism by reducing the physical world to a symbol of the divine, she underscored Taylor's Puritan separation of "divine metaphor" from "human metaphor (used by men to depict God's greatness)": "the Bible's basis in concrete reality" could not be permitted to "vanish" in loosely metaphorical interpretations that gave every event "a parallel spiritual meaning" (80). The tendency to lapse into the freer inventions of medieval allegorists, however, was a trap that even the scrupulously orthodox Taylor could not entirely avoid. Finding in the Second Series a movement toward suspect symbolic modes, Brumm suggested that Taylor's aesthetic orthodoxy was partly undermined by the rich Canticles imagery that occupied his later years, when his "fantasy bursts the confines of Puritan sobriety and succumbs to the charm of biblico-Oriental word pictures" (82). In the late Meditations, Brumm argued, Taylor enacted an "allegorization of the world," an "absolute spiritualizing of all images" that "far surpasses what the Puritan considered theologically permissible" (83). Because the most sacred poetic source available to Taylor had "led him to a sort of allegorical interpretation of the Scriptures, which Puritanism rejected as Catholic and medieval," Taylor never published his poetry (57). The German original of Brumm's study had been published soon after Grabo (1961a) argued for the Puritan acceptance of precisely the sort of images that Brumm found suspect, and soon after Murphy (1962) debunked the legend of Taylor's deathbed prohibition. And as Nicolaisen pointed out, Taylor's lush garden imagery did not constitute an allegorization of this world, but mimicked a biblically-sanctioned allegorization of the next world through earthly images (1966:136). Brumm's attempt to locate Taylor within a Miller-like progression from typology to symbolism may have prompted her to underestimate the artistic conservatism of a poet who refused even to contemporize the types as foreshadowings of New England's mission. Finally, she underestimated the importance and legitimacy of allegory within Protestant exegesis, especially in commentaries on the Canticles. Still, Brumm's work played a pioneering role in stimulating a vital investigation of biblical underpinnings for the poetry. Special issues of *Early American Literature* devoted to Taylor and to typology would soon follow her lead — and Nicolaisen's — in probing the imaginative structures of the Bible as keys to Taylor's art.

Taylor's anomalous status in early New England diminished greatly during the 1960s. Early in the decade Darrel Abel had called Taylor's verse "the finest esthetic flowering of the Puritan sensibility" but also "a departure from the Puritan formula of simple doctrine in prosaic language" (1963:87, 91). Five years later, in one of two anthologies of early American poetry prompted largely by Taylor's popularity, Kenneth Silverman claimed that the poet led a life "not at all different from that of many American Puritans" (1968:173). Indeed, even the rigid first generation would have found "instructive and exciting" his "ritualized struggle to grasp the mystery of communion" (174, 176). Harrison T. Meserole, editor of the second anthology, underscored Taylor's active involvement in the affairs of Westfield and New England and his orthodox use of the Bible and typology as a means of "seeing order in God's spiritual and material world" (1968:120). Active minister and private visionary, chanter of ritual and seeker of order, exemplary Puritan and unusual Puritan, English metaphysical and American proto-romantic — these oppositions illustrate the range of views still possible in the 1960s. But critical opinion was beginning to coalesce. At the start of the new decade, Grabo (1970:22, 1971:345) and Constance Gefvert (1971:xv) agreed that three distinct phases had marked the first thirty years of Taylor scholarship. In the 1940s critics tried to define Taylor's place in literary history; in the 1950s they explored his relation to Puritan aesthetics and theology; and in the 1960s they explicated individual texts in light of specific sources and influences. Although Taylor's phenomenal rise owed much to the popularity of the English metaphysicals, it was clear by 1970 that to read him required a reconstruction — as far as possible — of his uniquely Puritan mental world. The urgency of this task helped Taylor survive the decline of a New Critical aesthetic, even though his sudden entry onto the literary scene had been smoothed by the apparent capacity of his verse to satisfy that aesthetic, however unevenly. The gradual return to criticism of contextual approaches —

questions of authorial intention, source, audience, intellectual milieu, and other extratextual considerations — squared well with the realization that the nature of Taylor's Puritan imagination was only just beginning to be understood. Demonstrating the workings of that imagination in greater detail would become the central task of the decade ahead.

3: Maturation — The 1970s

BY 1970 THE SCHOLARSHIP had reached what Norman Grabo called a "post-adolescent, if not entirely mature, stage" (1971:356). In the following decade Taylor studies matured: the 1970s opened with extensive bibliographies by Grabo (1971) and Constance Gefvert (1971), reached midpoint with major critical studies by William J. Scheick and Karl Keller, and ended with Taylor's incorporation into important treatments by Robert Daly and Barbara Lewalski of American Puritan poetry and English devotional verse. Taylor scholarship began to come of age in 1969, when Everett Emerson, at the suggestion of Kenneth Silverman, devoted a special issue of *Early American Literature* to Taylor. Emerson's comment that "we think that there is much of value here" turned out to be an understatement: the essays in the Taylor issue (Winter 1969/70) mapped out major directions that would define the scholarship for years to come. The following issue (Spring 1970), devoted to biblical typology and guest edited by Sacvan Bercovitch, contained additional essays on the importance of this exegetical mode for understanding Taylor's verse.

Though widely varied in their topics and methods, the contributors to the *EAL* issues addressed an increasingly vexing problem: now that Taylor's religious orthodoxy was firmly established, how did he transform his beliefs into such vivid and engaging poetry? The scholars assembled by Emerson and Bercovitch took four basic approaches to the question: the nature of Taylor's rhetoric and language, the relation between the formal structures of the verse and his meditative activity, the influence of his biblical and exegetical sources, and his place at the beginning of an American tradition of symbolic thought and writing. Kenneth Ball and Gerhard Alexis took the first approach. Ball argued for Taylor's informed and purposeful appropriation of Renaissance rhetorical conventions as set forth in Thomas Wilson's influential *Arte of Rhetorique* (London: 1553) (1969/70). Agreeing with Peter Nicolaisen (1966) and Charles Mignon (1968) that amplification was Taylor's most frequent device, Ball maintained that Taylor used amplification not only to glorify Christ and deprecate man but sometimes to elevate both in a celebration of Christ's dual nature. Countering Donald Junkins's claim (1968) that Taylor eschewed traditional rhetoric as an ornamental distraction from his poetic aims, Ball integrated Taylor's skillful application of rhetoric with the poet's spiritual goals, citing the "elevating" images of Meditations 2.85 and 2.44 (84) and the "reducing" images of Meditations 1.31 and 1.40, in which negative amplification served as an apt rhetorical expression of Puritan humility (85). Alexis similarly defended the artistic purposes behind Taylor's difficult syntax. Focusing on the eighth stanza of the second "Christs Reply" in *Gods Determinations*, Alexis maintained that Taylor used "her games forth go" (*Poems*, 415) in the archaic sense of "she likes to go forth" (1969/70). The passage, Alexis argued, was typical of Taylor in its "intricate, if eventually rewarding, syntax" (100).

The four critics who centered on the relation between poetic form and meditative processes responded to Grabo's argument for a mystical Taylor (1961a) by confirming, in varying ways, Roy Harvey Pearce's comment that Puritan poetry reveals "a sense of composition as an on-going action" (1961:45). For Junkins, whose views came closest to Grabo's, Taylor's poetic was not so much mystical as vocational: his creative process could be understood only in the context of his calling as a Puritan preacher (1969/70: 67). Siding with Grabo (1962b:xli) against Robert Benton (1967:35-36) in the belief that Taylor based his poems on the doctrines of the corresponding sermons, Junkins blurred Grabo's distinction between the ratiocinative sermons and the affective poems by arguing for a greater overlap of the two modes in both genres. Because Taylor equated artistic with spiritual success, his "creative process" was inseparable from "his mystic Puritanism" (77). The religio-aesthetic unity of the verse was also confirmed by Karl Keller, who argued that Taylor saw his poems not as finished products but as part of an ongoing duty linked to his search for signs of his assurance as a redeemed soul (1969/70). Through the act of writing, Taylor, like other Puritans, was able to "re-enact the process of salvation and live in the illusion of development of self" (17). This ongoing contemplative and expressive process, by which Taylor was suspended between holy desire and an awareness of human limitations, made him an "exemplary private poet" whose isolation and independence defined his relevance for later American literature (22). Charles Mignon and Sargent Bush, Jr., related Taylor's religio-aesthetic process to spiritual paradoxes central to Puritan belief. For Mignon, the ongoing inner activity recorded in the Meditations accounted for their "interchangeable quality" over four decades of composition (1969/70:110). Citing Meditation 2.43, Mignon argued that the recurring tension between Taylor's varying surface strategies and his unchanging aims and larger structures reflected his "attempt to capture a certitude of eternity in the ambiguity of the present" and made possible his consequent "suspension of belief between doubt and certitude" (110). For Mignon, Taylor enacted a three-part pattern of self-scrutiny, the contemplation of doctrine, and an application of doctrine by which he tested his assurance and sought a closer relation to the divine. By continually internalizing and verbalizing spiritual paradoxes central to Puritan theology, Taylor confirmed his ability "to entertain eternal ideas in the single moment of controlled poetic time" (115). Bush found similar paradoxes of belief at the core of *Gods Determinations* (1969/70). Disputing Pearce's claim that "for all his concern with *discordia concors*, paradox interests Taylor little" (1961:47), Bush cited Thomas Hooker, Samuel Willard, Michael Wigglesworth, and the *Christographia* sermons to demonstrate that paradox was as central to *Gods Determinations* as it was to Puritan spirituality generally. Taylor's fascination with paradox emerged in his frequent posing of oppositions that could achieve harmony only within a gracious perspective, oppositions embodied in the two sets of characters who vie for Soul's allegiance and Soul's suspension between grace and damnation. The ending of *Gods Determinations*, Bush argued, embodied the greatest Puritan paradox of all: Soul clings to faith in spite of the convicting lessons of reason.

By describing a religio-aesthetic dynamic fully accountable within Puritan inner experience, Mignon and Bush offered implicit refutations of Grabo's mysticism thesis (1961a). Other contributors to the special issues reinforced this view by arguing that Taylor's meditative imagination was shaped more by specific biblical sources than by broad patterns of Christian spirituality. James T. Callow, for instance, insisted that Grabo's (1962b) and Junkins's (1969/70) arguments for the primacy of sermonic doctrines did not rule out the importance of the biblical headnotes (1969/70). Defining Meditations 1.19-22 as a unit in which Taylor dealt with the nature and efficacy of his attempts to praise Christ, Callow identified as the chief source of the poems not just their shared headnote but its context in Paul's command that "every tongue should confess" Christ's glory (Phil. 2:11). Paul's words, Callow maintained, forced Taylor to consider not just his duty to praise but his fallen inability to do so. Demonstrating how this theme unified the sequence, Callow concluded that critics "should not rely on the motto alone but check in the Bible for new leads" (94). The importance of biblical frameworks was reinforced by Kathy Siebel and Thomas M. Davis, who discussed Taylor's use of *aqua vitae* as an image of the cleansing power of grace (1969/70). Suggesting that Taylor's metaphorical equating of physical with spiritual corruption enacted Paul's exhortation to "cleanse ourselves from all filthiness of the flesh and spirit, perfecting holiness in the fear of God" (2 Cor. 7:1), Siebel and Davis argued that the image reconfirmed the fundamental unity of Taylor's callings as poet, pastor, and physician.

The most pervasive biblical source explored in these issues was typology, a richly symbolic structure that countered, as Bercovitch noted, the image of Puritans as "Ramist-bound scholastics who denigrated the imagination" (1970:6). Thomas Davis, Karl Keller, and Robert Reiter demonstrated the impact of this source on Taylor's poetry. In the typology issue Davis recounted the complex history of typological exegesis, beginning with the New Testament and such early commentators as the Jewish Philo and the Christian Origen, both of Alexandria (1970). The proliferation of allegorical readings in the Middle Ages prompted the Reformers' desire to recover a literal sense of Scripture, which propelled typology, with its preservation of the literal and historical dimensions of the biblical text, toward the center of Protestant exegesis. Tracing the growing use of typology by Tyndale, Luther, and Calvin as a means of avoiding the excesses of Alexandrian allegorizing and medieval scholasticism, Davis pointed out that vivid imagery like Taylor's had always been central to the tradition. This cast doubts on arguments by Mindele Black (1956:175-76), Ursula Brumm (1970:82), and others regarding the suspect nature of Taylor's language. Moreover, typology helped foster "an imagistic consciousness" that enabled Taylor and his contemporaries to clarify their place in providential history (41). In the Taylor issue Davis applied these traditions to the Meditations, arguing that the poet moved beyond "the limited type-antitype construct" toward a "broader" but still orthodox stance in the later typological poems (1969/70:28). Citing Taylor's use of the types in the *Christographia* and the anti-Stoddard *Treatise*, Davis maintained that Taylor's typology came closest to that of Origen, whom Taylor apparently considered orthodox despite his role in the development of Alexandrian allegory. Although the typological poetry, which Davis extended beyond Meditations 2.1-30 to encompass most of the first sixty-some poems of the Series, followed the general organization of Samuel Mather's *The Figures or Types of the Old Testament* (Dublin: 1683), Davis proposed that their deeper impetus came from Taylor's reaction to Stoddard's innovations concerning the Supper. As the Second Series progressed, however, Taylor moved beyond the types toward a "relatively freer mode of allegory" that was "more congenial" to poetry (36). Citing Taylor's later tendency to read the types less as history than as "reflections of his own spiritual state" (38), Davis concluded that even though Taylor's typological allusions were not original, he personalized them in "a symbology that is as vital and as intense as in any poet's work" (41).

In contrast to Davis's view that Taylor's personalizing of the types was consistent with traditional exegesis, Keller stressed Taylor's exceptionalism, depicting him less as a conservative typologist in the vein of Samuel Mather, Benjamin Keach, and William Guild than as an innovative forerunner of later symbolic modes (1970a). For Keller, Taylor's innovation emerged especially in the poet's playful assertion of "individuality within the closed system of thought that typology represented" (1970a:124). Taylor's meditative exuberance was embodied most directly in his witty manipulation of the types as a sacred "language game" (125). While most Puritans invoked the types to link New England with redemptive history and cosmology, Taylor sought to "slip himself into" the types and thus "into the plan of salvation by means of the vehicle of language" (130). Because he consistently focused on Christ as the fulfillment of all types, Taylor could both cherish the world and avoid the heresy of overvaluing it (136). Keller concluded that typology permitted Taylor to anticipate symbolic modes of thought and writing that would culminate in Emerson and the Transcendentalists. Reiter was more cautious in his discussion of Meditations 2.1-30 (1970). Agreeing with Grabo that the poetry represented the final stage of a devotional process that encompassed the sermons, Reiter traced the major typological themes through the sequence, stressing the importance of light/dark imagery as a device that unified Taylor's varied poetic uses of the types. Arguing that the poems revealed a three-part structure consisting of the confession of sin, the examination of the type at hand, and the affective application of its doctrinal significance, Reiter agreed with Davis that in the later typological poetry Taylor placed more emphasis on his spiritual state. For Reiter, the congruence of meditative and doctrinal concerns in the types allowed Taylor to make competent poems out of an otherwise "intractable" and "unpoetic" biblical subject (122).

Davis, Keller, and Reiter disagreed on the significance of the types for Taylor's poetry. For Reiter, typology provided useful but uneven material for the verse; if a particular type happened to synthesize Taylor's doctrinal and meditative concerns, he could develop it into a successful poem (1970:123). For Davis, typology took on greater significance: it was less a source of poetic matter than a structure informing Taylor's poetic manner, the basis of a rich "symbology" that surpassed mere ornament (1969/70:41). Keller went even further, though at some risk of ignoring Taylor's conservatism. While Davis argued that Taylor abandoned the types after having personalized them as fully as tradition allowed (36), Keller's view that the poet's typology went beyond Protestant standards rested on a broad definition that included "Canticles types" (1970a:130), even though most Puritans saw the Song of Songs as allegorical rather than typological because it was not rooted in historical events. Moreover, Taylor's stylized nature images did not square well with Keller's assertion that typology rehabilitated the created world: the poet did not "love" this world (136) so much as he subsumed it into a system of biblical pointers toward the next. Keller's broader reading of Taylor's typology stemmed in part from his interest in the poet's American identity as a forerunner of the Transcendentalists. On the most immediate level, Keller's twin concerns — typology and Americanness — seemed mutually exclusive. Bercovitch suggested that a preoccupation with "National Character" among Americanists had made them slow to appreciate typology, a decidedly "foreign" influence on colonial writing (1970:6). But as Brumm had demonstrated in the 1963 German original of *American Thought and Religious Typology* (1970), Taylor's fascination with the types could be located at the beginning of a national affinity for symbolism that peaked with the American romantics. In the Taylor issue Keller developed Brumm's approach by arguing that Taylor's poetry reflected a preoccupation with process and a consequent search for repeatable structures central to American writing and identity (1969/70). For Keller, Taylor's status as an American literary forebear emerged not from the few local allusions of a poet who seemed not "to know where he was at geographically" (11), but from a defense of New England piety that made him "a kind of nationalist" (13). Keller extended this argument in the typology issue by maintaining that in his self-awareness and his search for "correspondences" with nature, Taylor was "a first, small version of Emerson" who illustrated "a transcendentalized thaw of Puritan esthetics" (1970a:132). Arguing for broad continuities uniting Taylor's search for the divine in nature with the nineteenth-century "deification of Nature," Keller proposed that Emerson simply shifted the focus from Taylor's Christ to a Holy Spirit reconstituted as the "Over-Soul" (135). Seen within this framework, Taylor represented the start of a more secular typology in which faith and imagination would finally overcome their Puritan opposition and merge in romantic symbolism. Taylor, Keller concluded, was "closer to Emerson in his esthetics than to Calvin" (138).

The *EAL* issues ushered in an era marked more by consensus than conflict. Two scholarly and critical questions, for example, seemed largely settled. The first was Taylor's alleged mysticism. Accounting for the poet's religio-poetic experience within Puritan devotional traditions, Junkins, Keller, Mignon, and Bush argued so persuasively that the considerable value of Grabo's "mystical" reading was obscured. The second question was the effect of Taylor's frontier isolation on his art. All the contributors to the special issues, but especially Ball and Alexis, depicted Taylor as a conscious artist who succeeded in writing the way he wanted to, and not as a weak poet who failed in his attempts to write like the smoother metaphysicals. In their study of Taylor's biblical and hermeneutic sources, Davis, Keller, and Reiter implicitly cautioned against purely belletristic readings that ignored exegetical contexts inseparable from the poet's imagination. Two years later, when their essays reappeared in Bercovitch's *Typology and Early American Literature* (1972), typology emerged as the most compelling vehicle yet by which Taylor's artistry could be convincingly joined to his Puritanism. A related issue, though not settled, was clarified for further investigation. Keller's view of Taylor as a "version" of Emerson sparked a renewed search to define the poet's relevance for subsequent American literary history. The year after the Bercovitch collection appeared, Larzer Ziff argued that although Taylor was a "minor poet" when placed in the British context, he was important as one of the few early New Englanders to write "verse that lives beyond the occasion" (1973:258). For Ziff, Taylor's lack of audience and his dated poetic style produced the kinds of flaws usually associated with primitive artists. Calling Taylor "mystical well beyond the Puritan standard," he maintained that the verse was distinctly "unrepresentative of the main thrust" of the poet's culture (259). Most critics, however, argued that Taylor's poetry existed "because of," as Bush wrote of *Gods Determinations*, and "not in spite of, the Puritan milieu" (1969/70:53). Scholars working under this assumption began closer investigations of Taylor's place in that milieu, especially his intellectual, theological, and devotional sources.

Two years after the *EAL* issues, Reid Maynard summarized what had become the dominant opinion: Taylor's enthusiasm for the Supper was fully consistent with Puritan sacramentalism; his striking imagery reflected not only his biblical sources but their conventional exegetical and devotional application; and finally, Taylor's views on predestination and election were thoroughly orthodox (1972). Indeed, the more scholars learned in the 1970s, the more rigid the poet's orthodoxy seemed. Donald Stanford, for instance, revealed Taylor's censure of Benjamin Ruggles of Suffield for "Presbyterian" leanings, an episode reflected in the poet's attacks on "Young Cockerills" in his elegy for Samuel Hooker (1971a). Taylor's rabid anti-Catholicism emerged in David Sowd's discussion of his "answer" to a "Popish pamphlet" that blamed London's Great Fire of 1666 on England's persecution of Catholics (1975). Mukhtar Ali Isani, publishing and commenting on a letter from Taylor to his former college roommate Samuel Sewall, confirmed the poet's relish of spirited debate — in this case, over the proper interpretation of the pouring of the Sixth Vial in Revelation 16:12 (1971). While Sewall felt that the prophecy referred to the fall of Spanish America, Taylor held the more conventional view that it foretold the decline of the Ottoman Empire. Another letter to Sewall, which Davis published, revealed their shared denunciation of Jeremiah Dummer, who argued that the observance of the Sabbath was "exclusively ceremonial and therefore not perpetually binding" (1978a:107).

As Isani noted, Taylor "participated with remarkable fullness in the intellectual life of New England" (1972:123). New work on the Stoddardean controversy reinforced the poet's conservative activism. In his study of Puritan sacramental theology, E. Brooks Holifield argued that although Taylor agreed with Stoddard that many believers hesitated to become full church members because of their excessive scrupulosity, he was unwilling to tinker with the exclusive nature of the Supper in order to encourage their conversion (1974). For him, Holifield confirmed, the sacrament "was more than simply a sermon" or a converting ordinance (215). Paradoxically, however, there may have been something progressive about Taylor's reverence for the Supper as a seal of grace foreshadowed by the Jewish Passover. As Holifield suggested, Taylor's views may have reflected a general shift among Puritans in both Englands away from rational structures toward an increased emphasis on the religious affections. Indeed, Taylor provided prime evidence that many Puritans possessed a "remarkable sacramental consciousness" (224). James W. Barbour discussed an especially explicit poetic expression of this consciousness, the anti-Stoddard Meditations (2.102-111), in light of three decades of Taylor's prose defenses of an exclusive Supper (1975). Confirming his "essentially integrated sensibility" as poet and preacher by demonstrating the theological and imagistic unity of the poems and the prose, Barbour further undermined the view that Taylor was torn between art and orthodoxy (156). Taylor's conservative faith was also clarified by documents that Davis and other scholars published during the 1970s. The poet's growing opposition to Stoddardeanism could be seen, for instance, in the two versions of the "Foundation Day" sermon: an outline of the more aggressive 1690 revision was published with commentary by Dean Hall and Davis, who noted Taylor's "intensified concern for the misreading of scriptural language" (1975:207). Taylor's revised attack reflected the fact that although Stoddard proposed his changes in 1679, he didn't put them into practice until some ten years later; Davis (1974) and Davis and Jeff Jeske (1976) published Stoddard's declaration of his views, which Taylor had entered into his "Extracts" manuscript. Another sign of Taylor's uncompromising theology came from an early sermon on the "Day of Judgment" published by Davis and Virginia L. Davis (1972). Taylor's remarks revealed that his view of Doomsday was every bit as harsh as that of his seemingly sterner contemporaries, though conveyed with the same "imagistic intensity" that marked his poetry (526).

Other new material strengthened the bonds between the life and the art. Davis published the three versions of Taylor's "Valedictory" poem, an elaborate farewell to the world that revealed a poet more engaged with his surroundings — if only to repudiate them — than the otherworldly Meditations suggested (1972). As Davis noted, the "Valediction" reinforced Taylor's devotion to poetry as "the mode that had structured his personal relation to God throughout his life" (39). The centrality of the Bible in Taylor's spiritual and poetic vocations was also evidenced by his extensive verse paraphrases of Job and the Psalms. Citing Calvin's view of the Psalms as a sublime model for divine praise, Thomas and Virginia Davis suggested that Taylor's Psalm paraphrases comprised a "poetic workshop" in which the poet refined his meditative voice; indeed, the Hebrew Psalms may have constituted the most immediate model for his devotional verse (1977:469). The "Valediction" and the Psalm paraphrases shed new light on Taylor as a reviser — and sometimes a discarder — of his work. Additional evidence of his careful revising came from an earlier version of "A Fig for Thee, Oh! Death," published by Arthur Forstater and Thomas Davis (1976). Suggesting a source in Edward Pearse's *The Great Concern* (Boston: 1711), Forstater and Davis argued that the vivid struggle against death and the unifying sexual images revealed Taylor's creative modification of his source. Taylor's rarely examined role as a public poet was confirmed by his elegies on Richard and Increase Mather, the latter poem existing in three versions; the Mather elegies, Davis argued, lent further support to poetry's role in pulling together Taylor's doctrinal, social, and personal concerns (1976/77). Keller argued that the poet's lifelong involvement with the Mathers reconfirmed his "place among his contemporaries" (1978:135). Citing the incorporation of material from his letters into books by Increase and Cotton Mather, Keller suggested that the Mathers inspired Taylor's general poetic development as well as specific works. This ongoing contact with New England's first family, Keller observed, corrected "the stereotype of Taylor as the isolated, private poet of early America" (130). Finally, Charles Mignon confirmed a public and sermonic context for the typological Meditations when he announced the discovery of thirty-six corresponding sermons "Upon the Types of the Old Testament" (1977/78). When Mignon published the first of these sermons two years later (1980), the unity of Taylor's public and private expressions of faith was sealed.

Investigations into Taylor's wide and deep reading underscored the fact that he was neither a social nor an intellectual hermit. Although Stanford pointed out that the low assessed values of certain items in his library inventory indicated that he probably did not own complete sets of some of the works, especially those of Origen and Augustine (1971b), Thomas and Virginia Davis argued from citations in Taylor's prose that he had access to a number of works not listed in the inventory, including those of Origen, Tertullian, Cyprian, Augustine, and Justin Martyr (1971/72). Some of these works could even be identified by specific edition. Most likely, the Davises suggested, expensive multi-volume sets were dispersed among Taylor's survivors before the list was drawn up. Harrison T. Meserole, impressed with "the comprehensive range" of Taylor's reading, called for further investigation into his myriad sources, popular as well as learned (1973:126). Meserole stressed in particular the need to explore Taylor's use of folklore, as evidenced by some forty references in the Meditations to folk medicine, beliefs, and customs; also in need of investigation were the poet's technical and scientific allusions, for which Meserole cited Tobias Beuteln's description of the Dresden treasure house as a probable source in Meditations 2.56 and 2.109. Taylor's folk sources were taken up by Robert D. Arner, who maintained that the poet used folk proverbs, metaphors, and puns in Meditation 1.40 to create an underlying coherence that was not obvious if such sources were ignored (1973a). In addition to demonstrating Taylor's "linguistic virtuosity" in appropriating folk speech, Arner argued that such borrowings strengthened the "moral implications" of the gaming images (7). Elsewhere Arner discussed the influence on *Gods Determinations* of folk expressions and proverbs, which enhanced a colloquial tone appropriate to Taylor's purpose and audience (1973c). In addition to citing the role of folk speech in lending drama and vividness to the poem, Arner argued that Taylor's juxtaposition of folk and epic diction created an "uneasiness" in reading analogous to the spiritual "uncertainty" of his audience (3). Taylor also used folk proverbs to intensify his depiction of Satan and to clarify doctrine, thus fulfilling Puritan demands for a plain style in didactic writing.

Other scholars pursued Taylor's scientific interests. His fascination with natural history, reflected in his unfinished poem on "The Great Bones of Claverack," was confirmed by Lawrence Lan Sluder, who pointed out the presence in his library of several works dealing with medicine and natural science (1973). For Sluder, the surprisingly untheological poem reflected eighteenth-century "humor and rationalism" (271). Joel R. Kehler argued for Taylor's familiarity with the physiology of Galen from the medically accurate and poetically functional respiratory images in Meditation 1.3 (1975). Another glimpse of the Westfield doctor's scientific learning came in Ann Leighton's study of early American gardens (1970). Briefly acknowledging Taylor's knowledge of herbalism, astrology, and alchemy, Leighton observed that his manuscript "Dispensatory" merged biblical and Connecticut plants into "one whole," a procedure consistent with the biblical frame in which nature was usually portrayed in the Meditations (223). Donald Martin identified Taylor's "Garzia Horti" in Meditation 1.4 as a pun on the name of Garcia de Orta (ab Horto), author of a popular book on gardens (1978). But Taylor's scientific interests were not limited to the herbalism necessary for practicing medicine. Cheryl Oreovicz explored his knowledge of alchemy and its relevance to his conception of the saint's transformation through grace (1976). Arguing that the unity of matter and spirit central to alchemical theory informed Taylor's shifts from image to image, Oreovicz suggested that the poet could have learned the tradition from John Webster's *Metallographia* (London: 1671). William J. Scheick found a similar blend of science and theology in Taylor's allusions to comet-like phenomena (1976). Although Increase Mather's *Kometographia* (Boston: 1683), which Taylor owned, may have stimulated his depiction of comets as dire omens in Meditation 2.114, his more positive association of comets with Joshua in Meditation 2.10 suggested his view that such natural signs boded "well or ill depending on one's perspective" (37).

Scheick argued that Taylor believed in a "harmony between natural and biblical types," and thus held that the natural world, when seen with vision rehabilitated by grace, offered a consistent revelation of God's will. Finally, Karen Grube argued the influence of Augustinian numerology in her analysis of Meditation 2.80, which cited suggestive patterns in the number of words per stanza, the number of words allotted to each meditative stage recorded in the poem, and the number of syllables per line (1978/79).

Scholars who examined Taylor's literary sources in the 1970s generally stressed his imaginative use of such materials rather than holding them up as standards that revealed his poetic shortcomings. Stanford summarized Taylor's major sources in a general essay that reconfirmed the necessity of entering the poet's mental world in order to understand and appreciate the verse (1972). Stanford underscored the influence of English poets popular in Taylor's youth; the Bible, especially Canticles and Revelation; and rhetorical handbooks of the day, which accounted for the poet's fondness for such devices as amplification, meiosis, ploce, and paradox. Suggesting that the episode recorded in "The Experience," "The Return," and "The Reflexion" may have prompted Taylor's decision to undertake a regimen of periodic meditation through poetry, Stanford argued that *Gods Determinations* was more "an anthology of poems" than a unified work (86). As Stanford conceded, the historical and theological contexts of the poetry posed a formidable barrier to modern readers, for whom "an act of the historical imagination" was necessary in order to appreciate Taylor's artistic achievement (89). Because of his spiritual goals, for instance, Taylor did not visualize his figures in any literal sense, which led him to mix his metaphors. Stanford similarly argued that typological correspondences often provided structural coherence to the seemingly random associations in the Meditations, which served as "a kind of spiritual diary" (79). Elsewhere Stanford cited the influence of a decidedly nontheological source, English satirical poet John Cleveland, on Taylor's "Verses on Pope Joan," a bawdy retelling of the legend, popular among Protestant polemicists, of a young Englishwoman who died in childbirth on the way to her Papal coronation (1973). Cleveland's two "Hermophrodite" poems, Stanford argued, lay behind Taylor's scurrilous gender puns. A minor adjustment to Stanford's claim that Taylor lacked Milton's "wide-ranging humanism" (1972:60) was suggested by Isani's publication of an English translation of the Daedalus story in Ovid's *Ars amatoria* found in the binding of Taylor's "Commonplace Book" (1975). Attributing the fragment to Taylor and dating it at about 1700 (Thomas Davis later judged the handwriting to date from the early 1670s [*Minor Poetry*, 327]), Isani suggested the poet's familiarity with popular English translations of Ovid by Arthur Golding and George Sandys. Isani presented another unexpected facet of Taylor's learning, his participation in the era's "taste for the exotic," as revealed in the poet's notebook of curiosities relating to Eastern cultures (1972). Taylor, Isani maintained, incorporated some of this material into such poems as the *Metrical History of Christianity*.

New comparisons with English devotional poets paid greater attention than formerly to the distinct cultural and intellectual outlines of Taylor's world. Scheick argued, for example, that differences between Taylor's poetry and George Herbert's stemmed from the contrasting ways in which each applied typology to his verse (1975). Scheick held that because Herbert's typology was less conservative and historically bound than Taylor's, the Anglican poet was able to make freer and more personal elaborations on the types. Herbert's participation in a literary culture that allowed such creativity accounted for this difference, as did Taylor's rigid "contraction of the poetic self in his work" — a contraction from which he occasionally strained for "release" (85). Donald Davie cited socio-literary rather than exegetical differences to explain the contrasts between Taylor and British hymnist Isaac Watts (1976). While Watts's verbal restraint stemmed from his participation in a literary community influenced by Dryden, the isolated Taylor adhered to an outmoded metaphysical wit. Unlike Watts, Taylor never "sank" his style for the benefit of external readers (507). Davie argued for the individualistic Taylor's place at the start of an American tradition of "unsociable" and even "antisocial" poetry (510), as opposed to the tendency among British poets to address their verse to society at large or to specific societal groups. Albert Gelpi agreed that Taylor's frontier isolation accounted for the rougher, distinctly American cast of his poetry (1975). Taylor's roughness relative to Herbert and Philip Pain was confirmed in Donald Stanford's study of the theme of death in the three poets (1976). Arguing that Pain exhibited more affinities with Herbert than Taylor did, Stanford cited Meditations 1.34, 2.92, and 2.112 as evidence of Taylor's cruder but more powerful apocalyptic sensibility.

When arguments for a "baroque" Taylor reasserted themselves in the 1970s, the term no longer suggested a specific formal classification that evidenced his lapses in taste, but instead described verbal extremes artistically appropriate to his emotional intensity. Walter Reinsdorf, for instance, argued that Taylor was a metaphysical poet who occasionally employed a baroque style necessitated by "an extreme intensity of religious feeling" that was sacramental rather than mystical (1970:34, 36). Like Donne and Crashaw, Taylor used verbal excess to make his imagery less representational, thereby reinforcing his metaphoric ties with the divine. Harold Jantz, complaining of an anti-baroque prejudice among literary historians weaned on tighter metaphysical structures as well as "old Victorian standards," linked Taylor with Edward Johnson and John Fiske as practitioners of an intentionally baroque art that was actually a New England innovation rather than a relic of Old World forms (1976:6). Although Jantz argued that Taylor's baroque traits rendered the term "metaphysical" too narrow and reductive to account for the verse, the relevance of both terms, derived as they were from canonical British literature rather than the poet's religio-aesthetic practice, had diminished. Karl Keller called Taylor both a "Puritan metaphysical poet" and the practitioner of a "wilderness baroque" in which verbal excess was consistent with the meditative intensity he sought (1975a:73, 163). And in the fullest discussion to date of Taylor's British literary contexts, Barbara Kiefer Lewalski argued the need to get beyond such "familiar and very elastic categories" as "metaphysical, meditative, baroque, Augustinian" in order to perceive biblical precedents shared by Taylor and his English counterparts (1979:ix).

Another important "literary" influence on Taylor was more visual than verbal. Extending observations by Grabo (1961a:154-58) and Thomas E. Johnston, Jr. (1968/69), Alan B. Howard argued for the impact on the poetry of emblem writers like Francis Quarles, Geoffrey Whitney, and George Wither (1972). Comparing the Meditations to "blind" emblems, or emblems without accompanying pictures, Howard maintained that it was Taylor's emblematic method, not his conservative typology, that confined him to an "essentially closed and conventionalized system of correspondences" (371). Because the emblem tradition subordinated images to their doctrinal significance, Taylor illustrated a "tragedy and failure" in Puritan art stemming from an insistent polarizing of "natural and supernatural, language and truth" (384). Not everyone, however, saw such visual elements as harmful to Taylor's work. Jeff Hammond and Thomas Davis argued that iconographic sources, including emblem books, tombstones, and funeral broadsides, helped sharpen Taylor's image of a death's head in Meditations 1.34 and 2.112 and "A Fig for Thee, Oh! Death" (1973). Dickran and Ann Tashjian also connected Taylor's images of death to tombstone iconography in their defense of the ubiquity and power of visual symbolism in early New England (1974). Objecting to Allan Ludwig's assumption that iconophobia informed Puritan visual traditions, the Tashjians cited Taylor's "typological perception" as an "exegetical analogue for the poetic conceit" (1974:181). For Taylor, they argued, language was more than a mere vehicle for ideas: "Upon Wedlock" illustrated how the "suprarational configuration" of language shaped the symbolic form that ideas took (134). Late in the decade Lynn Haims took the opposite view, arguing that a Puritan impulse to visualize the divine resulted in a "furtive aestheticism" that ran counter to accepted artistic practice (1979:18). Combining iconographic and psychological approaches, Haims cited Taylor's images of God's face as evidence that Puritans both "needed" and "needed to deny" such visualization due to their deep-seated ambivalence toward art (21). *Gods Determinations* in particular reflected Taylor's search for visual and concrete forms that would satisfy a "childlike" Puritan desire to visualize God, a desire that was also embodied in tombstone carvings and jeremiads (26). Taylor's image of God's smiling/frowning face conveyed this ambivalence toward visualization as well as the anxiety reflected in the Puritan habit of depicting God as a parent. The quest for "visions and voices" to counter the ineffability of the divine (34) resulted in maternal portrayals of God illustrated by the gentle Christ of *Gods Determinations* as well as the Puritan search for schematized and repetitive structures like the *ordo salutis*. "Such absolute forms," Haims suggested, compensated for a Puritan "overload of uncertainty and ambiguity" (40).

Puritan iconography derived many of its images from Taylor's most pervasive source, the Bible and Protestant exegesis — a fact symbolized by Francis Murphy's discovery of the poet's Bible, a 1634 edition bound with a 1628 Sternhold-Hopkins metrical Psalter (1971), and Gordon E. Slethaug's discovery of his copy of Thomas Taylor's *Christ Revealed* (London: 1635), a popular handbook on typology that influenced the organization of the typological sequence in the Second Series of the Meditations (1973). In keeping with a growing interest in the impact of the Bible on the poetry, most critics argued that Taylor's images gained in depth and coherence once their exegetical import was understood. Judson Boyce Allen, for example, maintained that "Upon a Spider Catching a Fly" invoked a psychomachia stemming from a medieval commentary tradition preserved well into the seventeenth century (1970). Citing a parallel to Nicholas of Lyra's commentary on Wisdom 12:8, Allen argued that the death of the fly symbolized the transcendence of "carnal desires" as the poem moved from legal fear to gracious praise (260). Hartmut

Breitkreuz soon proposed an alternative source for the scene, the exempla of Odo of Chriton (1971). Robert N. Boll and Thomas Davis suggested the influence of Augustine's *On Christian Doctrine* on Taylor's assertion in Meditation 2.138 that the teeth of the Canticles Bride (Cant. 4:12) represented a digesting of the Word by faith and meditation (1971). Such biblical and exegetical underpinnings were reinforced by Karen E. Rowe, who cited Canticles commentators to support her view that the erotic images in Taylor's late poems were "sacred" and not "profane," thereby countering Brumm's argument (1970:82-84) that such images carried Taylor beyond strict doctrinal and artistic limits (1974). Confirming that mainstream Protestant commentators considered the Song to be wholly allegorical, Rowe argued that Taylor's Canticles poetry exhibited conventional Protestant ways of reading such enigmatic scriptural texts. Consistently and deliberately subordinating the Canticles images to their spiritual meanings, Taylor turned to the Song as a supreme example of divinely inspired poetry written in praise of Christ. Rowe confirmed the special appropriateness of the Song for the later Meditations, in which Taylor's focus on Christ's reconciling love provoked less self-doubt and a greater sense of intimacy with the divine than in the earlier poems.

William J. Scheick, Peter White, and Michael Schuldiner underscored the importance of such extratextual contexts for recovering the imagistic and structural coherence of the poetry. Taking issue with Howard's claim (1972) that the Meditations lacked such coherence and Keller's denial that Taylor's poems "*mean* very much" (1975a:94), Scheick defended Taylor's "elusive" transitions in light of the private nature of the Meditations and the modern reader's unfamiliarity with "commonplace facts or daily details" that Taylor and his contemporaries easily recognized (1977:164). Demonstrating the presence of unifying artistic structures in Meditations 1.39 and 2.3 through an analysis of themes, images, puns, and allusions from daily life, Scheick called on critics to be more cautious in assuming "randomness of imagery" in poems that often derived their coherence from the speaker's ongoing tension between assertion and restraint (173). White argued for similar coherence in the introductory poem of the typological sequence, Meditation 2.1 (1978). Focusing on the coat imagery derived from Exodus and the blood imagery by which Taylor united the sacrament with Christ's sacrifice, White defended Taylor's "metaphoric" portrayal of "transcendent realities" in human terms (20). That same year Schuldiner agreed that Taylor's "problematic" images could frequently be clarified with reference to sources that lay beyond "a strictly defined literary tradition" (1978:92). The "Mammulary Catch" of Meditation 1.3, for instance, referred to the sense of smell and not, as Joel Kehler maintained (1975), to both olfaction and respiration. Similarly, the elaborate lock images of Meditation 1.49 represented Taylor's consistent and successful attempt to give concrete expression to his spiritual themes. Arguing that biblical associations often provided patterns by which Taylor's imagery cohered, Schuldiner maintained that the seemingly inconsistent images of ascent in Meditation 1.20 — a ladder associated with Christ's divinity and a chariot linked with Christ's humanity — were linked by Psalm 104. The use of both images enabled Taylor to stress Christ's theanthropic duality.

As this work made clear, scriptural contexts could be ignored only at the risk of seriously misreading the poems. Taylor's immersion in biblical traditions received the fullest treatment from Barbara Kiefer Lewalski, who described the poet as the last practitioner of a "Protestant poetic" that encompassed Donne, Herbert, Vaughan, and Traherne (1979). Like most scholars in the 1970s, Lewalski placed Taylor in an English tradition without making older claims that he somehow failed to exploit it. Countering Grabo's view of a Catholic-like devotion informing Taylor's poetry by arguing that the verse owed "more to contemporary, English, and Protestant influences than to Counter Reformation, continental, and medieval Catholic resources," Lewalski proposed a biblical poetic as a means of bridging the "Anglican-Puritan divide" that had marked Taylor studies from the beginning (ix). At the heart of English devotional poetry, she argued, lay a Pauline redemptive paradigm that shaped how sixteenth- and seventeenth-century Protestants read the poetry of David and Solomon. From the Psalms and the Song of Songs poets derived their conceptions of genre, their notions of sacred rhetoric, and their central tropes for the devotional life. Typology and allegory suggested the symbolic possibilities of language, history, and spiritual experience. Among secondary influences Lewalski cited Protestant meditation as probably the most important to Taylor, especially meditation preparatory to the Supper and the growing seventeenth-century practice of "Heavenly Meditation" (165). Other influences, Lewalski confirmed, included emblem writing, especially the Jesuit "school of the heart" tradition adapted to English use by Christopher Harvey's *Schola Cordis* (London: 1647), and homiletic theory, which helped shape the Protestant poetic voice.

In her chapter on Taylor, Lewalski dismissed the "Metaphysical-Puritan dichotomy," agreeing with Kathleen Blake (1971) that the Meditations were informed by a more broadly defined "Protestant" poetic based on biblical and soteriological structures. Reconfirming the orthodoxy of Taylor's sacramental themes, Lewalski agreed with Mignon (1968) that Taylor deliberately enacted artistic failure in order to emphasize God's glory. Less confident than Herbert that any human praise was adequate, Taylor grounded himself in the Word by writing sermon-like contemplations of specific biblical texts. Although a few poems, such as "The Experience," seemed occasional, Lewalski agreed that the First Series was consistent with a meditative program set forth in Taylor's Lord's Supper *Treatise*, while the Second Series generally followed the "classic Protestant paradigm" of spiritual life in its progression from the typological Meditations through more directly Christological poems to the final sequence on Canticles texts (397). The apparent "plateau of assurance" that Taylor achieved in such late poems as Meditation 2.156, however, was "tentative and partial," in keeping with the poet's orthodoxy. Although she agreed with Keller (1969/70; 1975a) that Taylor's recognition of the futility of his poetic goals resulted in "a meiotic, secular language of non-praise which is nevertheless devoted to the glory of God" (405), Lewalski also insisted on Taylor's typological conservatism in his consistent focus on the Christic Antitype. Concurring with Davis that the application of the types became more personal as the Second Series progressed (1969/70), she underscored the orthodoxy of Taylor's typological theory and methods. And although she agreed with Howard that Taylor often used emblems with a "directness and rigidity" that suggested the "exhaustion of a literary mode" (1972:212), she resisted Howard's conclusion that the poems were diminished by and reducible to doctrinal abstractions. More important than the influence of emblems, she argued, was Taylor's obsession with rendering praise to Christ, a dilemma he resolved by using the subjunctive mood to indicate how he would sing if graced and the future tense to anticipate how he will sing in heaven. Since both modes depended on the sanctification he wished to confirm through poetry, Taylor turned to the Psalmist and the Canticles Bride as artistic "models for heaven, not for earth" (249). The Song of Solomon in particular defined his ideal of sacred poetry attainable only "in the millennium and in heaven" (69). After discussing the *Christographia* poems (Meds. 2.42-56) as Taylor's attempts to apply various aspects of Christ to his own spiritual state, Lewalski cited the final Canticles sequence (Meds. 2.115-153) as further evidence that the poet's religious response was neither mystical nor "ecstatic"

(411), even though the very last poems (Meds. 2.154-165) suggested an unusually confident appropriation of the Bride's voice.

As Lewalski's discussion of this sophisticated biblical aesthetic suggests, most critics in the 1970s agreed with Martz that Taylor's poetic roughness was at least partly deliberate and not the unintended product of an artistic primitive (1960:xix). The artistic integrity of the poems was also stressed early in the decade by Thomas Davis, who argued that the Meditations began not as a "mechanical" ritual but out of "psychological release" necessitated by disturbing events that occurred in the summer of 1683 and were recorded in several occasional poems (1970/71:25). Countering Grabo's view that the poems were closely tied to the sacrament day sermons (1962b), Davis argued that the irregular intervals between poems in the First Series were inconsistent with a regular celebration of the Supper. Because a regular pattern suggestive of the sacramental context emerged only around 1700, Davis maintained that the early Meditations were best seen as "Occasional Meditations." Keller soon agreed (1975a:292), and as we have seen, Stanford suggested that the spiritual episode recorded in the three titled poems of the First Series may have inspired Taylor's lifelong meditative project (1972:70). But while most critics remained unwilling to divorce the early poems from the sermons or the sacrament, general agreement with the aesthetic implications of Davis's argument was evident in the decade's many stand-alone explications. The effectiveness of Taylor's technique in "Huswifery," for example, was underscored by John Higby, who demonstrated the appropriateness of the image of the fulling mill for conveying the Supper's transforming power (1972), and by Francis A. Simonetti, who argued that the poem's prosody offered a formal and phonic equivalent to Taylor's search for union with the divine (1973). Defending the interconnectedness of sound, structure, theme, and imagery, Simonetti argued that diphthongs, soft consonants, nasals and liquids aptly conveyed the movements of a spinning wheel and that the end rhymes in the last stanza successfully tied together the entire poem. C. R. B. Combellack argued that Taylor achieved similar unity in "Upon Wedlock" with the image of the marriage "knot" (1970). Sanford Pinsker argued that although "Upon the Sweeping Flood" suffered from Taylor's inability to control the ironic reversals he invoked, the poem suggested an intriguing balance in the dual purgation of earth and heaven (1975). Caroline Zilboorg, identifying sources in 1 John 2:1 and Matthew 22:38 for the legal metaphors of Meditation 1.38, defended their accuracy and thematic consistency within the poem (1978).

These explications reflected the growing critical agreement that Taylor's difficult language was more lucid than it first seemed. Kent Bales and William J. Aull, for example, cleared up a problem in Meditation 1.6 by pointing out that "overly" in line six did not mean "excessively" but "superficially," a reading that exposed Taylor's pun on the Latin *super facies* and his hope for a faith that was more than skin-deep (1970). Dale Doepke clarified a difficult passage in "The Preface" to *Gods Determinations* by pointing out that the antecedent for "it" and "its" in line eleven was "earth" and not "Sea's" (1970/71). Broader discussions of Taylor's language also stressed underlying logic and artistic purpose. Gene Russell applied computer techniques to a defense of Taylor's rhymes, agreeing with Johannes Hedberg (1960) that the apparent off-rhymes were often consistent with the poet's probable Leicestershire dialect and pointing out that many suspect rhymes deviated "in only one phonetic feature" (1971:171). In contrast to Mignon's view that the Meditations were essentially interchangeable (1969/70), Russell suggested that Taylor's experiments resulted in a style that became "less dense" as time went on (179). Russell extended his views two years later in an essay that prefaced his computer-generated concordance to the Yale *Poems* (1973). Maintaining that Taylor used off-rhymes consistently and systematically as a means of avoiding monotony of sound and spirit, he argued that the poet was a deliberate artist who employed his own "idiom" (xxiv). Although the concordance itself proved useful for closer studies of Taylor's language, its inconsistencies in spelling and capitalization prompted Scheick's warning that it had to "be used with caution" (1974b:231).

Taylor's imagery, frequently criticized in earlier studies as evidence of bad taste, was also increasingly redefined in terms of artistic function. Sybil Jacobson, for example, argued that the images were not merely decorative but indispensable to the poet's goal of praising Christ (1973). Jacobson maintained that container/containment images suggested Taylor's desire to be encompassed by and united with Christ. Images of growth conveyed the effects of grace, and images of "expression or dispersion" articulated the poet's gratitude for Christ's love (60). For Jacobson, Meditation 1.28 illustrated the "aesthetic vitality and integrity" of Taylor's work (67). Karl Keller also countered the charge that Taylor lacked taste by arguing that the poet's "bawdry" intensified a pervasive contrast in the poems between the human and divine realms (1970b). Keller, citing the Bible, Augustine, Luther, and Calvin, confirmed the traditional nature of Taylor's scatological images as depictions of human depravity. Taylor's use of erotic images to depict grace had similar precedent, from the Song of Songs and John's gospel to Calvin, Thomas Hooker, and Richard Sibbes. Reflecting a longstanding Christian tradition of portraying divine love as an antidote to a fallen world, such images served to reinforce, especially in "The Reflexion," Taylor's gracious assumption of an "active, masculine role" as Christ's lover (401). For Taylor, Keller concluded, "Being able to love amounts to salvation" (404). In an essay prefatory to Russell's concordance, Keller extended Clark Griffith's thesis that Taylor's metaphors took on a life of their own (1966) by arguing that the poet's exuberant metaphors pushed language beyond rational and perceptual limits in a religio-aesthetic "ritual" that validated verbal play (1973:xvi). In contrast to Roy Harvey Pearce's comment that "For Taylor technique is little or nothing" (1961:53), Keller argued that "ideas play little or no part" in the verse (xix). For Keller, words constituted the real core of Taylor's art: by stretching their significance through unexpected juxtapositions, the poet celebrated language as a means of realizing his identity as a soul in union with Christ. Linguistic excess — puns, hyperbole, "leaps" of logic and metaphor — "liberated" Taylor "within the system of his beliefs" and raised his language to a "sacramental" level. Additional evidence for such verbal exuberance came from Thomas Davis, who suggested the scatological "Waftings" instead of Stanford's "Castings" in line 37 of Meditation 1.48. As Davis wryly noted, Taylor seemed to acknowledge "more than one way to 'Make a joyful noise unto the Lord'" (1978b:234).

Such defenses of Taylor's conscious artistry were at root processual. Lewalski's examination of biblical and exegetical sources, for example, related these sources to an ongoing inner dynamic that transcended individual poems. This emphasis on process, which began with Martz, Grabo, Junkins, Mignon, Keller, and Bush, peaked during the 1970s. Although most critics insisted on a distinction between Taylor's religio-aesthetic process and classic mysticism, Grabo's early argument for a mystical Taylor was not so much repudiated as it was recast in explicitly Protestant terms. Franz H. Link, for example, argued for a three-part meditative structure that both articulated and stimulated Taylor's affections as he moved from sin through grace to praise (1971). Confirming Taylor's equation of grace and singing, Link noted Taylor's use of biblical models, especially Psalm 150, in anticipation of full praise in heaven, and argued that his exclusive concern with praising God distinguished him from the English metaphysicals. Erdmute Lang, finding the three-part pattern in

Meditation 1.42, similarly argued that Taylor's desire to arouse his memory, understanding, and will surpassed his concern with traditional poetic form (1971). An especially important process-based defense of Taylor's artistry, one that anticipated Lewalski's focus on Protestant spirituality, was Kathleen Blake's argument that Taylor differed from Catholic devotional writers in his Puritan insistence on the "metaphoric" nature of the Supper as an outward "Signe" of the divine "Signatum" (1971:4). In their rejection of Catholic transubstantiation, Protestants retained the integrity of the sign and its separateness from the thing signified, thus giving metaphor a "special but limited capacity" to bridge the divine-human gap (11). For Blake, the inherently metaphorical nature of sacrament and Scripture informed Taylor's use of sensory language. Seeing the power of his own words as "analogous, if not identical" to that of the Word (11), the poet viewed metaphor as a "kiss" (2) between God and man by which flesh and spirit could become conjunctive rather than oppositional. Through art, Blake concluded, Taylor could reach "touching distance of the spiritually real" (14) without risking a Catholic-like "ego and world-obliterating consummation" (24). Michael D. Reed offered a similarly Protestant rather than mystical reading by arguing that the Meditations intensified Taylor's desire for heaven even as they reaffirmed his earthbound separation from it (1974:308). Reed stressed the inherent futurity of poems that did not merge the earthly and celestial realms but situated the poet between them in a "hypothetical" mode by which he managed to avoid both "pride and hypocrisy" (311). For Reed, Taylor's focus on the hypothetical, clearest in the proposed exchanges of praise for grace with which many of the poems conclude, defined his distinctively American voice (312). At the end of the decade Michael North reconfirmed the futurity of the poetry by arguing that Taylor's images consistently reflected his underlying faith in the covenant and the Supper as metaphors of "promise" and a "physical assurance of Grace" (1979:3). Confirming that Taylor sought metaphors by which he could extend the promissory themes of the sacrament, North linked Taylor's use of the types as promises of redemption with his ultimate goal of arriving at heaven. Like Lewalski and Keller, North argued that "the esthetic arrangement of images, words, or syllables" (15) was less important to Taylor than his desire to internalize the covenant by participating in its "regenerating metaphors" (16). Taylor's seeming indifference to his poems as artistic products was supported by Jesse C. Jones, who pointed out discrepancies resulting from his insertion of unnumbered poems in the First Series, his habit of repeating and omitting numbers throughout the Meditations, and the difficulty of determining whether some poems were drafts of others (1974). Jones concluded that any figure given for the actual number of *Preparatory Meditations* was necessarily tentative.

The focus on Taylor's religio-aesthetic dynamic culminated at mid-decade in the work of William J. Scheick and Karl Keller. Grounding his approach in redemptive and faculty psychology, Scheick argued for the key role of the will in Taylor's art and thought (1970). Although the will was passive in redemption because the Fall had rendered it a "viper's nest" of corrupt passions, its partial regeneration at conversion brought it a renewed freedom that made possible the believer's choice to glorify God. In the Meditations Taylor repeatedly sought signs that his will was conforming to the divine will. Although complete congruity was impossible in this life, he strove to achieve "momentary and fleeting experiences" of such "attunement" (53). Elsewhere Scheick explored an analogy that Taylor drew between the Trinity and the regenerate faculties, with the enflamed will corresponding to the workings of the Holy Spirit (1971a). Just as the Spirit expressed the "will" of the Father and the Son, so Taylor's words — the reflections of *his* will — conveyed the state of his reason. In keeping with a logocentric notion of piety that defined his ongoing response to the divine *Logos*, Taylor's childlike "lisping" could be corrected only by Christ as Word (53). Constantly seeking evidence that "the Word's art" was "mirrored" in his own language (52), Taylor wrote to involve his entire being in acts of praise. In a third essay Scheick pointed out the shortcomings of terms like "mystical," "meditative," and "metaphysical" to describe a poetic based on Christ's mediating role as the *Logos* spoken by God to man (1971b). Because Taylor could not presume upon his own election, he neither sought nor thought it possible to achieve mystical resolution. "Meditative" also failed to account for verse that did not adhere to Ignatian patterns. And because Taylor's search for metaphoric links to the divine made him indifferent to mere ornament, he was not a true "metaphysical." Scheick also countered Keller's focus on Taylor's "act of desiring" (1969/70:19), arguing instead that the meditative process was less important to the poet than its results: an ongoing suspension between "presumption" and "despair" as he intensified his spiritual life through circular images conveying the mutual love of Christ and the saint (175). In another essay Scheick focused on the self projected in the Meditations (1972). While Grabo had argued that Taylor sought a loss of self in union with the divine (1961a:82), Scheick countered that the poet's real goal was a closer scrutiny of self for signs of a regenerative process that would end only in the next life. Far from abandoning the world and the self in the manner of the classic mystics, Taylor found within himself and his surroundings valid and legible expressions of divine love.

Taylor's optimistic view of the world was central to Scheick's full critical study, *The Will and the Word* (1974a). Scheick argued that Taylor adhered to an Augustinian tradition of piety that granted more efficacy to human faculties and the physical world than Calvin allowed. Within this tradition, the understanding, though corrupted by the Fall, was partially restorable through grace. To a soul who experienced this renovation, nature could offer spiritual lessons in a validation of the physical anticipated by the gracious conjunction of matter with spirit in the Incarnation. Augustinian optimism enabled Taylor to use poetry to articulate the "saving knowledge" that unified the natural and supernatural realms (21). Poetry thus offered a potential revelation of the effects of grace on his ability to find divine truth in the Bible and the world. Taylor's corporeal element shared this potential for rehabilitation: it was, Scheick argued, "the *fallen condition* of nature and the body" and not physicality itself that Taylor and other Puritans denigrated (27). Because grace restored the saint's entire being, Taylor did not seek a mystical release from the body but sought to "realign his body and soul" in imitation of the harmonious balance in the Incarnation (36). For Scheick, the faculty that made this possible was the will, which Taylor saw as the "integrating power" of the elect soul's identity by virtue of its particular association with the Holy Spirit (51). Once the will passively consented to God's will, it regained the freedom "to offer more than mere consent" (71). Following Puritan demands "to act *as if*" his preparatory efforts were efficacious (87), Taylor sought signs of his "saving attunement of the heart" with God's will in his poetic quest "for conversion, that is to say, for love and identity" (89).

For Scheick, the Incarnation set the mediating precedent for Taylor's attempts to bridge earth and heaven with words. Because Taylor saw the Christic Word as "God's artist" (97), he was able to achieve some sense of conformity to God's will and to communicate with the divine by shaping "active verbal assertions of love" into meditative poems (101). Despite their elaborate surface, these poems met Puritan demands for a plain style because their language was not mere ornament; rather, it invoked Taylor's whole being as a believer whose affections were properly checked by a rational faculty restored by grace. An analogy between human "words and the Word" (103) justified Taylor's *imitatio Christi*, based on Scripture and embodied in his ongoing verbal exercising of a renewed will. Seeking his identity as an aroused saint who found the "Word's art mirrored in his own words" (114), Taylor invoked self-deprecation not just on a personal level but as a reflection of universal depravity. For Scheick, the label of artistic "primitive" did not fit an artist who consciously strove to achieve "poetic excellence" as a sign of spiritual renewal (124). Instead, Taylor's poetic roughness was a deliberate extension of the will's role in verbalizing an underlying human-divine unity. Taylor's attempt to fuse these planes through metaphor was patterned on Christ as the "supreme metaphor" that linked the two realms and informed the poet's verbal confirmations of unity with God (136). Scheick found this unity in Taylor's nature images, which were usually filtered through the Bible, and images drawn from human activity and daily experience, especially images of exchange between earth and heaven. Because Taylor's style was rooted in redemptive psychology and not belletristic tradition, Scheick argued that a better term than "metaphysical" for describing the poetry was Rosemond Tuve's "principle of decorum," which suggested the seventeenth-century search for images and forms appropriate to the subject and the author's intent. Like Mignon (1968), Scheick argued that the Meditations were artistically successful in that they usually satisfied a private poetic decorum based on the mediating Word. In pursuing this decorum, Scheick argued, Taylor never sought to abandon his personal identity or the physical world. In answer to Grabo, Scheick conceded a mystical "element" in a poet who nevertheless exercised "*practical* piety" in this life (153). Actively asserting his will rather than absorbing it into the divine, Taylor ended his poems in "petition" and not mystical "resolution" (156). His *imitatio Christi* did not end in contemplative ecstasy but dramatized an ongoing search for a spiritually rejuvenated self in the here and now. Enacting a cycle of hope and despair that underscored the eternity of God's plan, the Meditations exhibited a sameness that mirrored Taylor's "irresolution" as a self whose assurance could never be final (167). Scheick concluded that Taylor's ongoing assessment of his relation to the idealized self of the elect soul anticipated later American writing, especially its moral themes, propensity for symbolism, and concern with identity.

Scheick's Taylor was an American *Puritan*; Keller's was more a Puritan *American*. While Scheick restricted his focus to the Meditations as expressions of redemptive psychology, Keller related Taylor's entire poetic corpus to his public vocation in the New England frontier (1975a). The figure who emerged in the opening chapters of *The Example of Edward Taylor* was an orthodox, even reactionary defender of the New England Way. But the rest of the study argued that this very rigidity made possible a striking degree of poetic freedom. Although Keller stressed at several points Taylor's artistic exceptionalism, this was less a return to the unorthodox poet of earlier studies than it was an attempt to read the poetry in light of current theories regarding the reality-shaping power of language and verbal myth. For Keller, Taylor was an "example" not only in his integrity as poet and believer but in his ability to create an identity from the ambiguities of speech. Keller maintained that in the private Meditations "Taylor is only a voice," a "discursive function" divorced from external experience (9). Invoking a proto-modern Taylor who chose "to live in an *illusion* of reality" (9), Keller found a "mythic quality" in his doctrinal conservatism and precedent for American nationalism in his defense of New England orthodoxy (33). And although Keller argued that Taylor saw his public and pastoral role in aesthetic terms, he maintained that the poet and the preacher lived "separate lives": while the poetry "*created* a life within," the sermons merely "reported or pointed to one" (42). Taylor's wide reading, his family life, and his active leadership of frontier Westfield thus did not intrude upon the Meditations. What frontier life did contribute, Keller argued, was a "rough hewn" quality and a folk "primitivism" reflected in Taylor's wide-ranging curiosity as "a poet of oddities" (63).

In contrast to Scheick's portrait of a deliberate and sophisticated artist, Keller argued that Taylor wrote not from a "well-developed esthetic sense" but from spiritual and expressive "necessity" (70). Initially prompted to write by the Lord's Supper controversy, the poet later wrote as part of a spiritual exercise in imagining an identity that was not mystical but "hyperbolic — and perhaps mythic" in his desire to create "a Self above oneself" (74). While this much squared with Scheick's view of a "sacred" self in the verse (1974a: 161), Keller suggested an escape from theological structures in Taylor's self-fashioning. The speaker of the Meditations, he argued, was "the Taylor of his desires," an "illusion" by which the poet "could make a meeting with the divine forbidden by his theology" (74). Arguing that Taylor wrote in the belief that his illusion of Christic intimacy would become a reality, Keller suggested that he suppressed his poems simply because their purpose as private devotional aids had ended. The public poetry and the prose, however, exhibited another aesthetic altogether, one that focused on "definitions of truth" rather than self-regeneration (112). While Taylor was a born poet, he thus fully exercised his gifts only in private. Still, Keller saw a public dimension to Taylor's verse that enhanced his importance as a forerunner of American poetry. Keller had previously argued that Taylor's typology anticipated American symbolic discourse of the nineteenth century (1970a). Now the poet's relevance for a later America lay not so much in his verbal progressivism as in a theological conservatism embedded in the "myth structure" of the Connecticut Valley, "antirationalist" and preparationist in contrast with the more reserved Puritanism of Boston (228). For Keller, this structure encouraged Taylor to pursue an intense self-examination later manifested in Dickinson, Hawthorne, and Melville. Citing Taylor's participation in a "wilderness baroque" shared with Cotton Mather and Jonathan Edwards (163), Keller argued that the exercise of wit played a distinct role in the development of "an American individualism" that compensated for Calvinist austerity (167). Most important for Taylor's American identity, however, was his preoccupation with a meditative process that centered on "writing about writing" and "self-discovery" (93). For Keller, this process, which brought Taylor "to the point of mystical union without crossing the line over into sensuality, pride, antinomianism," suggested that Taylor's poems "do not *mean* very much" except as dramatizations of the self "in the *act of desiring*" (94). While Taylor's endless variations on a single unifying activity suggested his most American trait, Keller depicted a poet who was more exceptional than exemplary within his own time and place. Despite Keller's insistence on the cultural "vitality" of early America (10), his Taylor was an exception proving the rule that Puritan poetry was "an artistic embarrassment" (101). What made Taylor's verse unusual was his aestheticizing of the faith: while the poetry written by his contemporaries merely expressed theological truths, Taylor "read (misread?) the theology *as* esthetics"; they thus "became dull apologists and he became a real poet" (102).

Keller agreed with Scheick that Taylor's "metaphysical" traits were not merely ornamental but reflected a vital epistemology of faith. For Keller, spiritual joy propelled the poet beyond the conventions of the Ignatian meditation toward an anticipation of Edwards's view that "primary beauty" consisted of delight in conforming to God's will (180). This primary beauty, Taylor hoped, would stimulate his creation of effective praise. Puns, analogies, conceits, and metaphorical leaps took Taylor beyond the merely intellective toward an Emersonian pursuit of divine beauty in the world by which he could assert himself "within the rigid system of his piety" and achieve "an illusion of oneness with his God" (188). Reiterating his earlier argument that Taylor's balance of excremental and erotic imagery was inseparable from his faith (1970b), Keller insisted that the poet's "semi-Dionysian" stress on Christ as joyful Lover reflected no deviation from Puritan theology (207). Moreover, Taylor's consistent humility checked any tendencies toward un-Puritan mysticism, especially in his Meditations based on the Song of Songs and the gospel of John. Taylor did not stress the physical Christ, as in Catholic devotional writing, but "the beauty of the idealized self" that he wished, through grace, to become (216). For Keller, Taylor was a genuine poet because he managed to violate his rigid theological system just "enough to make room for himself in it" (231). Invoking Saussure's distinction between *langue* and *parole*, Keller argued for a "disparity between mythic *language* and individual *speech*" in Taylor. While the language of the myth gave the poetry its power, Taylor's own speech — "something added, something of the man himself" — afforded him "a kind of creativity within the system of his beliefs" (232). Poetry thus helped him assume a place within his theology while ensuring sufficient "freedom within form" (236). In this sense, Keller suggested, poetry may have been a *"liberating* art in Puritan culture": Taylor's "ideology was perhaps livable without such a device, though perhaps not yet alive in *him* until he wrote" (236).

As the progenitor of "an indigenous American poetry" (235), Keller's Taylor exhibited a primitivism based on memory rather than representation. Calling the poet "the Grandma Moses of American literature," Keller asserted that although Taylor tried to imitate the poetic conventions of his day, he was most interesting when he failed to do so and thus unwittingly revealed "his own personality" (245). While Keller conceded that Taylor's roughness may have been a "deliberate" expression of his fallen state (252), he generally saw the strained images, choppy meters, forced rhymes, and difficult syntax as the unplanned products of the poet's ruthless self-honesty. For Keller, this individualism, based on a human dignity inherent in Taylor's focus on the Incarnation, reflected an optimistic "humanism" that offset Puritan pessimism (264) and was articulated in the preparatory thrust of poetry written "as a means of perfecting human behavior and through human behavior purifying church and state" (272). Despite his comment that Taylor's preparationism was a form of "pathology" (275), Keller insisted that writing helped the poet forge "a greater affirmation of his humanity than the conventions of Christian humanism could" (276). Agreeing with Scheick that poetry helped Taylor "express the fact that he does have a will, that he can will, that he is willing" (279), Keller concluded that the deepest significance of the Meditations derived simply from the process of writing them: "Poetry for Taylor is in part theanthropic (the word is also the Word) and in part preparatory (language is action) but mainly it is existential, autonomous, self-sufficient" as "a human action that affirms itself" (280).

These two important studies had more in common than might first appear. Scheick read the Meditations in light of "Puritan theological thought, psychological notions, and literary traditions" (1974a:167); Keller similarly placed Taylor's "wit back into the context of his theology where it belongs" by illuminating the "esthetic extensions of his theology" (1975a:188, 173). In addition, both scholars stressed what Scheick called Taylor's attempt at "defining his self through words" (162) and Keller termed "the picture of the man that is created by his poetry" (257). Finally, both related the formal features of the verse to the spiritual processes it embodied, even though both were somewhat ambiguous regarding the precise nature of Taylor's spiritual exercises. Although Scheick emphasized Taylor's post-conversion search for an "assurance" that was "rarely, if ever, maintained while the saint lives on earth" (86), he repeatedly referred to Taylor's "quest for saving love or conversion" (79; see also 25, 89, and 120). Keller's "preparationist" aesthetic was even more problematic. Attesting to the poet's "quest for signs of an assured salvation" (91), Keller nonetheless argued that the poems showed "Taylor *in the process* of preparation" (92), a process that strictly applied only to those who still sought their initial conversion. In an earlier article Keller had alluded to the poet's quest "to be disposed for saving grace" (1969/70: 17); the reprinting of this article in Bercovitch's typology collection prompted Norman Pettit, whose own study had stressed the preparationist emphasis on pre-conversion experience (1966), to point out that Taylor was preparing not for grace but for a sacrament that sealed the prior reception of grace in the soul (1975:290). Moreover, while Keller cited Taylor's search for a "perfect preparation" (92), it was unlikely that so orthodox a Puritan would have seen preparation as a means of "perfecting human behavior" (272). A clear difference between Scheick and Keller emerged, however, in how each connected Taylor's life with his art. By reading the Meditations in light of redemptive psychology, Scheick more convincingly integrated the concerns of the poet, the preacher, and the Puritan. By contrast, Keller invoked a split between Taylor's private and public identities by treating the sermons and public poems in terms of what they *didn't* do relative to the Meditations. As a result, his view that Taylor was a genuine poet was based on only about one-fourth of the extant verse. And despite his attempt to locate Taylor's aesthetic "*within* Puritanism rather than at its limits" (3), Keller actually placed the poet outside those limits by calling him the only "real poet" of his time and place (102). Nor was his stress on Taylor's "ecstatic optimism" convincingly reconciled with the rigid Puritan depicted in the biographical sections of the study (269). Finally, Keller asserted that poetry helped Taylor "make a meeting with the divine forbidden by his theology" (74), even though, as Grabo and others were suggesting, such intimacy was mandated rather than proscribed. A contradiction inherent in game-like verbal exercises that were nonetheless "a matter of spiritual life or death" (91) emerged perhaps most clearly in Keller's discussion of Taylor's meditative speaker. Despite arguing for the presence of "something of the man himself" in the verse (232), Keller came close to suggesting a literary or spiritual persona by stressing the "roles" of a poet who cherished the "illusion" of a relationship with God (78). In his self-articulated identity, Keller's Taylor seemed to play his verbal game as much by modern as by Puritan rules.

Another difference between Scheick and Keller centered on the longstanding debate over whether Taylor's artistry was deliberate, as Martz had claimed (1960:xviii-xix), or accidental, as Pearce believed (1950:44-46). While Scheick saw Taylor as a sophisticated poet who developed a style expressive of faculties partly restored by grace, Keller's Taylor was a true primitive whose poetic achievement was less a matter of artistry than of personality. Although the question of whether Taylor's eccentricities were intentional could be addressed through the public poetry, where his assumption of an external readership would presumably make him ply his craft to the best of his abilities, this lead was rarely pursued despite Michael Colacurcio's pioneering study of audience in *Gods Determinations* (1967). As Grabo noted at the beginning of the decade, *Gods Determinations* was being unfairly "excluded" from newer discussions (1970:23). Although Grabo may have contributed to this neglect by focusing on Taylor as a contemplative and by citing the poem as evidence of his inability "to sustain a work of any length" (1961a:168), he rightly observed that critics were ignoring "the dynamics of the work itself." Dismissing Colacurcio's stress on readers, Grabo suggested that no other Taylor poem was "so clearly and exclusively motivated by artistic, uncompromised poetic impulse" (1970:24). Precisely because Taylor was "nowhere" in the poem, *Gods Determinations* offered an opportunity for a truly aesthetic reading rather than a mere biographical or theological gloss. If given proper attention, the poem could even become "the fixed star in Taylor's critical firmament." Scheick and Keller did little to bring about Grabo's prediction. *The Will and the Word* mentioned *Gods Determinations* only in passing, and *The Example of Edward Taylor* was surprisingly brief and unsatisfying in its treatment of all the non-meditative verse. Keller argued that although *Gods Determinations* was an "appealing" treatment of conversion, it was "esthetically disappointing" relative to the Meditations (1975a:129, 135). For Keller, Taylor's gifts for private meditation overshadowed any skill he may have developed as a public poet because his conception of public verse was "too low, too issues-oriented, quite provincial" (137). The *Metrical History of Christianity*, for example, was written by a "different Taylor from the Taylor of the Meditations" and was therefore "all the less interesting" (143). Unable to reconcile the public poet's vision of "man's ugliness as God's art" with the private poet's deeply affirmative "humanism," Keller concluded that the *History* was merely "embarrassing" (159).

Although Grabo and Keller posited an artistic separation of *Gods Determinations* from the Meditations, other scholars in the 1970s underscored experiential continuities that united the two sequences, following Colacurcio and Bush in defending the poetic form of *Gods Determinations* in terms of spiritual processes recorded in the Meditations. Robert D. Arner, for instance, related the poem's structure to "theological and psychological" rather than "conventionally dramaturgical" frameworks, thus confirming the interdependence of Taylor's poetic practice and Puritan beliefs (1973b:29). Relating the poem's two "Prefaces" to Taylor's covenantal themes, Arner defended the theological necessity of the second preface as a signal of the believer's shift from the private throes of conviction to his "participation in the community of visible saints" (29). John Gatta, Jr., confirming Colacurcio's emphasis on the poem's consolatory effects (1967) and Stanford's view that it was written as a "handbook or guide" for congregation members (1972:79), examined *Gods Determinations* as evidence of Taylor's rhetorical sensitivity in countering "scrupulous melancholy" with a poem that was essentially "comic" in its overall design and execution (1975:122). Gatta identified comic strategies in Taylor's broad portrayal of Satan, dialogues that satirized the reader's despair, a standard comedic "social integration" conveyed through church membership, the invocation of music as an antidote to melancholy, and a "comic resolution" achieved in the soul's election (124). The poem's "comic spirit," Gatta concluded, transcended the "strictures of dogma" (141). Gatta later argued that these consolatory structures derived from the case divinity of Thomas Hooker, especially as formulated in *The Poor Doubting Christian* (London: 1629) (1979). Gatta noted not only the similar doubts that Hooker and Taylor countered, but also their portrayals of Satan as a cynical disputer, their use of dialogues to expose spiritual doubt, and their shared belief in a "protracted model of effectual calling" more accessible than the sudden conversion stressed by John Cotton and by Taylor's nemesis, Solomon Stoddard (5). In contrast to Hooker, however, Taylor chose a more comforting approach appropriate to his pastoral experience and purposes. David L. Parker similarly contrasted Stoddard's views with Taylor's blending of "preparation and effectual conversion" as illustrated in *Gods Determinations* (1976/77: 263). Correlating the salvific process devised by Justice and Mercy with descriptions given in Taylor's "Spiritual Relation" and "Profession of Faith," Parker cited additional evidence for Taylor's opposition to the sudden-conversion model in Meditations 1.39-41, written just after Stoddard began practicing open admission to the Supper. Parker concluded by suggesting that Taylor's notion of gradual conversion, shared by Cotton Mather, would eventually lead to the Arminianism opposed by Edwards during the Great Awakening (273). At the end of the decade Scheick agreed with Grabo that such purely theological readings tended to overlook the poem's artistry (1979:38). Extending the covenantal dichotomies cited by Bush (1969/70), Scheick argued that the artistic unity of *Gods Determinations* was based on a "jawbones schema" designed to squeeze readers between the forces of damnation (Satan, Justice, the Law) and redemption (Christ, Mercy, the Gospel). Satan, who played an unwitting role in the salvific process by serving as "an inverted Christ," repeatedly appealed to natural law and fallen reason as a means of provoking despair (42). Scheick concluded that Taylor's use of a house/church motif to structure the journey to conversion resulted in a unified poem and not, as Stanford had suggested, a loose "anthology of poems" treating a single subject (1972:86).

Still, the *Preparatory Meditations* received the bulk of the commentary in the 1970s, not only because they seemed to shed more light on Taylor's spiritual processes but because they suggested more clearly his importance for American literary history. Hyatt Waggoner had observed that Taylor either seemed "hardly worth reading" or a "poetic pioneer," depending on whether he was seen in an Old or a New World context (1968:24). Although this assessment suggested more about critical predilections than about the poetry itself, Waggoner was correct in underscoring Taylor's doubleness as an Englishman in frontier America. Typology soon figured in the debate over Taylor's American identity. Lewalski placed the poet not at the beginning of an American tradition but at the end of an English tradition destined to wane with the decline of dogmatic Christianity and the falling prestige of the Bible (1979:425). As we have seen, Keller (1970a; 1975a) took the opposite tack, following Brumm (1970) in linking Taylor's exegetical vision with his American romantic and Transcendental successors. Brumm soon distinguished between typology's meaning for Taylor and its "timeless" aesthetic implications, citing Meditation 1.10 to illustrate the "esthetic adaptability" of the types in Taylor's art (1972:193). Arguing that Taylor used typology as a means of bridging the gulf between divine glory and human sin, Brumm connected the exegetical significations of the "Aqua-Vitae" image with the poem's visual and phonic effects. Taking issue with Keller's stress on Taylor's playful wit, Brumm underscored the poet's serious belief in correspondences between "the name and the thing" based on Christ's dual nature (201). The types offered Taylor "a rich structure of symbolic relations," some of which acquired an archetypal significance that enriched their strictly theological import (202). Comparing Herbert's freer poetic application of typology with Taylor's refusal to remove Christ from the typological equation, Brumm confirmed that Taylor used the types as "a roster of symbolic equivalents of grace" (206). The following year Brumm published an overview of Puritan writing, including an introduction to Taylor, that did much to stimulate interest in Taylor among German scholars (1973).

While Brumm suggested the archetypal significance of Taylor's symbolic structures, Albert Gelpi stressed their national import in his study of American poetry through Whitman and Dickinson (1975). Defining the history of American poetry in terms of the poet's persistent "crisis of place and role," Gelpi argued that isolation from the mature literary culture of England forced the American poet to "justify and comprehend the poetic act" before finding an authentic voice (10). For Gelpi, as for Keller, Taylor was an artistic anomaly who gave Puritanism "its majestic (and uncharacteristic) poetic statement" in poems that "violated" early demands for plain expression and later demands for neoclassic restraint (21). Agreeing with Keller that Taylor's American identity lay in his development of repeatable, processual structures that anticipated Whitman, Williams, and Pound, Gelpi combined Scheick's view of the primacy of the Incarnation with Keller's emphasis on the erotic, especially the poet's use of Canticles themes and images to transcend rational and earthly paradoxes. Finally, Taylor foreshadowed a dialectic involving a poetry of vision and a poetry of creation that ran throughout American literature. For Gelpi, Taylor contributed to a distinction in American poetry between "types" as figures of divinely-authored truth and "tropes" as figures of the poet's creativity (51). With the rise of more secular modes of thought, the American poet became identified less as a "religious seer" than as a conscious artist who "manipulates or resists the otherness through which he moves" (53). Keller similarly reiterated Taylor's relevance for later American writing by drawing parallels with Dickinson and with an even more "modern version" of Taylor, Joyce Carol Oates's 1964 story "Upon the Sweeping Flood" (1975b). Besides sharing a title, the Taylor poem and the Oates story both dealt with human presumptuousness (324). At the end of the decade Keller elaborated on the Taylor-Dickinson connection by locating both within the sustaining "myth" of "Connecticut Valley Puritanism" (1979:41). By fostering a "more sensationalized piety" than that practiced in Boston, this myth enabled both poets to articulate unique identities within rigid cultural structures. American visionary continuities were also invoked by Donald Barlow Stauffer, who depicted Taylor as a precursor of a Transcendental symbolism whose "fusion of mysticism and intellectual power" often gave modern readers a mistaken impression of frontier "charm and quaintness" (1974:30, 32). But Taylor's spirituality could suggest even broader parallels, as when Mohan Lal Sharma compared his images of colors and clothing, often reinforced by light imagery, with analogous figures in the mystical writings of Indian Bhaktas and Persian Sufis (1970).

Despite growing interest in Taylor's spiritual and literary heritage, not much work was being done on his relation to his literary contemporaries. There was, to be sure, general agreement with Stanford, Grabo, and Scheick that Taylor as minister and believer was fully in step with Puritan social and spiritual codes. As Everett Emerson observed, Taylor's religious "satisfactions" were "not necessarily different from what other Puritans felt" (1977:115). Taylor the poet, however, remained on the margins of the Puritan fold, if not outside it, largely because of the still-prevalent presumption of a bias against art in early New England. But Keller's gap between this "real poet" and the "dull apologists" who wrote the rest of Puritan verse (1975a:

102) began to close as scholars started to incorporate Taylor into thematic studies of early American thought and writing. In his discussion of sea imagery in Puritan texts, for example, Roger B. Stein cited Taylor's treatment of Noah as a personal type in Meditation 2.29 as an articulation of an "archetypal dread of a return to chaos" widespread in the literature (1972:29). The significance of the sea as an emblem of disruption, Stein argued, united seventeenth- with nineteenth-century American writing. This fear of nature was confirmed by John Seelye, who cited a widespread "walling-out of the New England landscape" by Puritan poets and underscored Taylor's determination to exclude the external world from his contemplations (1977). Asserting that Taylor's metaphors have "the intensity of personal expression" but were "in reality highly conventionalized expressions of devotion" (314), Seelye placed this withdrawal from the physical New England within a broad Renaissance abhorrence of "inchoate, hence chaotic and therefore evil aspects of nature" (315). More explicitly literary comparisons also began to establish Taylor's commonality with other Puritan poets. As we have seen, Harold Jantz united Taylor with John Fiske and Edward Johnson within an essentially baroque aesthetic (1976). James Bray similarly joined Fiske and Taylor in a baroque tradition embodied in their incorporation of the Tree of Life image into "systems of apocalyptic metaphor" (1974:33). Because Fiske developed his images more logically, his work lacked Taylor's imaginative association of images, which anticipated "symboliste poetry" (33). Another parallel to Taylor was New England exile David Dunster, whom Harrison Meserole described as a comparably gifted poet, especially in the "metaphrase" of Canticles contained in Dunster's 1683 manuscript *Gospelmanna* (1976:39). Though less allusive and more conventional than Taylor, Dunster showed greater metrical variety. Finally, Robert Daly joined Taylor with his contemporaries in a poetic reconstructed from elements in Puritan thought which, "though not explicitly literary, have literary implications" (1977:137). Arguing that critics consistently overstated the degree and nature of Puritan iconophobia, Daly confirmed that images promoting and intensifying religious experience were not only tolerated but encouraged. While Ramism fostered a Puritan focus on "perception and articulation" rather than poetic "creation" (146), the restricting effect of Ramist structures on the poetry had also been overestimated (145). Agreeing with Scheick (1974a) that the Puritans saw the world as a legible "book written by God" (147), Daly concluded that the Puritan poet was more like a Roman seer (*vates*) than a Greek maker (*poeta*).

The following year, in the fullest response yet to Grabo's call for a revaluation of Puritan aesthetics, Daly published the first book devoted to American Puritan poetry (1978). The result was not so much a new view of Taylor as a new view of other Puritan poets based on what Taylor was revealing about the Puritan literary imagination. Reacting against the critical tendency to read Bradstreet and Taylor as "exceptions" to a "Puritan rule" based on untested generalizations (222), Daly attacked the old assumptions of Puritan hostility toward art and a dismissal of "the physical world and the concrete images needed to render it" (4). Arguing that Puritans saw the physical world as a "system of metaphors made by God and explicated in the Bible" (19), Daly pointed to widespread Puritan appeals to the senses as a backdrop for reading Taylor. Pointing out that Puritans placed no prohibition on using images for devotional purposes, especially images derived from Scripture, Daly argued that their divine authorship shifted such figures from Ramist *elecutio* to *inventio* as signs left by God for man to read. Because divine glory lay beyond human comprehension, meditative writers like Richard Baxter promoted "anthropomorphic" conceptions of the divine as a "psychic necessity, not a metaphysical fact" (78). Puritan poets thus condemned this world only in relation to the next, freely drawing upon the former to represent the latter. By applying these symbolic structures to Puritan poetry in general, Daly made Taylor seem less an exception to an aesthetic tradition than its ideal spokesman and fulfillment. What made Taylor different from his contemporaries was not his aestheticizing of doctrine, as Keller claimed, but his more uncompromising dissatisfaction with metaphor as a bridge to the divine, a dissatisfaction that resulted in his anticipation of a celestial realm where he would finally "sing well the songs he has sung badly through a lifetime of frustrated effort" (172). Because Taylor found the bridge to God afforded by metaphor "necessary but ultimately unsatisfactory," he yearned for the "second bridge" — physical death — "to unlock his poetry as the first had not" (176). Daly argued that biblical metaphors clarified Taylor's grasp of a "divine tenor only dimly apparent in nature" (180). Reiterating Scheick's emphasis on the mediatory power of the *Logos* (1974a:97), Daly identified metaphorical writing as Taylor's vehicle for enacting an *imitatio Christi* central to his devotional life. But because the poet found metaphors unsatisfactory, he used them to depict divine glory "not by similarity, but by opposition" (188). This, Daly argued, accounted for his deliberate choice of "preposterous" figures and his halting prosody in poems "revised to make clear the inadequacy of his metaphors"

(190). While this procedure helped Taylor avoid pride, it freed him to probe the limits of metaphorical expression in poetry that was "always in process, never completed" (198). While Wigglesworth's near-Gnosticism prompted him to eschew metaphor and Bradstreet's firmer belief in the world's metaphoric value allowed her to link earth with heaven, Taylor's conviction that such metaphors became legible only through grace resulted in his focus on struggle and vision sought rather than stasis and vision achieved.

Michael Clark soon countered Scheick's and Daly's view that Puritans could read the world clearly as a God-written text, arguing instead that worldly signs were ambiguous concealers as well as revealers of divine truth (1978/79). Grounding this ambiguity in the uncertainty of assurance and the unbridgeable gap between earth and heaven, Clark argued that Puritan contemplation did not move smoothly from the creatures to the Creator but was repeatedly frustrated by the separation of the corporeal sign from the divine Signified that was effected at the Crucifixion. But redemption reasserted continuities between earth and heaven, and the resulting "dialectic" of meaning and unintelligibility gave Puritans "a sense of the meaning of things and of their persistent refusal to make sense" (291). At root, Clark and Daly were proposing different answers to Grabo's early call for an aesthetic treatment of Puritan art (1962c). Grabo now argued that the search for signs of sanctification created a "holiness impulse" in Taylor, who articulated a "lyric inclination" embedded in "colonial theology itself" (1978:85). While Daly joined Grabo in seeing Puritan writing as a symbolic expression of religious experience, Clark argued for a purer form of linguistic isolation, an extrapersonal intertextuality in which Puritan texts — including Taylor's — were readable mainly in relation to a system constituted by and within other Puritan texts. Keller had anticipated Clark in his emphasis on verbal play and his view of Taylor's language as a semi-autonomous medium answerable chiefly to its own rules (1973, 1975a), while Kathleen Blake had suggested the semiotic focus in her discussion of the Puritan distinction between sign and signatum in the Supper (1971). But for an increasing number of theory-oriented critics in the late 1970s, including Clark, literary discourse was beginning to undergo an even greater isolation from referentiality. Language was increasingly seen as a hermeneutic system complete unto itself, a web of signs that was far less personally expressive than biographical and historical critics had traditionally assumed. As the decade ended, it remained unclear whether Taylor, whose participation in the historical and cultural structures of early New England was just emerging, was ready to be ushered into the era of poststructuralism.

By the end of the 1970s, the chief contexts for reading the poems had been defined. Brumm (1970), Gelpi (1975), and Keller (1970a, 1975a) had suggested Taylor's place in American literary history. Scheick had probed the connections between the poetry and an inner world shaped by Puritan perceptual and redemptive psychology (1974a). Daly had placed him in the company of his fellow New Englanders (1978), and Lewalski had tied him to his literary and spiritual predecessors in England (1979). In an excellent introductory survey, Jane Donahue Eberwein summarized these frameworks, stressing the importance of seeing Taylor for what he tried to be: "a versifying Puritan minister or even a frontier psalmist" (1978:71). Placing the poetry in the context of his ministry and underscoring the strength of his assurance in celebrating the human/divine relationship, Eberwein cited the influences of meditative and rhetorical traditions, metaphysical poetry, everyday life, and especially the Bible on poetry written not as polished art but as "a tool for examining the soul and directing it toward God" (70). Still, these frameworks were yet to be explored in sufficient detail. The precise nature of Taylor's spiritual experience was still not clearly defined. The impact of the Bible and scriptural exegesis on the verse was only generally understood, especially the question of how Taylor managed to turn his biblical models into vivid poetry. In addition, another Edward Taylor remained virtually unknown: a poet whose public and didactic verse seemed distressingly "Puritan" in the worst sense of the word, so at odds with the Meditations and *Gods Determinations* that critics barely acknowledged it. Finally, there remained, as Grabo pointed out, a profound ambivalence regarding Taylor's achievement as an artist. What did the critical commonplace that he wrote good poetry really mean? This issue, as Joseph M. Garrison noted at the start of the decade, had important implications for the classroom as well as for scholarship. Commenting on the infrequent teaching of "early American literature *as literature*," Garrison called for such texts as Taylor's to be taught as "conscious art" (1970:487, 488). But in whose consciousness? There was an uneasy sense that Taylor's intentions and the modern reader's responses did not match — that those traits which critics valued most about his work were precisely what Taylor would have dismissed as evidence of his fallen self and art. Although the maturation of Taylor studies in the 1970s reinforced the view that he was an orthodox Puritan as well as a genuinely gifted poet, these two critical commonplaces remained curiously isolated from each other. The whole Edward Taylor — presuming such an entity was recoverable — was not as clearly understood as the scholarship suggested.

4: Consolidation — The 1980s

BY 1980 THE TAYLOR BOOM was over, and the new decade would see only about half as many items as the 1970s. The most obvious reason for this was perhaps inevitable: Taylor's bloom as a "new" poet had faded, and with it, the sensationalistic fervor of the early years. Second, work on Taylor declined because his potential for revitalizing early American literary studies was finally being realized. Armed with insights derived in part from his verse, scholars began turning to other figures in need of fresh readings and assessments. As this new work began to revitalize the field, it no longer seemed that every early Americanist was — or needed to be — a Taylorian. Finally, the dramatic progress of the 1970s made it seem as if all the important questions had been answered. Not only had Taylor become less mysterious, but he was beginning to seem as worked over as any other major writer. The 1980s accordingly saw a consolidation and extension of structures lined out in the preceding decade. More details of Taylor's intellectual milieu came to light, especially his use and modification of sources. New work also focused on his emotional milieu as part of a larger revaluation of Puritan spiritual experience. In addition, the decade saw fresh insights from literary theory: like other scholars, Taylorians were increasingly forced to reconsider their poet's importance in light of new theoretical and methodological challenges to traditional literary study. Ironically, no sooner was Taylor established within the American canon than the assumptions validating that canon began to erode. As a vigorous proponent of New England and Puritan traditions whose dominance in American studies was being questioned, Taylor seemed in danger of changing overnight from the freshest face in the anthologies to early America's Milton, a defender of an increasingly suspect and elitist artistic and spiritual tradition. It was easy enough in the 1960s and 1970s to assert Taylor's importance for American literary history; it became less so when the very definitions of "American," "literary," and "history" were becoming problematic.

The most important work of the decade, however, came not from theorists or critics but from editors. In their three-volume *Unpublished Writings of Edward Taylor* (1981), Thomas M. and Virginia L. Davis forced a timely reconsideration of the popular image of an exclusively introspective poet. Two years later the Davises and Betty L. Parks issued Taylor's most systematic exegetical work, the unfinished *Harmony of the Gospels*, in four volumes (1983). Another important addition to the Taylor corpus lent exegetical ballast to the typological poems of the Second Series: Charles W. Mignon's long-awaited two volumes of *Upon the Types of the Old Testament* (1989). At the decade's end, nine thick volumes of new material awaited — and for the most part still await — scholarly investigation.

The first volume of *The Unpublished Writings*, the *"Church Records" and Related Sermons*, included professions of faith and public relations given at the founding of the Westfield church, the two versions of Taylor's "Foundation Day" sermon, records of nearly fifty years of disciplinary cases, and two disciplinary sermons — all of which underscored, as Thomas Davis noted in his introduction, Taylor's strict adherence to New England's founding principles (1981a). Davis confirmed that the minister behind the poetry was "addicted to order and process" in his determination to record "the ecclesiastical history of the orthodox at Westfield" (xiii). Citing the six-year delay in the founding of the church and tensions with neighboring communities, Davis revealed that Taylor used father-in-law James Fitch's *The first Principles* (Boston: 1679) in preparing his "Profession of Faith," though the poet-preacher was more emphatic than Fitch in linking the Lord's Supper with conversion narratives and fuller in his comments on the Judgment. Reviewing the exchange of documents from 1688 to 1690 between Taylor and Stoddard, Davis argued that Stoddard did not actually admit the unconverted to the sacrament until 1690. Taylor, revising his "Foundation Day" sermon in response, continued the battle in the *Treatise* sermons and the unit of Meditations dealing with the sanctity of the Supper (2.102-111). The disciplinary cases also revealed a strict spiritual leader willing to suspend the sacrament if necessary to ensure Westfield's conformity with the New England way. In his pastoral dealings, Davis observed, Taylor imposed exacting moral standards although he well understood the "human weaknesses" of his congregation (xxxiii). The second volume of *The Unpublished Writings* contained letters exchanged between Stoddard and Taylor, Stoddard's "Arguments for the Proposition" and sermon on Galatians 3.1, and Taylor's "Animadversions," anti-Stoddard syllogisms, and "The Appeale Tried." Reviewing the history of the controversy, Davis underscored the gradual evolution of Stoddard's views (1981b). At first seeking only to modify the Half-Way conditions and not to redefine the

Supper as a means to conversion, Stoddard worked for over ten years trying to persuade his ministerial colleagues of his views. Convinced that New England's declension required drastic action, Stoddard finally preached his sermon on Galatians in which he defined the Supper as a converting ordinance. As Davis suggested, Stoddard's final view may have been prompted by his own especially intense conversion. In the late 1680s Taylor began the counter-struggle that took its most explicit form in the revised "Foundation" sermon and the *Treatise*, which Davis called "the most successful of Taylor's extant prose" (38). Taylor never published this work, Davis maintained, because his respect for the Supper found its deepest articulation in his private devotional life rather than in the public forum. Taylor's thirty-year fight reflected an obsession with form also evident in the unvarying stanzaic pattern of the Meditations, his verbal celebrations of a sacrament that united his concerns as "person, pastor, and poet" (48). The Stoddardean controversy also suggested the pluralistic nature of a New England Puritanism that was "large enough," as Davis noted, to accommodate both Stoddard and Taylor, "the activist as well as the visionary."

The third volume of the *Unpublished Writings*, which included verse paraphrases of Job and the Psalms that the Davises painstakingly recovered from fragments in the bindings of the manuscript books, reinforced the central role of poetry in the life of a man who wrote, as Davis pointed out, "twice as much poetry as Milton, four times that of Donne, five times that of Bradstreet, and six times Wigglesworth's total" (1981c:xi). The minor poems that comprised the bulk of Taylor's output were important, Davis argued, because by addressing "the immediate, the occasional, the public" they allowed the poet "to focus upon his own identity in the Meditations." They also revealed the artistic beginnings of a young poet "unable to find his own voice" (xii) but determined to "recreate the New England past" in poetry (xiii). Suggesting that the Hebrew Psalms stimulated Taylor's search for an open-ended mode of writing that stressed "process and not product" (xiv), Davis argued that *Gods Determinations*, an embodiment of Taylor's poetic experimentation and his involvement with King Philip's War and the Half-Way dilemma, reflected this new sense of artistic purpose, especially its closing lyrics and their anticipation of the poet's meditative voice. As Taylor's "song of the self," the Meditations allowed him to unite the sacramental and historical frameworks of Puritanism in a form that transcended linear time and permitted extensive revision. Through this form, which was "responsive to the immediate and yet modified in reflection" (xvii), Taylor internalized and personalized New England's promise, reacting to the spread of Stoddardeanism by transferring "the wilderness errand into the creation of the self as garden" (xviii). This inward shift, Davis suggested, was reinforced by the Job paraphrases and their reminder that "individual steadfastness" was still possible even though the collective mission seemed in decline (xix). As the connections between New England and New Zion became increasingly obscure, Taylor found the *Metrical History* less reassuring; as a result, he dropped it and several other projects in order to concentrate exclusively on the Meditations and the "womblike bower" of the Song of Songs. For Davis, Taylor's heightened interiority did not reflect a shutting out of the world so much as his direct reaction to it. Davis later published a new Taylor poem discovered too late for inclusion in the *Minor Poetry*, an elegy on David Dewey, deacon at Westfield (1986). The elegy, published around 1713 in a commemorative pamphlet, again challenged the image of the otherworldly poet which dominated the criticism. As Davis observed, all of Taylor's elegies, including this sole elegy that found its way into print, were "published" poems in that they circulated in manuscript: in this sense Taylor was "a public poet and known as one" (81).

In the introduction to the four-volume *Harmony of the Gospels*, Taylor's exercise in the ancient practice of constructing parallels among the synoptic gospels, Davis reconfirmed the poet's extensive learning (1983). The *Harmony*, which Taylor apparently began in the mid-1680s and worked on sporadically over the next thirty years, drew heavily on Origen, Augustine, Theophylact, and Matthew Poole's compendium of Bible commentary, the *Synopsis Criticorum*. As Davis noted, Taylor's was only the second harmony in English (the first was John Lightfoot's 1644 *Harmony of the Four Evangelists*) and the first by a colonial American. Correcting Karl Keller's assertion that Cotton Mather had tried to get Taylor's *Harmony* published (1975a:82) (the work in question was actually Mather's own *Biblia Americana*), Davis argued that although Taylor completed only the first year of Christ's ministry, enough of the work existed to show his individual adaptation of the genre and his remarkable "integrity of thought" (xxxviii). The *Harmony* not only shed light on individual poems but established a framework for important image clusters in the poetry. Finally, Davis maintained that the *Harmony* joined the *Christographia* in reconfirming the impact of the dichotomous Christ on Taylor's thought and writing, especially his characteristic propensity to frame striking juxtapositions of "the concrete and the abstract, the physical and the spiritual" (xxxvii).

Taylor's wide reading was equally evident in the thirty-six sermons on Old Testament types corresponding to the typological Meditations that opened the Second Series. Charles W. Mignon, who later told how the sermons came to light when a Taylor descendant donated them to the Nebraska State Historical Society (1990), had announced their discovery in *Early American Literature* (1977/78) and published the first sermon, preached in 1693, in the *William and Mary Quarterly* (1980). Henry Wyllys Taylor's biographical sketch of his great-grandfather, which was discovered with the Nebraska manuscript, was soon published by Deborah Koelling (1982). Judge Taylor, who traced the family line back to one "Taillefer," a Norman minstrel killed at Hastings, took considerable pride in his poetic ancestor. As Koelling suggested, the genealogical information contained in the document could lead to the discovery of additional manuscripts. Mignon's two-volume *Upon the Types of the Old Testament* featured a substantial introduction and a full textual apparatus, including notes explaining Taylor's sources and allusions and an appendix containing his marginal notes. Relating the sermons to Taylor's life and other works, Mignon traced the historical and biographical influences on the sermons, from Taylor's boyhood pastor, silenced by the Nonconformity Act of 1662, through his education at Harvard and his familiarity with such commentators as Origen, Augustine, and Poole (1989). Citing the sermons as evidence of Taylor's dual roles as scholarly exegete and warm exhorter to the faithful, Mignon confirmed the preacher-poet's careful structuring of sermonic uses to address his hearers' spiritual needs. Agreeing with Davis's early view that Taylor was both conservative and innovative in his poetic use of the types (1969/70), Mignon confirmed that the poet, avoiding a historical application of the types, confined himself to traditional correspondences but developed them in new ways. Citing the treatments of Samson and David, Mignon argued that the three basic kinds of sermons in the collection — doctrinal, disciplinary, and confirmatory — were united by Taylor's underlying goal of expounding doctrine "by teaching the congregation how to read the Old Testament" (xl). Although Taylor's most immediate sources were Thomas Taylor's *Christ Revealed* (London: 1635), Samuel Mather's *Figures or Types of the Old Testament* (Dublin: 1683), and Benjamin Keach's *Tropologia* (London: 1681), his distinctive sermonic approach lay in his emphasis on Christ as the link between the types and the individual believer. Mignon traced a progression in the sequence from doctrine (sixteen sermons) through discipline (thirteen sermons) to confirmation (seven sermons), a movement corresponding to Taylor's thematic focus on Christ, the church, and the soul. The first of these three groups stressed the typology of Matthew (the new Israel as Christ's kingdom), the second that of Paul (the church as Christ's body), and the third that of Paul and John (Christ in the sacraments and in the believer's spiritual life). Demonstrating that Taylor arranged his sermons to strengthen their thematic and sequential coherence, Mignon suggested that while he was probably drawn to typology by the Lord's Supper controversy, his deeper motive was his realization that the types "could have tropological meaning for his congregation" (li). Finally, Mignon confirmed the unity of the sermons with Taylor's other writings by explicating Meditation 2.26 in the context of typological themes developed in its corresponding sermon. The sermons reconfirmed that nothing in Taylor's poetry could not also have been expressed publicly through preaching. As Mignon noted, Taylor's was a "preaching ministry" (lxxi) — a fact with important implications for the poetry no less than the prose.

Davis and Mignon both underscored Taylor's engagement with the culture of early New England and its precedents in Reformed England. Other scholars in the 1980s similarly contextualized Taylor by confirming his informed and active participation in the mental world of the seventeenth century. The standard critical assumption was no longer that the poems embodied some deviation from that world, whether spiritual or artistic, but that they exemplified it fully. This filling in of Taylor's mental map took many forms, including reexaminations of his relation to Anglo-European literary culture, studies of his familiarity with the science of his day, and more detailed probings into the impact on his verse of the Bible and Protestant biblical exegesis. Taylor's devotional practice also received a closer look, though from two distinct standpoints: the first consisted of current theoretical frameworks of self/text interaction, and the second consisted of historical frameworks derived from Puritan identity and redemptive psychology. Finally, Taylor's relation to other Puritan poets also received fuller treatment, as did his role as a forerunner in the development of American writing. The problematic nature of his American identity, however, began to challenge common formulations of his historical and national significance. This question, along with the equally difficult problem of assessing his poetic achievement without invoking anachronistic aesthetic criteria, began to unsettle the scholarly consensus that had been developing for over a decade.

The broadest perspective on Taylor's literary affinities came from A. Owen Aldridge, who argued that early American literary study "need not (and perhaps should not) be confined exclusively to the American continent" in his discussion of Taylor in the context of the European baroque (1982:18). Aldridge claimed that Taylor, when seen in a European framework, exemplified a cultural lag that Bradstreet managed to escape. Countering Harold Jantz's argument for a widespread and vital baroque aesthetic in the English colonies (1976), Aldridge saw Taylor as the sole practitioner in British America of an "exuberant style" exemplified by Italian poet Giambattista Marino and Spanish poet Luis de Góngora, a style that differed from the English metaphysical use of "conceits that communicate intellectually" through irony and paradox (60). Taking issue with William J. Scheick's view that Taylor's language was linked to his conception of the divine *Logos* (1974a), Aldridge argued for a more ornamental poet who sought brilliant and novel "verbal effects" designed to "dazzle the reader's mind" (63). For Aldridge, Taylor sought God in "nature, not metaphor or any other aspect of language" (65). Arguing that Taylor surpassed English and Continental poets in his use of sexual images and his innovative diction, Aldridge maintained that Taylor's contemporaries would have considered his diction "a fashionable display" consistent with baroque expectations of verbal virtuosity (71). Echoing Keller's opinion (1975a) that Taylor was a poet of language rather than ideas, Aldridge maintained that what distinguished him from other poets in English was not his frontier isolation but his use of "exotic" images from the Bible, a trait that linked him with eighteenth-century visionary poet Christopher Smart (85). Arguing that Taylor's verse was never published because it violated the neoclassical decorum of the era, Aldridge attributed the poet's twentieth-century popularity to a modern resurgence of interest in the baroque.

Similarly broad contexts for reading Taylor came from Norman Grabo, Harrison Meserole, and John Shields. Grabo briefly suggested parallels between Taylor and seventeenth-century Mexican poet Sor Juana Inés de la Cruz (1988:118), whom Aldridge had paired with Bradstreet (1982:25-52). Meserole underscored European precedent for Taylor's art by arguing that the late medieval "mechanical wonders" listed in Meditation 2.56 served to contrast art and nature with divine glory (1989:119). Taylor's allusion to "Regiamont" referred to Johann Müller, the fifteenth-century mathematician and astronomer who built a mechanical eagle in honor of Maximilian I (120). Shields pursued an older influence not examined since Willie Weathers's early studies (1946, 1954). In contrast to Aldridge, who concluded that Taylor's chief difference from European baroque poets lay in his avoidance of all classical elements except a "pastoral" mode based on the Old Testament (1982:79-80), Shields argued that Taylor, after an early outburst of zeal, became highly tolerant toward his Renaissance classical inheritance (1984). Comparing Taylor's attitude toward the classics with Jerome's "humanistic response" (162), Shields maintained that Taylor's classical references became more frequent after 1700. Citing allusions to Alexander the Great (Med. 2.150, "Upon Wedlock"), Midas (Med. 2.155), and Prometheus and Pandora (Med. 2.79) as evidence that Taylor was able to tell the story of sin with classical rather than Christian figures, Shields concluded that except for his negative association of Rome with the Papacy, Taylor was "a humanistic Puritan — a colonial New England Jerome" (168). Donald Stanford, John Shawcross, Harold Jantz, and Anna Maria Pellegrini invoked literary comparisons much closer to home. In an excellent general survey of Taylor's life and work, Stanford reiterated the poet's participation in the intellectual and artistic traditions of his own time and place (1984). The psychological turmoil set forth in *Gods Determinations*, for example, owed much to the case divinity of William Ames and to John Downame's *Christian Warfare* (London: 1633). Although Stanford called *Gods Determinations* "the best long poem written in seventeenth-century America," he reconfirmed that Taylor's major poetic achievement consisted of the Meditations, a "private spiritual diary" rich in rhetorical and exegetical traditions (314). While the Meditations often lacked the "closely knit logical organization" of Donne's and Herbert's best work (315), they fully exhibited Taylor's poetic gifts and the remarkable range of his expression, from "religious ecstasy" to "quiet Herbertian piety" (317). Shawcross, briefly and favorably comparing Taylor's prosodic skill with Herbert's, agreed that comparisons based on Anglo-American literary contexts need not invoke "the odiousness of observing that Herbert did it better" (1988:47). Jantz cited this pitfall as well, countering Louis Martz (1960) and Aldridge by renewing his attack on the assumption that a "cultural lag" existed in colonial America (1985). Arguing that the widespread belief in colonial backwardness had prompted critics to underestimate Taylor's achievement, Jantz maintained that Taylor and other New England poets, if read in the context of the literature of their own day, articulated "not simply the ruinous fragments of an old but the creative coming together of a new diction unheard of in Old England" (270). Taylor's English precedents were also cited by

Pellegrini, who classified Taylor as a late metaphysical in a general essay written to introduce the poet to Italian students of American literature (1980).

By now, however, it seemed clear that Taylor was not a narrowly "literary" poet: his conviction that everything under the sun could be enlisted in God's praise precluded that possibility. An especially valuable result of work on nonliterary sources was the recognition of Taylor's creative ability to incorporate secular material into his devotions. Taylor's poetic use of scientific knowledge, for example, emerged in Scheick's discussion of two competing optical theories that the poet skillfully adapted to thematic purpose in the Meditations (1983b). Scheick argued that the Aristotelian theory, which held that light originated from luminous bodies, became Taylor's emblem of a postlapsarian vision dependent on Christ's luster; the Platonic theory, in which the eye was considered the source of light, represented the rehabilitated vision of the saint, whose inner eye was struck by Christ's light and thereby gained clearer spiritual sight. Citing Meditation 1.16 as an especially full expression of Taylor's optics, Scheick confirmed not only that such intellectual sources revealed a coherence that lay "beneath the surface chaos" of the poetry (234), but that Taylor believed in a profound compatibility of the natural and supernatural realms. Scheick extended his defense of an artistically accomplished poet in a study of Taylor's herbal images and their "precise aesthetic contribution" to the poetry (1983a:64). Through a close reading of Meditation 2.62, Scheick not only confirmed the accuracy of Taylor's herbal images in light of seventeenth-century medical practice, but demonstrated the poet's incorporation of these images into a coherent aesthetic structure that supported a movement in the text from spiritual sickness to salvific health. Jes Simmons defended the botanical appropriateness of Taylor's plant images in "Upon Wedlock," finding in the mix of Old World and New World plant names evidence of the colonial goal of forging "a separate identity in breaking from England" (1983:18).

Catherine Rainwater further revealed the artistic relevance of Taylor's science for the poetry in her study of his accommodation to the new astronomy of Copernicus (1984). Rainwater argued that Taylor's ambivalence toward the shift to Copernican cosmology was based on aesthetic grounds rather than any fear that God's biblical order was being threatened. Maintaining that he invoked both the medieval and the Copernican model in various poems, depending on his artistic and meditative needs, Rainwater found in Meditation 2.21 an integration of scientific and biblical discourses within a "Copernican emblem" by which the poet inserted himself into cosmic and redemptive structures. For Taylor, the new science did not contradict the Word but offered an alternative means of confirming it. By combining older and newer cosmologies, the poet was able to extend his "expansive typological vision" (15). Anthony Damico, Joan Del Fattore, Cheryl Oreovicz, Ursula Brumm, and Cora Lutz confirmed a similar blending of natural and biblical orders in the poetry. Damico explicated Meditation 2.1 not simply as an introduction to the types but as a typological poem in its own right, based on the natural "type" of scarlet dye made from Mediterranean shellfish, the "Created Shells" of the poem (1982/83:228). By skillfully developing this type into an elaborate treatment of atonement, Taylor revealed that the "glory of the world," the scarlet dye used in royal robes, was an inferior prefiguration of Christ's blood. Suggesting Pliny the Elder as a possible source, Damico argued that the image supported Taylor's extensive but generally neglected interest in natural history. Del Fattore suggested a source for such alchemical images as liquid gold (Med. 2.47), the golden tree (Meds. 1.29, 2.31, and 2.37) and the saint's transformation (Med. 1.7) in John Webster's *Metallographia* (London: 1671), which Taylor copied out for his own use (1983/84). Oreovicz, incorporating Taylor into a survey of the influence of alchemy on Puritan poetry, demonstrated his use of alchemical metaphors to convey the soul's transformation (1985:108). Stressing his considerable alchemical learning and his obsession with God as divine chemist, Oreovicz argued that Taylor exploited such "chemical images" to depict "the comfort and consolation attendant on a state of grace" (109). Brumm explored Taylor's fascination with numerology (1982). Citing Augustine's appropriation of ancient number schemes into a symbolism reflective of divine wisdom, Brumm related Taylor's six-line meditative stanza to the widespread significance of six as the number of creation and redemption. In Meditation 1.28 Brumm found numerical correspondences involving the number of words in the poem, the frequent doubling of key words, and structural designs created by the distribution of key terms in the poem. "Vessell," for instance, was repeated with increasing frequency per stanza, resulting in a vessel-like shape with a narrow neck and broad base. For Brumm, Taylor's attempt to shape his poems in harmony with divine number systems reflected popular Renaissance traditions of a musically and mathematically harmonious cosmos. Lutz, suggesting that these scientific interests became something of a family trait, used Taylor's poem on the "giant's" bones discovered in New York as a springboard for discussing grandson Ezra Stiles's interest in natural history (1982).

In general, these studies confirmed Taylor's search to reconcile the created world with his most pervasive source: the Bible and Protestant biblical exegesis. At the start of the decade Mason I. Lowance, Jr., followed Brumm (1970), Karl Keller (1975a), and Albert Gelpi (1975) in placing Taylor's biblical turn of thinking within an evolving American symbolism that culminated in the Transcendentalists (1980). His study also complemented Barbara Lewalski's *Protestant Poetics*, which had appeared the previous year (1979): while Lewalski investigated a biblical aesthetic that Taylor shared with his English predecessors, Lowance linked Taylor's biblical imagination to his American successors. For Lowance, Taylor's symbolism embodied a transition from the conservative typology of Samuel Mather to later and more personalized applications of biblical figuralism. Like Davis (1969/70) and Lewalski (1979), Lowance argued that Taylor did not alter the typological tradition but enhanced its personal application through his hopeful identification with Christ as Antitype. Noting that Taylor used allegory and typology as "different vehicles for expressing the same essential substance" (90), Lowance maintained that Taylor's poetry was "exegetical, not mystical" (94) as the poet applied the types to his personal salvation and to redemptive history. The *Christographia* poems and sermons revealed how Taylor merged "personal, figural, and historical theology" into "an aesthetically satisfying, doctrinally sound statement of individual spiritual fulfillment" (105). Lowance concluded that because the poet identified with historical as well as eternal processes embodied in the types, the "language of Canaan" retained "real metaphorical value" for his inner life even though communal and historical applications of typology to New England's mission were on the wane (111). By internalizing the structures of collective prophecy, Taylor contributed to an American tradition of prophetic nationalism that culminated in another poet who expressed a similarly "personalized sense of manifest destiny," Walt Whitman (294).

Most scholars examined the impact of the Bible on the poetry itself rather than connecting Taylor's biblicism to later American writing. Dennis H. Barbour, for example, demonstrated the influence on *Gods Determinations* of the "hexameral" tradition, a Renaissance adaptation of the six-day creation narrative in Genesis exemplified by Guillaume Du Bartas's *Divine Weeks and Works* (London: 1605) (1981/82). Barbour argued that Taylor drew from the tradition creatively, abandoning the usual Genesis chronology for more "impressionistic" structures that stressed "doctrine rather than narrative" (215) and omitting Adam's name from the "Preface" as a means of encouraging the reader's convicting identification with postlapsarian humanity. Barbour concluded that the hexameral tradition helped Taylor confirm the inevitability and glory of providential history. Other biblical influences on the Meditations emerged in Old Testament poetry. Extending the work of Lewalski (1979:249) and Davis (1981c:xiv), Rosemary Fithian Guruswamy demonstrated the impact of the Psalms, an impact based on the widespread view that in his varying moods David foreshadowed "the typical Christian soul" (1985:90). Guruswamy maintained that Taylor appropriated not only Psalmic themes of lament (Med. 2.26), supplication (Med. 1.21), and praise (Med. 1.9), but such rhetorical devices as amplification and antithesis, many of his central images, and his preference for "earthly, common figures" (107). Speaking in a voice that was at once personal and representative, Taylor adopted a search for humility and assurance foreshadowed in the seven penitential Psalms. Guruswamy concluded that in his devotion to David's art as the pattern for all Christian meditation, "Taylor wrote his own Book of Psalms" (110). Building on work by Karen Rowe (1974), Jeffrey A. Hammond discussed the influence of Taylor's other chief biblical source, the Song of Songs (1982/83). Agreeing with Rowe against Brumm (1970:82-84) that Taylor's use of Canticles was consistent with standard Protestant practice, Hammond argued that Taylor considered the Song's imagery to be totally "spiritualized" by virtue of the text's status as timeless allegory (200). Its allegorical presentation of eschatological themes gave the Song a special appropriateness for the aging poet, whose growing concern with heaven and glorification reinforced his identification with the Canticles Bride in the late sequence of poems based on texts from the Song (2.115-165). This biblical identity reflected the poet's increasing focus on the celestial Christ, a figure foreshadowed most fully and engagingly by the Canticles Bridegroom. Serving as Taylor's *ars moriendi* in his declining years, the Song of Songs stimulated and intensified his meditative preparation for death and union with Christ, when he would "sing the song of the Bride with an unfettered voice" (209).

David Watters stressed the role of Canticles-based eschatology in his study of a prophetic dimension of Puritan aesthetics and iconography that enabled believers to transform "the facts of death into images of personal and communal triumph" (1981:11). Stressing Taylor's optimistic invocation of millennialist frameworks to strengthen his identity as a member of Christ's mystical body, Watters maintained that Taylor's shifting "surface intricacy" was balanced by his solid faith in a prophetic self-as-Bride (172). This faith assumed visual form in Puritan tombstone carvings, where eschatological hope informed the practice of "representing the face of the spouse as the face of the resurrected saints" (185). Lynn Haims also explored Taylor's relation to patterns of visualization in Puritan art (1985). Arguing that in *Gods Determinations* Taylor subtly "reconstituted in his poetry the images his theology abhorred" (84), Haims maintained that his desire to "visualize his religion and his God" was sufficiently strong "to exact a compromise with the prohibitions against making 'similitudes' of things religious in Exodus 20.4-5" (1985:84, 96). Reviewing the structure and central images of *Gods Determinations* as an accommodation "of religious sanctions and aesthetic strivings" (96), Haims argued that Taylor used dark/light imagery and musical imagery to give his theology artistic form. Although this dichotomistic structure corroborated earlier readings by Sargent Bush (1969/70) and William Scheick (1979), Haims overlooked Robert Daly's warning against overstating the nature of Puritan iconophobia (1978) and as a result, suggested that Taylor's verse succeeded in spite of, and not because of, his solidly Puritan beliefs. Arguing that Taylor's imagery resulted from expressive needs fundamentally at odds with the dictates of the theology, Haims saw Taylor as an underground artist "whose imagination found a partial outlet in the rich visual imagery of scripture" (96).

Most critics, however, agreed with Daly that biblical images were not sources of a covert aesthetic but legitimate signs of divinity, part of an interpretive framework inseparable from the images themselves. The importance of this framework for reading the poetry was the central argument of Hammond's analysis of Meditations 2.25 and 2.149 (1982). Commentary traditions, Hammond maintained, often revealed Taylor's artistic choices to be less arbitrary than the poetry itself suggested. Exegetical frameworks also shed light on Taylor's view of his own poetic process as a gracious recapitulation of Old Testament ceremonies. The burnt offerings contemplated in Meditation 2.25, for instance, offered biblical precedent for his verbal praise as a fulfillment of the sacrificial types. Hammond also discussed the erotic imagery of Meditation 2.149, citing the standard commentary view that the Canticles Bride's navel represented the spiritual nutrition that the Church offered spiritual infants. By stressing the importance of commentary traditions in revealing an underlying thematic coherence in Taylor's imagery, Hammond opposed the

New Critical isolation of his texts that sometimes informed assessments of his artistry. At mid-decade Lowance and Rowe summarized indispensable theological contexts for all Puritan verse, including Taylor's. Lowance reaffirmed the Augustinian and Protestant assumption that the Bible, with its parabolic and metaphorical language, did "not always plainly express what God is" but adapted "the understanding of him to human capacity" (1985:39). Because the Holy Spirit had made rich use of figures and metaphors, "the universe of language and imagery was available to the poet who sought to reconcile art and truth in his verse" (39). As Lewalski's "Protestant poetic" (1979) and Lowance's "language of Canaan" (1980) also confirmed, the "plain style" — especially in poetry — was not all that plain. Rowe discussed a key to Puritan symbolic discourse in her concise survey of the literary implications of typology (1985). Arguing that the types provided "a God-sanctioned myth" that "placed the Puritan migration and each saint's journey within providential history and millennial revelation" (64), Rowe traced the communal and private uses of the types into the eighteenth century, when the "language of Canaan" gave way to "the rhetoric of Federalism and the Enlightenment" (56). Like Davis and Lowance, Rowe noted that Taylor's refusal to practice a recapitulative typology that related the types to New England history was consistent with his search for celestial and not "historical immortality" (63).

Rowe developed these views in *Saint and Singer: Edward Taylor's Typology and the Poetics of Meditation* (1986). Making substantial use of the typology sermons that Charles Mignon was preparing for publication, Rowe expanded early work by Davis (1969/70, 1970) and Robert Reiter (1970) into a full-scale treatment of the Meditations in light of Taylor's use of the types. Rowe argued that for Puritans, the types did not merely offer an intellective structure for reading Scripture but stimulated the believer's "superior mystical insight derived from faith" (50). Confirming the Puritan belief that the insightful typologist was necessarily aided by grace, Rowe connected Taylor's typological practice with his search for religious assurance, a connection reinforced by his use of the personal types — the Old Testament bearers of faith — as models for his meditating speaker. For Taylor, as for other Puritans, these examples of the faith were more accessible than "the *exemplum exemplorum* of Christ Himself" (87). The ceremonial types similarly foreshadowed Taylor's meditative process. Like Hammond (1982), Rowe saw Taylor's poetry as a new ritual of inner obedience adapted to the gospel dispensation. The self-purgation effected by this ritual was modeled on the purification types: Taylor's "apparent surety about his election" was based on a process by which an acute awareness of sin could instill true repentance (132). The sacramental types similarly shaped Taylor's conception of the Lord's Supper and his opposition to Stoddard's modified admission requirements. By probing correspondences between the Testaments, Taylor could both connect with Christ and assert Christ's clear difference and superiority, thereby forging a meditating self that was at once personal and representative. Meditation 2.58, for example, voiced "everyman's" deliverance (148), and the overall sequence of the poems reenacted "the morphology of conversion" (163). Suggesting an archetypal dimension of Taylor's "inward journey — one paradigmatic of every Puritan saint's aspiration for spiritual transcendence" (223), Rowe saw the Meditations not simply as "personal exercises" (219) but as conflations of Taylor the individual with extrapersonal redemptive patterns that he sought to animate within. Rowe agreed with Scheick (1974a) that an *imitatio Christi* made possible by Christ's theanthropic nature stimulated Taylor's pervasive duality as a self poised between "rationality and heightened affections" (275) and between "outward sinfulness" and inner grace (276). Writing as "both saint and singer" (276), Taylor saw the poetic imagination as "virtually synonymous with God-given spiritual insight and creative power" (268).

Rowe offered the most persuasive and detailed discussion yet of Taylor's biblicism. But the more scholars learned about the Bible's influence on Taylor's poetic practice, the less clear they were about the poetic results. To be sure, Rowe, Lowance, Guruswamy, and Hammond made his poetic eccentricities seem less arbitrary in light of biblical traditions familiar to him and his contemporaries but obscure to modern readers. But if his artistic decisions were tied to biblical structures inseparable from the Puritan imagination, could he really be called a conscious artist at all? As the best practitioner of the biblical approach, Rowe also best revealed its shortcomings. She made astute analyses of scriptural precedents for the poet's metaphors, rhetorical devices, tropes and conceits, and generic models such as Canticles, Isaiah, the Psalms, and Job. But revealing these precedents was not the same as judging their artistic impact on the poetry. Although Rowe demonstrated that Taylor's poetic aims were not those of a post-romantic poet, she hesitated — as did Lowance, Guruswamy, and Hammond — to pursue the aesthetic implications of this insight. Commenting on Meditation 2.24, for instance, she conceded that Taylor's fondness for the "labored conceit may at times stretch our patience" even though his dogged pursuit of such parallels was consistent with his "search for universal truths grounded in particularities" (124). And despite her insistence on Taylor's typological poetic, Rowe's assessment of the poems seemed based on modern expectations of formal unity and personal expressiveness. Taylor's summary of Exodus types in Meditation 2.59, for example, "recycles rather than shapes the various metaphors into a cohesive conceit" (156). For Rowe, Taylor was a poet of "limited skill, but glorious ambitions" (270), even though artistic skill and spiritual ambition were inseparable within the typological poetic that she described.

The difficulty of assessing Taylor's artistry — of negotiating oppositions posed by historical knowledge and critical judgment — became one of two themes that threatened to disrupt the broad critical consensus of the 1980s. The other, as we shall see, was Taylor's "American" identity. While most critics were silent on the issue of artistic assessment, Scheick noted that a truly aesthetic accounting of the poetry was being neglected. Responding to John McWilliams's comment that no Taylor poem seemed "wholly successful" and that undue critical attention was being paid to Taylor and to Philip Freneau as America's first real poets (1983:132), Scheick countered that Taylor was "more original and inventive" than commonly thought in his active creation of "coherent rather than chaotic" poems (1988a:3). As we have seen, Scheick had incorporated Taylor's science into demonstrations of the artistry of specific poems (1976, 1983a, 1983b). Scheick now restated the need to read the poetry "aesthetically" by citing Meditation 1.8 as a poem embodying an "aesthetic logic" and as an illustration of the fact that Taylor failed only when his language became overly "discursive rather than poetic" (1988a:2, 8). Focusing on word play and the unifying "arching" forms in the poem, Scheick maintained that Taylor's skillful fashioning of emblems hardly revealed "an unenergetic rehearsal of worn-out patterns embodied in verse that lacks tension" (10). Like Grabo's earlier call for an aesthetic reading of early American texts (1962c), Scheick's defense of the poems as poems went largely unanswered. Most critics continued to focus on Taylor's intellectual sources or his spiritual process rather than the artistic results of either. When Keller reiterated his process-centered approach in his last essay on Taylor, he illustrated both its strengths and its weaknesses (1985). After a witty survey of the history of Taylor scholarship, Keller argued that Taylor repeatedly and deliberately enacted artistic failure because "the process of writing his poetry" interested him far more than "his finished products, since they represented his fallen state" (189). Taylor enacted verbal failure, Keller asserted, "to *show* he needed the help of his God. Not the critic's help — God's." Taylor, "the great Acting Poet (both as stand-in and as self-dramatist in a role) of early America" (190), played a role encouraged by preparationism and necessitated by Puritan views regarding the insufficiency of language. The result was a persona liberated by his theology, a speaker free to assume various roles in his search for signs of grace. For Keller, Taylor was "the first American to discover language as a way out of some of the oppressiveness of the Fall, even while the way out was indigenous to the system of the Fall itself" (194). While this argument squared well with Taylor's constant denigration of his poems, Keller's emphasis on verbal play suggested a modern (or perhaps postmodern) view of verbal discourse that understated Taylor's fundamentally serious motives for writing. Taylor was working out his own salvation in fear and trembling — not that of a fictive or ludic self. Although Keller's Taylor was attractive from the standpoint of current theoretical perspectives on the autonomy of literary discourse, it seemed unlikely that the poet saw such earnest spiritual work as "his own game, not God's at all" (188).

Affinities between Taylor's self-creation and poststructuralist theory were more systematically asserted by Michael Clark, who had pioneered a semiological approach to Puritan texts in the late 1970s by arguing that Puritan signs simultaneously provided and blocked access to the divine (1978). Clark now applied the tools of semiotics to a discussion of heaven/ earth dichotomies central to the Puritan imagination (1985a). Agreeing with Scheick (1974a) and Daly (1978) that Puritanism had been unfairly associated with a gnostic dismissal of the physical world, Clark argued that for Puritans, symbolic and linguistic mediation had been effected by the two chief articulations of the divine, the Incarnate Word (God/man) and the Revealed Word (divine truth/human language). The primacy of the Bible encouraged a Puritan obsession with signs that both revealed and concealed the divine realm that they signified. By describing the world as a text that both represented (because divinely created) and could not represent (because fallen) the divine framework, Puritan semiology did not eschew language but centered on it as a vehicle for bridging the heavenly and earthly realms even as they remained "ontologically distinct and epistemologically antithetical" (75). The gap between historical and aesthetic agendas in the criticism, Clark suggested, found potential closure in the theory of signs. Such an approach suggested a reading of Taylor that underscored the universal problems of expression as well as the solutions specific to *Puritan* expression. In another essay Clark argued the relevance of semi-autonomous linguistic structures to Taylor's speaker (1985b). Complaining of a lack of theoretical sophistication in early American literary studies, Clark pointed to the prevalence of biographical readings as evidence of a general neglect of Foucault's call for the study of language as an "object of knowledge" rather than as a mere medium for the expression of ideas (122). The usual assumption of biographical critics — that texts simply express the author's meaning — also ignored Lacan's "symbolic order of experience" and the constructed nature of textual "subjectivity" (123). Texts, Clark argued, reveal "discursive strategies that constitute the individual as author or speaker" rather than the reverse (124). Applying this view to Taylor, Clark maintained that the Meditations were best seen as a "discursive gesture" by which Taylor tried "to situate himself as subject in and to the order of discourse" (125). Taylor constructed a grammar of his relation to Christ in speech-acts that were neither rhetorical nor autobiographical but discursive in that they located his textual identity within "a broad network of social relations and theological hierarchies" (129). In accordance with Heidegger's dictum that "language speaks man," the "grammar of grace" set forth in the Meditations created their speaking subject (129). Alan Leander MacGregor soon found similar linguistic autonomy in Taylor's use of metaphor (1988). Building on Clark, Michael North (1979), and Clark Griffith (1966), MacGregor applied a deconstructive approach to the Meditations, "de-theologizing" Taylor's poetic by stressing "his linguistic production of transcendence" through a "disparity" of images that was "constitutive, not disruptive, of their meanings" (351, 337). Applying Paul Ricouer's theory that metaphor invokes "*heuristic* fictions" that subvert referential ties to reality and thus constitute new discursive "meanings" (338), MacGregor argued that Taylor enacted such "cognitive redescription" as a means of opening up a "new predication" of the divine (338). Recasting Griffith's argument for the "momentum" of Taylor's metaphors in poststructuralist terms, MacGregor argued that Taylor's metaphors simultaneously asserted their own power and conceded the infinite superiority of God's metaphors. In the "Preface" to *Gods Determinations*, for instance, the disparity of vehicle and tenor in the image of the bowling alley forced Ricouer's "semantic *im*pertinence" in a leap beyond the rational (342). Linking the "Prologue" to *Gods Determinations* rather than to the Meditations, MacGregor argued that Taylor's juxtaposition of "pen" and "crumb" created a similar fiction that projected God as an ideal reader capable of grasping the transcendent "new pertinence toward which the poet gropes" (349). Enacting a conventionally Christian "ritual decomposition of the self," Taylor saw himself and his language as "signs pointing elsewhere" (358). Jerome DeNuccio similarly argued from the "Bright Beams" of Meditation 1.22 that Taylor followed Richard Baxter's "semiotic lesson" in seeking a "concrete sign" of the ineffable (1988:10). By moving from "mere cognition to the perceptible level of affection," Taylor invoked "a semiotics of God's glory" (11).

Such overt applications of contemporary theory were rare, perhaps because most critics remained unconvinced that Puritan conceptualizations of expression and self had been sufficiently applied to Taylor's work. Most critics leaned toward theological rather than theoretical structures to explain how Taylor "fashioned" an identity without deliberately doing so — without adopting a spiritual persona, as Keller suggested, in order to "deceive God" into saving him because he was so "good at being no good" (1985:193). That Taylor's speaker embodied inner processes inseparable from Puritan psychological, linguistic, and devotional structures was a central critical assumption in the 1980s. But those structures had become considerably broader and more pluralistic then they had seemed in the 1960s, when Grabo proposed his view of a mystical Taylor. Since Grabo's monograph (1961a), historians had been developing a far more volatile model of Puritan inner life, one in which Taylor seemed less an exception than an especially articulate spokesman. Edmund Morgan (1963), Norman Pettit (1966), Owen Watkins (1972), Sacvan Bercovitch (1975), Philip Greven (1977), David Leverenz (1980), Charles Hambrick-Stowe (1982), Patricia Caldwell (1983), John Owen King (1983), Charles Lloyd Cohen (1986), Ann Kibbey (1986), David D. Hall (1989), and Andrew Delbanco (1989) were lining out a surprisingly rich emotionalism in Puritanism. For Bercovitch, Taylor exemplified a "ritual celebration-exorcism" suggesting that despite their scholasticism, "the Puritans exalted will above intellect, experience above theory, precept, and tradition" (21). Leverenz cast Taylor's turmoil in psychoanalytic terms, citing his excretory images as expressions of Puritan anality and his images of food and drink as reflections of the parental aspect of the Puritan God (111, 124). Taylor's private poems, Leverenz argued, reflected an "American tradition of redeeming contaminated society by retreating into solitude" at the "breakup of shared fantasy and shared community" (199). King argued for the formulaic rather than literally autobiographical nature of confessions of sin by such "benign" seventeenth-century ministers as Taylor (57). Delbanco similarly cited Taylor's use of a

Puritan "language of ceremony" that compensated for the sensory plainness of Puritan worship (140). And in his important study of Puritan devotional life, Hambrick-Stowe called the Meditations "characteristic of common practice" (20) as expressions of Taylor's preparation for the Supper, for renewed assurance of his election, and "for the perfection of sainthood in eternity" (208). Suggesting that Taylor sometimes contemplated physical objects like the communion loaf and cup, Hambrick-Stowe argued that the poems were not self-contained texts but were completed only in the administration of the sacrament. The fact that the poems, offered as "interim praise" in anticipation of celestial music (215), became "more mystically erotic" after 1700 showed that Puritans could achieve progress in their spiritual experience.

Such psychological and devotional paradigms figured prominently in studies of *Gods Determinations*. George Sebouhian drew the clearest parallels between the poem's structure and the morphology of conversion (1981/82). Building on Michael Colacurcio (1967) and David Parker (1976/77), Sebouhian outlined a five-part sequence, leading from election through conversion, that was dramatized by the poem's agonistic themes and by the heightened affections of its final lyrics. The preparationist Taylor, focusing on the Second and Third Ranks as representations of hesitant believers, stressed the salvific agency of preaching by depicting Soul's dependence on the advice of the experienced Saint. Appending a detailed chart correlating individual lyrics with the stages of conversion, Sebouhian argued that Taylor's careful structuring revealed a "complex orchestration of form" frequently overlooked by critics (236). J. Daniel Patterson modified Colacurcio's conclusions by arguing that Taylor's audience in *Gods Determinations* was not limited to Half-Way members but encompassed all of the elect (1987). Reading the poem as a dramatization of an *ordo salutis* applicable to all believers, Patterson saw in the figure of Saint a reflection of Taylor's belief that the converted should help their unconverted brethren, a view consistent with the poet's liberal views regarding evidence for salvation. For Patterson, the chief feature of Taylor's preparationism was a "consistently positive, optimistic" hope of the potential for grace (77). Elsewhere Patterson addressed several textual and interpretive difficulties in the poem. He untangled the difficult syntax of "The Preface" by arguing that "Sea's" should be read "sea as" (1985), and clarified a crux in stanza eight of "Christ's Reply" complicated by Taylor's inconsistent revising of the passage (1989b). Finally, he took issue with the text in the Yale *Poems*, arguing that three of the fifty-six emendations that Stanford made to the version in the "Poetical Works" were unnecessary (1989a).

Patterns of Puritan identity had the greatest impact, however, on readings of the Meditations as critics began to revaluate Taylor's spiritual experience in light of revised views of the Puritan psyche. Extending Louis Martz's focus on Taylor as a meditative poet (1960), Ursula Brumm contributed to the study of the poet's devotional processes by underscoring Thomas Hooker's role in promoting a meditative intensity in New England that was clearly embodied in Taylor's verse (1983). She later stressed Taylor's struggle between sin and sanctity, a struggle reflected in his juxtapositions of images of decay and disease, as in Meditation 1.34, with images of light and sparkling gems (1987). Brumm now saw Taylor's use of such images as far less unusual for a Puritan than she had previously argued (1970:82). Maintaining that Taylor derived "ideas and their visualization" from traditions of Puritan meditation, she compared his devotional methods with those of Hooker and Edmund Calamy (1985:331). Taylor, following Calamy's advice to meditate on the Word and the world, exploited both sources in poems that confirmed a circular relation between effective praise and grace. In her defense of a distinctive and original Protestant meditative tradition that was not merely derivative of Catholic practice, Brumm distinguished between "meditative" and merely "contemplative" verse, arguing that Taylor wrote truly meditative poetry while Bradstreet did not (324). But given the emerging richness of Puritan spiritual life, this distinction, as well as the careful separation of Catholic from Protestant devotional practice, seemed more problematic than such arguments would have appeared ten years earlier. In a substantial introduction to selections from Bradstreet and Taylor published in the Paulist Press series on "Sources of American Spirituality," Hambrick-Stowe presented Taylor as a poet solidly grounded in traditions of Christian meditation encompassing Catholic and Puritan alike (1988). Although he distinguished Catholic meditative practice from a Puritan spirituality of "householders" rooted in the here and now (19), Hambrick-Stowe painted Catholic-Puritan devotional continuities with a broad brush that balanced an overly narrow emphasis on a strictly "Calvinist" Taylor. Confirming that Bradstreet and Taylor wrote to strengthen their faith, not to assert sectarian affiliations or to create polished works of art, Hambrick-Stowe followed Martz, Grabo, and Keller in underscoring the primacy of devotional processes in the poetry. Still, his suggestion that Taylor never wrote with readers in mind seemed to ignore many, if not most, of Taylor's poems, including some that were included in the collection. Although he stated that Taylor did not write *Gods Determinations* "or any poem for publication but as part of his own spiritual exercises" (143), he conceded that this "didactic" poem revealed Taylor in the decidedly public roles of preacher and theologian.

Grabo, the earliest defender of a contemplative Taylor, had met with considerable opposition in the 1960s and 1970s from scholars who argued that the poet's moods were accountable within a decidedly non-mystical Puritanism. In retrospect it seems that Taylor's orthodoxy needed to be more firmly established and widely accepted before critics were willing to acknowledge the devotional elements that Grabo stressed. Moreover, by the 1980s the existence of some form of "mysticism" seemed more probable within the Puritan experience of the faith. By mid-decade Larzer Ziff could argue that Taylor deviated from metaphysical practice because his meditative pattern was "not that of metaphoric elaboration but of mystical contemplation — awakening, purgation, rapture, and union" (1986:41). It was thus ironic that as other critics began to reconsider the devotional aspect of the poetry, Grabo modified his earlier position. In the revision of his 1961 monograph he conceded that "earlier claims for Taylor's personal mysticism were possibly overstated" and argued that the poet "could operate within a mystical literary tradition without himself being a mystic" (1988:xi). "Speaking for the representative soul," Grabo maintained, "Taylor used the contemplative way to intensify more ordinary Protestant religious experiences" (51). Taylor's purpose, Grabo repeated from the first edition, was "to produce a vision, not perhaps for his physical eyes, but for the eye of the soul that is the mirror or image of God in him" (40). In 1988, however, this statement — in retrospect not so different from Scheick's argument against Taylor's mysticism (1974a) — did not seem so radical. Nor did Grabo's retention of the traditionally Catholic distinction between Taylor's "active" and "contemplative" life. Where Grabo continued to part company with most critics, however, was his insistence that Taylor "passes beyond" particular selfhood to achieve "a state of complete mystical union with Christ" (51). Yet at the end of the study he concluded that Taylor's meditative speaker "defines and measures himself against a mystical pattern that he can admire, approach, and use, even if he can never realize the mystical ecstasy in person" (117). This ambivalence aside, Grabo joined Rowe in conceding that Taylor's devotional processes did not always enhance his poetic achievement, arguing that his focus "on the idea or the underlying logic rather than the image itself" often prompted him to develop his images inconsistently (82). While the revised *Edward Taylor* retained all the strengths of the original as a comprehensive discussion of the poetry in light of Taylor's life and thought, Grabo's revisions, consisting mostly of cuts from his discussion of the earlier poems, were extremely light. Rather than incorporating recent scholarship on Taylor and Puritan devotional life generally into a defense of his original thesis, he both conceded too much and altered too little.

John Gatta soon offered a less ambivalent defense of Taylor's devotional intensity. Early in the decade Gatta had argued that Taylor accepted the "mildly heterodox" idea that glorified saints resided higher than the angels in the cosmic hierarchy (1982). Finding precedent for Taylor's views in the Bible (Heb. 2:16 and Eph. 2:6), the Greek Fathers, Richard Baxter's *The Saint's Everlasting Rest* (London: 1650), and Increase Mather's *The Mystery of Christ* (Boston: 1686), Gatta argued that this "super-angelic anthropology" accounted for Taylor's unusual "optimism" (367). Indeed, Taylor's emphasis on "the miracle of *theosis*" reinforced a "mystical impulse" throughout the Meditations (368). In *Gracious Laughter* Gatta developed his emphasis on Taylor's spiritual joy, linking Keller's stress on verbal play (1985) with seventeenth-century meditative structures by arguing that the poet's exercise of metaphysical wit enacted a "reverent parody," a "distorted imitation of Holy Writ" that articulated his sense of unworth (1989:14). Taylor's awareness that he could not render effective praise invoked a "comic disparity between earthly vehicle and divine tenor" (18) that enabled him to become a "holy fool for the sake of Christ" (23). Arguing that Taylor repeatedly attacked his sins rather than "his own person" (20), Gatta thus found joyous affirmation at the heart of Taylor's self-deprecation. Such verbal exuberance countered the stasis of religious melancholy as each poem moved "from splenetic torpor to sanguine delight" (49). In this manner, Taylor achieved a gracious — because fully engaged — participation in biblical promise. Helping him to generate and maintain a strong religious assurance, Taylor's self-attacks as poet and sinner intensified "a barely disguised confidence in the speaker's redeemed status" (60). Agreeing with Rowe that Taylor wrote as an "Everysaint," less "the romantic solitary than a representative self" (76), Gatta argued that the Meditations assumed social significance from their sacramental focus and from the poet's search for a "festival frame of spirit" appropriate to all covenanted believers (94). This devotional affirmation also informed *Gods Determinations*, a "counterjeremiad" (103) aimed at instilling "a final comic vision of rebirth and recovery" by which Taylor's readers could take delight in the redemptive schema (111).

For Gatta, Taylor's private expressions of holy delight were in some sense mystical. Agreeing with Donald Stanford (1972:70) that the specific "episode of mystical illumination" recorded in "The Experience," "The Return," and "The Reflexion" may have prompted Taylor's decision to write the numbered poems (1989:142), Gatta defined the poet's spirituality broadly, as a "deification" of the soul through the "promise of union with God in love" (145). Still, he connected "the self's alchemical refashioning" in the poetry to a decidedly Puritan search for assurance (155). Reiterating Scheick's view (1974a) that Christ's dual nature gave Taylor access to sanctity, Gatta aligned himself more closely with Grabo and Keller in his stress on Taylor's contemplative joy. Arguing that Taylor saw "glee" as "the emotional incarnation of grace" (149), Gatta defined spiritual exuberance as Taylor's primary meditative response to the Supper, the biblical types, the Canticles allegory, and the created world. Unlike Keller, however, Gatta did not push Taylor's joy toward proto-modernity. His was neither a modern nor an "American" Taylor, but "a real Puritan as well as a real poet" (207). Spiritual joy also figured prominently in Parker Johnson's view that Taylor's poems recorded neither a "doubt-stricken conscience" nor "traumatic spiritual experience" (1988:85). On the contrary, Taylor's constant anticipation of his transfiguration into a glorified saint gave the poems a futurity that allowed him to fail without dire consequences. Biblical rhetoric, a partial corrective to fallen speech, became the source of Taylor's delight in his correspondence with the divine, especially in the later Meditations. For Johnson, as for Keller, Taylor was liberated by the inherent futurity of his religio-aesthetic practice: as "preparatory tunings" in imitation of the "more accurate instrument" of the Bible, the poems reinforced the poet's optimistic anticipation of celestial glory (96).

Gatta and Johnson placed Taylor's self-deprecation within an inner ritual shaped by theological and psychological paradigms of self. Taylor's self-attacks, as Charles Mignon had observed twenty years earlier (1968), were inseparable from his self-affirmation as an assured believer. In this context, too, his seeming lack of imagistic coherence and development assumed artistic purpose. As articulations of an extrarational dimension in Taylor's verbal ritual, imagistic leaps mirrored the playfulness of affections heightened by an assurance of salvation that Charles Lloyd Cohen called "a reiterated experience of weakness transubstantiating into power" (1986:108). As this renewed interest in Taylor's extrarationality suggested, the debate over his mysticism had stemmed in part from the unavoidably ambiguous terminology of religious experience. It was also becoming apparent, however, that the debate had been linked to theoretical issues involving textual subjectivity and self-construction. In the 1980s, what "really" went on in Taylor's mind when he wrote was beginning to seem less important — or perhaps simply less recoverable — than what he *thought* was going on. In short, Taylor's "real" self in a literally biographical sense seemed less accessible than before, except perhaps, as Clark argued, as a discursive construct shaped by Puritan theories of language and psychology. Although the scholarship did not directly acknowledge it, Taylor was beginning to undergo something of the "death of the author" posed by Roland Barthes. The result, as was the case in literary studies generally, was a birth of interest in Taylor's discursive speaker. If the poet behind the poetry seemed unreachable, the poet *in* the poetry might be dealt with on "his" own terms.

Although few critics went along with a thorough deconstructing of Edward Taylor, the growing emphasis on extrapersonal structures derived from Puritan psychology, soteriology, and discourse countered a view of the Meditations as naively or literally autobiographical texts. Groundwork for seeing an extrapersonal element in Taylor's speaker had been laid by Scheick, who noted Taylor's "incessant endeavor to assert his self and to appraise that self's relation to the 'Sacred selfe'" (1974a:161), and by Keller, who found in the Meditations a "mythic Taylor" and a "Self above oneself" (1975a:74). Critics focusing on Taylor's biblical models, including Lewalski (1979:397), Hammond (1981/82), Guruswamy (1985), and Rowe (1986:223), identified a similarly paradigmatic dimension in Taylor's voice, as did Clark, who eschewed a literally expressive function in the verse in favor of a "subject" whose coherence reflected semiotic rather than psychological unity (1985b). At the end of the decade Jerome DeNuccio argued that in Meditation 1.22 Taylor learned from the impossibility of adequate praise his need to enact a "self-emptying" (1989:21). By writing, he intensified his faith that "he will himself become a perfect poem" (23). At mid-decade Michael Schuldiner took a theological and archetypal approach to selfhood in Taylor, arguing that extrapersonal patterns emerging in the First Series of the Meditations reflected the four parts of Calvin's first stage of redemption as well as the epic journey of the Christianized classical hero (1986). Schuldiner maintained that in his progression toward assurance and Calvin's "Christian Liberty" (114), Taylor experienced "illumination" in "The Experience" and "The Return," confronted his pride in Meditation 1.24, underwent the classic "faith-doubt dilemma" in Meditation 1.36, and reached a crisis in Meditation 1.40 resulting in his subsequent focus on "a paradigm in the life of Christ" that led to the full assurance voiced in Meditation 1.41 (120). Proposing the classical journey as "an alternative, secular means of access for the modern reader" (121), Schuldiner traced Taylor's progress, guided by the Holy Spirit, past dangers of arrogance suggestive of Calypso, a confrontation with Siren-like sin, an inner dilemma recalling the passage between Scylla and Charybdis, and a replication of Theseus's escape from the Labyrinth, guided by the "Clew of Wonders" of assurance in Meditation 1.41.

Such clearly articulated reflections of Puritan theology and psychology further diminished Taylor's anomalous status in early New England. By the 1980s most critics agreed that Taylor did not differ from other Puritan poets in kind but in degree. He became an "example" not in Keller's sense of a poet striking out on his own (1975a), but as a poet who pushed the imaginative structures of his time and place toward expressive limits made possible by his relentless interiority. As Peter White stated in his introduction to an important collection of essays on Puritan verse, early New Englanders were emerging as people "in love with language and ideas" (1985:1) — a view that Taylor had done much to stimulate. Armed with bases for comparison firmer than merely assuming that Taylor was a better poet, a number of critics followed Scheick (1974a), Jantz (1976, 1985), and Daly (1978) in solidifying Taylor's place in New England literary culture. Scheick incorporated Taylor into a study of the Puritan funeral elegy, citing his poem on Samuel Hooker as an example of the elegy's power to provoke the reader's self-examination in light of the deceased's example (1985). Ritamarie Sargent, comparing Bradstreet and Taylor, maintained that Taylor's elegies not only expressed personal loss but reflected his ministerial duties as he moved "from passive obedience of the fate to active involvement in the cure" (1984:157). Jeffrey Walker saw the typically Puritan acrostic structures in Taylor's elegies on Charles Chauncy and Francis Willoughby as "examples of the visual and verbal fireworks" that he abandoned in his poem for first wife Elizabeth (1985:254). Daniel Patterson argued that "Leaden heeld" in Meditation 2.1 recalled biblical descriptions of God's slowness to anger, a popular theme among Puritan poets (1984). Agnieszka Salska placed *Gods Determinations* and the diary-like Meditations on opposite sides of a public/private divide characterizing all

Puritan writing (1984). The Meditations, more emotional than the sermons and the public verse and fuller in depicting the mutuality of the saint's relationship to the divine, reflected a Puritan impulse toward confession and self-expression consistent with Taylor's relative lack of concern with poetic form and craft. Taylor also figured in Klaus Weiss's argument that Puritan religion and artistic mimesis were not antithetical, as commonly assumed (1984). Reiterating the views of Scheick (1974a) and Daly (1978), Weiss cited a twofold mimesis in Puritan writing: an imitation of the world and an imitation of Christ. Because Puritans saw the world as a copy of a pre-existing idea in the divine mind, the *imitatio Christi* also encompassed an imitation of nature. The order that God had stamped upon the world — from elemental and vegetative life up through man and the angels — defined the Puritan conception of aesthetic beauty. Taylor, Weiss argued, was more directly involved than his contemporaries in an imitation of Christ, especially in his stress on Christ as theanthropic mediator and in his images drawn from the arts, which suggested God's role as an artist of both the created world and the revealed Word. Scheick reconfirmed a Puritan Taylor by arguing that the poet effected a simultaneous assertion and effacement of self that was part of normal Puritan spirituality (1983c:1412). Toward the end of the decade Scheick placed Taylor among contemporary poets in their shared fascination with emblems, citing his creation of multiple bowl-like emblems in Meditation 1.8 and his use of his own face as an emblem in Meditation 2.3 (1988b:94). Confirming that Taylor was similar to but not derivative of the metaphysicals, Scheick argued for a "deliberately executed decorum of imperfection" in the verse (95). A balance of self-assertion and self-effacement resulted in Taylor's being "curiously within and outside his poem at the same time" as he occupied a "liminal space between despair and presumption" (95). For Scheick, Taylor was not only a true Puritan but an accomplished poet whose seemingly random associations stemmed from his use of facts "commonplace" in his era but obscure to modern readers (97).

As the seventeenth-century Taylor waxed, the proto-American Taylor began to wane. A few critics in the 1980s continued to see the poet as a precursor of American literary traditions. At mid-decade, for example, Weiss argued that Puritan mimesis, as practiced by Taylor and his contemporaries, influenced such later American thinkers as Edwards and Emerson (1984). Lewis Putnam Turco called Taylor the first American "amateur" poet, arguing that his value lay not so much in the poetry itself as in his foreshadowing of Emerson

(1986:10-11). And Carter Martin, who compared Taylor with Donald Barthelme, commented on Taylor's method of "linguistic fantasy" in Meditation 2.48 and its role in forcing readers to transcend the rational in order to achieve awe at divine mystery (1985). Although Martin stressed thematic and generic rather than nationalistic ties between the two writers, claims for Taylor's American identity began to assume a tentativeness that reflected broader changes in American literary historiography. To be sure, traditionally "American" patterns — a penchant for symbolic language, a concern with identity, visionary or quasi-visionary aims, an attraction to cyclical or episodic structures — could be found in the poems. Yet it became more and more difficult to find such patterns without imposing aesthetic or nationalistic structures determined by contemporary cultural and political agendas. Hayden White, Stephen Greenblatt, and others were arguing that the past could not be reconstructed, or even viewed, free from the ideological narratives of the present. Gatta's comment that Taylor was not an "American" poet but a Puritan one (1988:207) reflected a growing reluctance to assert his importance for American literary history. On a practical level, this goal had always been problematic. Was it possible to argue literary influence, at least in the usual sense, for someone who had no readers among later American poets until the 1930s and thus no direct literary heirs? Taylor's work could certainly be located within a progression of symbolic thought and writing in America, as Lowance had argued at the beginning of the decade. But Lowance conceded that such a view was inevitably shaped by later historical, critical, and political trends when he remarked that early New England's "language of Canaan" would be reincarnated in America's "articulation of imminent fulfillment," in its "work-ethic and the impulse to make the world safe for democracy" (1980:295). Keller, the most forceful proponent of an "American" Taylor in the 1970s, scarcely mentioned this theme in his last Taylor essay, and then only in terms of the poet's ludic self responding to the relative freedom of the New World (1985).

The growing critique of nationalistic undercurrents in the practice of American literary history began to shatter the scholarly consensus that marked the 1980s, not just among Taylorians but among American literary scholars generally. Michael Colacurcio had raised the issue for early Americanists in the late 1970s when he argued that the usual historical models merely reflected "our own geometric (or other metaphorical) arrangement of all texts within a given field" (1978:130). Writing American literary history, Colacurcio remarked, usually meant "creating some putative whole by reading texts in sequence" (130) in accordance with a pervasive belief in the "mystery" of America (131). Summarizing a growing critique of an aesthetic and nationalistic bias that some critics found in American literary historiography, David D. Hall argued that the traditional history of early American literature had been shaped by a "fusion of modernism and nativism" implicit in the search for American precedents in colonial writing (1983:325). The modernist bias was attacked by Hammond, who maintained that post-romantic preferences for the obviously expressive or confessional poem had rendered critics unable to deal with "the central traits of the Puritan poem: its didacticism and its conventionality" (1987:126). The nationalistic bias was attacked by John McWilliams, who argued that in the "classic" studies of early American literature, the search for "distinctly American" traits "took precedence over the study of transatlantic patterns"; as a result, early texts were valued only as "prototypes" of nineteenth-century American writing (1983:129). Carl Kropf (1983) and William Spengemann (1983) issued similar critiques. Spengemann, arguing for closer attention to the nonbelletristic texts of "British America," agreed with McWilliams that the longstanding dominance of early New England writers had contributed to a neglect of the transatlantic contexts that prevailed at the time. The critics' need to isolate early American writers from British literary culture, Spengemann later argued, stemmed from a fear that these writers, if placed within an Anglo-American context, would "lose not only their American identity but the literary virtues we attribute to them" (1989:142). Grabo questioned not only the dominance of New England Puritanism in early American studies but the very concept of Puritanism as traditionally defined. Puritan culture, less monolithic than commonly assumed, had been unduly stressed because of its presumed connections with the nineteenth-century American canon (1987). Philip Gura agreed that a 1950s American Studies search for nationalistic forerunners, especially in New England as the presumed birthplace of national identity, continued to distort the reading of early American texts (1988). R. C. De Prospo, restating the issue as the decade drew to a close, similarly lamented the "perennial supporting role" of early American literature as "the first and least articulation of what will be said later, and more fully, and better" (1989:249). The source of the problem, De Prospo argued, was a "foundational ethnocentrism" that imposed a "hegemony of modern humanism" on the writing and teaching of American literary history (249, 255).

Early Taylor studies had reflected just such a tug-of-war between nationalism and aesthetic elitism: one group of critics enlisted Taylor in the broader effort to put American writers on a par with British as suitable objects of professional literary study, while another argued his artistic inferiority to seventeenth-century English poets who seemed to embody modernist aesthetic values presumed to be universal. By the 1980s, as McWilliams suggested, literary nationalism had won out. "Are we writing so assiduously on Taylor," he asked, "because he is a New England Puritan belatedly fitted into the tradition we all teach?" (1983:132). Taylor's rise, of course, had been accelerated by his perceived affiliations with English metaphysicals who preceded him and American symbolists who followed. But it was becoming difficult to validate either group — let alone the man in the middle — by appealing to aesthetic traits innocent of twentieth-century cultural predilections and the historical development of professional literary study. The consolidation of Taylor studies began to dissolve, but not from the pressure of deconstructionists, whose self-professed inability to shed steady light on texts prompted a return to cultural, historical, and psychological frameworks and the construction of unitary readings. Instead, the consensus broke with the more pragmatic recognition that reading is always political, that ideological choices determine critical methods and the results that they achieve. As pluralistic social perspectives and historicized aesthetic perspectives began to influence the profession, it became harder to see Taylor as representative of an "American" literary tradition. Which America? Whose literature? And finally, Which Taylor? The scholarship in this sense came full circle: the many Edward Taylors who populated the 1940s and 1950s were poised to return with the 1990s, as scholars and critics realized that the Taylor they saw depended on the choices they made. If Taylorians became less sure of themselves and if the answers they provided were more tentative as a result, the scholarship was about to assume a new and exciting diversity.

5: Prospects — Since 1990

BY 1990, AFTER A HALF-CENTURY of scholarship and criticism, it was time to take stock. This retrospective mood marked a collection of essays that appeared in the inaugural issue of *Studies in Puritan American Spirituality*, edited by Michael Schuldiner. In their accounts of how Taylor's texts had been edited, Donald Stanford, Norman Grabo, Thomas Davis, and Charles Mignon confirmed that the poet's rise was no mere accident; on the contrary, a talented and diverse group of critics had established his importance in a process inseparable from their aesthetic preferences and the scholarly choices they had made. Given recent and profound changes in the practice of literary history, however, especially the growing awareness of the difficulty of assessing Taylor's artistic achievement and national relevance, it was inevitable that future work would reflect different preferences and choices. Although the new eclecticism of the early 1990s made it difficult to predict where those choices would ultimately lead, the consensus of the preceding decade fragmented into five basic strands. The first approach was aesthetic, as Taylor's poetry was incorporated into an artistic reappraisal of Puritan writing that was sensitive to the historical nature of expressive goals and literary taste. The second was biographical, as the poems were linked with greater precision to Taylor's artistic development as he responded to personal and social turmoil in his life. A third approach was to investigate a variety of Taylor's sources, not simply to discover his precedents but to demonstrate his artistic integration of these materials into viable poems. A fourth approach connected the poetry with Puritan patterns of self-experience and literary codes that underscored the historical distance of Taylor's work. Finally, gender criticism aligned Taylor with an American tradition of thought and writing that no longer represented rugged individualism and visionary intensity, but psychic repression and social reaction. Although these frameworks for reading — aesthetics, biography, sources, theology, and psychology — overlapped at many points, they marked out distinct and promising directions for future work.

The theme of reassessment was implicit in another publication that ushered in the 1990s. In her selections for the *Heath Anthology of American Litera-*

ture, Karen Rowe contextualized Taylor as a poet steeped in historical and aesthetic otherness (1990). Her inclusion of two of his Psalm paraphrases emphasized his biblicism; these were followed by six lyrics from *Gods Determinations*, four "occasional" poems, nine Meditations, selections from the "Valedictory" poem, and the second version of "A Fig for thee, Oh! Death." Most unusual, perhaps, was the appearance of only three early Meditations, a sharp contrast to the usual anthology emphasis on ostensibly "metaphysical" early poems like "The Experience" and "The Reflexion." Other anthologies edited by George Perkins (1985), George McMichael (1989), and Emory Elliott (1991) continued to encourage a relatively context-free explication of the poetry by stressing the occasional poems and the better-known Meditations, although Nina Baym's selections in the *Norton Anthology of American Literature* included a Psalm paraphrase and brief selections from a *Treatise* sermon (1989). The headnote in Perkins still maintained that the "metaphysical" Taylor forbade publication (97), while the McMichael headnote stated that the poet probably considered his verse "too sensual for a clergyman" and that his "mystical, even occult intensity" looked forward to Dickinson and Whitman (148). The headnote in Elliott, citing precedent for Taylor in the metaphysicals, called Taylor both "thoroughly Puritan" and "distinctly non-Puritan," asserting that "it is for their exception to practically every rule of Puritan poetry" that Taylor's poems are "most highly prized" (151). Rowe's Taylor, by contrast, was not slicked up for undergraduates; she insisted that his "occasional lyrics" appealed to modern tastes because of historical accident rather than aesthetic inevitability (344). In classrooms as in scholarly journals, the quality of the poems could no longer be asserted without confronting their alienating difference and with it, the historical nature of artistic goals and standards. As we have seen, William J. Scheick had pointed to a general failure to account for Taylor's artistry (1988a). The difficult intersection of aesthetics and history, together with the issue of Taylor's "American" identity, continued to provoke questions that fostered the new scholarly diversity.

The American Taylor, on the wane during the preceding decade, reappeared in Richard Ruland and Malcolm Bradbury's history of American literature as a double "story": the literary historian's account, and "the fable a country told itself as it tried to understand its own becoming in writing" (1991:xix). Although Ruland and Bradbury considered Taylor a solid Puritan, they found "something occult and Platonist" in his thought and an unusual "baroque intensity" in his style (23). Citing a fundamental compatibility of Puritan and metaphysical sensibilities, they saw Taylor as a precursor of "the moral, psychological, and symbolic intensity that comes to characterize so much of the richest American writing" (26). The view of America as a narrative written and rewritten in the process of settlement was supported by Stephen Fender, who underscored the profound illegibility of the land to European newcomers (1992). Fender cited Taylor's *Diary* as evidence that the typical Atlantic passage narrative was a "lively prose record of surface phenomena" that was only later "turned into a story" with narrative significance (123, 126). Few other critics, however, chose to confront Taylor's Americanness. Even though the 1988 *Columbia Literary History of the United States* had been offered as a progressive revision of the field, R. C. De Prospo claimed that the book perpetuated a traditional "cult of continuity" based on a "presentist marginalizing of the past" (1992:235). Arguing the need to see the past as "*difference*, not continuity" (256), De Prospo called for the recreation of "a more mobile early American literature" in the interest of "deconstructing American literary nationalism" and its traces in the scholarship (258). One attempt to avoid modern assumptions of artistic worth and national identity, as we have seen, was to connect Taylor's art with poststructuralist discursive models, an approach taken up by Karl Keller (1975a, 1985), Michael Clark (1978/79, 1985a, 1985b) and Alan MacGregor (1988). But for most scholars, the contexts of history, culture, and theology were too insistent for Taylor to be deconstructed so easily. Clark's discussion of Taylor's subjectivity as a tissue of linguistic and semiotic structures embedded in Puritan discourse (1985b) prompted the strongest reaction to what some critics saw as excessive or reductive theorizing. Calling Clark's views a form of "textual autism," David Shields argued for a return to the poetic text as a valid "object" that revealed something of Edward Taylor as a real person responding to his faith as a real force in his life (1990). Shields maintained that the poet was not "trapped in discourse" but used language to express recoverable theological and psychological concerns (314). Countering Clark's Heideggerian view that "language speaks man," Shields argued that language "can speak to us of man" — in this case, of the spiritual concerns of a believer who hoped to internalize "the divine presence" (311). Robert Daly issued a different response to the theorists' challenge (1990). Conceding that the goal of finding a "defining essence" in American writing had proved elusive, Daly argued for a shift from the essentialist terms of the older historiography to an anthropological view of American culture as "a collection of epistemological templates" (193, 194). Such connections as liminality, which Daly proposed as an American "family resemblance," could be asserted without invoking the "reductive or distorting continuity" that theorists were attacking (197).

Shields and Daly were not the only critics impatient with theory-oriented assertions of a fundamental unintelligibility in early American texts. Thomas Davis and William Scheick both reconfirmed, though in different ways, authorial intention and artistic design in Taylor's work. Scheick called attention to Taylor as a deliberate artist by demonstrating the poet's skillful integration of thematic and structural elements into coherent poems (1990). Citing a general "evasion" in critics' "desire to explain away, rather than to explain, Taylor's poetry" through unsupported generalizations (34), Scheick attacked the frequent assumption of "internal disorder" in the verse by arguing that the poet was more "original, inventive, and poetically accomplished" than generally acknowledged and that his work displayed a "play of these qualities" that was "coherent rather than chaotic" (36). Scheick had argued for the unifying function of emblem-like structures in Meditation 2.3 (1977) and *Gods Determinations* (1979). Now he selected Meditation 1.19 as an example of "a text of partially recoverable authorial intention" that demonstrated Taylor's meaningful integration of theological patterns, classical and biblical allusions, and a structurally unifying emblem into a poem whose underlying spiritual process was successfully reflected in "the hope-engendering perfect circle suggested by all the artistic elements in the poem" (1990:37). A theological progression from Creation through the Incarnation to the Judgment was reinforced by Taylor's manipulation of light/dark imagery and Christ/serpent oppositions. A second set of correspondences, based on allusions from Genesis and Revelation, conflated the classical Hercules with the triumphant Christ. These elements were united by an emblem of a pit, which transmuted into a meteor crater, a grave, the pit of hell, the depths of sin, a stomach that consumes the fleshly exterior of the elect, and a serpent's mouth. The coherence of these images, Scheick argued, reflected Taylor's desire to "maintain hope" (54) by achieving a "balanced account" of these elements through which he could restore cosmic order in anticipation of the Second Coming and a final uncoiling of the serpent in Christ's triumph. Countering charges by Barbara Lewalski (1979:388-426), Alan Howard (1972), Karen Rowe (1986:270), and John Gatta (1989:207) that Taylor's poetic skill was limited, Scheick argued that the poet sought "God's attention" not with humble artistic failure but genuine artistic accomplishment (57).

Scheick soon expanded his view of the Meditations as "artistic texts designed, like emblems, to be read" (1990:59) into a study of Puritan aesthetic structures that did not simply fold Puritan art into a vague "American literary tradition" (1992:4). Arguing that the "aesthetic dimension" of Puritan texts (1) lay in the "logogic" intersections of "secular and divine meanings" which pervaded Puritan language (2), Scheick proposed these "cruxes" or "sites" of tension as points at which Puritan authors and readers could "hesitate and contemplate the duality of signification in the temporal world" (3). These cruxes in Puritan discourse reflected a dynamic tension between the Renaissance validation of speech and the Reformed distrust of any speech not solidly rooted in biblical and allegorical contexts. Taylor, Scheick maintained, exploited these dualities in *Gods Determinations*, not merely in the contrast between Christ's speech and Satan's but in a dichotomy inherent in Satan's words themselves, in which a crux centering on the "hand" stuck between two fighting rams (*Poems*, 404) revealed signs of grace even in fallen speech. For Taylor and his contemporaries, Scheick argued, all postlapsarian language was, by virtue of its mediation of the sacred and the secular, a kind of "double-talk" (29). Bradstreet's and Taylor's skillful management of emblems as logogic cruxes produced a fundamental coherence concealed beneath a deliberately disordered surface. Scheick reprised his discussion of Meditation 1.19 as an example of such design, arguing that the poem revealed artful construction rather than naive expression blindly shaped by spiritual or biblical demands. The "aesthetic design" of such a poem was no accident, but the deliberate "work of Edward Taylor, a poet nervously hesitating over and playing at the logogic site where eternal definitions and temporal meanings (the corrupted dispersion of divine denotation) intertwine" (67).

Thomas Davis also argued that Taylor was a deliberate artist who was fully aware of "a general audience — not solely Christ — for his poetry" (1992:17). Placing the Meditations in the context of the changing conditions of Taylor's life in Westfield, Davis countered the critical tendency to ignore important shifts in the poet's artistic aims and attitudes. Taking issue with Charles Mignon (1968) and Karl Keller (1975a, 1985), who both stressed an unchanging process embodied in the Meditations, Davis argued from manuscript evidence that Taylor's practice of periodically recopying blocks of poems revealed the poet's view of his verse as "not in process but completed" (15). For Davis, the intervals of recopying and the final order of the poems suggested an evolution in spiritual and artistic goals shaped by Taylor's early life in Westfield, biblical and exegetical traditions, and the turmoil surrounding the New England mission, especially King Philip's War and the controversy over the Supper. In Davis's view, Taylor's highest artistic aims and achievements came early in the First Series of the Meditations. Those aims changed, however, as the Series progressed and Taylor gradually linked the poems more directly with the sermons and the sacrament in a deliberate reining in of his verse. Davis argued that Taylor restricted his initial ambitions because of his love for Christ and the recognition of his own limitations that this love brought (202). The poet's extreme biblicism also helped shape his rage for order: in his desire to activate the rich metaphors of Scripture within New England and himself, he sacrificed an earlier artistic individualism in order to achieve an increasingly neobiblical identity and integrity. Davis maintained that Taylor's initial poetic vocation, grounded in his ordination and the founding of the Westfield church, was marked by a shift from the elaborate acrostics of his early work to the "Coarse Iämbick" of the Meditations (23). At this point, too, Taylor — possibly in collaboration with wife Elizabeth — began the Psalm paraphrases, thus moving from the more secular forms of acrostic and elegy to David's biblical precedent, from poetic ingenuity to a biblical fidelity appropriate to a poet who would devote the rest of his days to meditating on Scripture. For Davis, *Gods Determinations* played a crucial role in this shift. Relating the two major sections of the poem to the Indian war and to debates surrounding the Half-Way Covenant of 1662, Davis argued from the relative unimportance of the Supper in the poem as well as in the original Foundation Day sermon that the sacrament emerged only later as an institutional framework for the verse. Despite its uneven quality, *Gods Determinations* represented a breakthrough in Taylor's poetic development, especially its final lyrics, which articulated the believer's "true freedom within the structure of the church" (44).

Citing the variety of voices and prosodic forms in *Gods Determinations*, Davis argued that the *Preparatory Meditations* actually reflected Taylor's "radical limiting of the range and scope of his poetry" (47). Carefully ordering his poems and periodically recopying blocks of poems, Taylor intended to create a poetic "artifact" by "imposing an order, adjusting experience to some sense of structure in his own mind" (50). The First Series, Davis maintained, was just such an artifact. Reiterating his early argument that the earliest Meditations were "occasional" rather than sacramental (1970/71), Davis pointed out that a regular interval suggestive of sacrament days emerged only later in the Series. In early poems like Meditation 4, Taylor did not yet see his poems as finished artistic products; instead he was obsessed with exploring the complex interplay of scriptural analogies, parallels, and correspondences. For Davis, this early exuberance, also evident in the occasional poems, emerged in the development of the first-person voice of the Meditations, Taylor's "extended Psalter" (64). At this point, the new minister gradually began to focus on the Supper as an articulation of "the emotional intensity that even ordinary Puritans often brought to the Sacrament" (65). Davis suggested that New England's increasing focus on post-conversion experience, prompted in part by Stoddardeanism, provided a context for the event recorded in the three titled poems — "the one 'experience' in all of Taylor's poetry that reflects a mystical vision," though not the kind usually associated with traditional mysticism (58). That Taylor at this point linked his self-deprecation more to his "inability to offer adequate praise" than to a deeper depravity reflected an optimism consistent with the spiritual intensity of "The Experience" (68). Davis cited Meditations 7 and 12 as illustrations of this early artistic confidence. But while subsequent poems revealed Taylor's growing artistic proficiency, such poetic pride could not continue without a Fall. In Meditations 19-22, Davis argued, Taylor recognized the sad contrast between his ambitious goals and the disappointing results. At this point the poet's equation of flawed art with inescapable sin became more frequent and insistent, until in Meditation 26 he confronted the implications of the "grace/poetry identification" implicit in such confident expressions as Meditation 7 (101). The loss of his wife, discord within his congregation, a major smallpox epidemic, and growing disputes with Stoddard soon culminated in the outburst — "My Sin! my Sin" — that opens Meditation 39. Davis argued that Taylor found antidotes to this despair in the Christic Advocate of Meditations 39 and 40 and the institutional ritual of the Supper. Chastened, Taylor recopied the preceding poems and began anew. The results of this crisis were reflected in the poet's greater emphasis on order, sequence, and interlocking themes as well as a closer connection between images and the biblical headnotes. This new stress on structure and regularity, Davis argued, allowed Taylor to continue his Meditations despite the distraction of "external events" (127).

Ten years after meditating on the Advocate, Taylor recopied the remaining poems of the First Series and began renumbering with a new Series and a new sequence on the biblical types. For Davis, the overall progression of the

Second Series from highly structured typology to the more open mode of allegory continued to reflect Taylor's external life. Events of the early 1690s, including the poet's marriage to Ruth Wyllys and the growth of his new family, salary disputes with Westfield, the addition of two deacons to assist him in his duties, and the relatively more stable politics of the colony, made Taylor more self-consciously "ministerial" (134). An even more crucial impetus for this shift toward poetic ritual was Stoddard's decision to institute his relaxed admission requirements for the Supper. With the sermons *Upon the Types of the Old Testament* and their verse counterparts, the close poem-sermon connection reflected in the poems following Meditation 1.41 became fixed. The external artistic and meditative structures offered by the types resulted in poems that were relatively less inventive, spontaneous, and expressive of "the poet's immediate experience" (139). For Davis, the Job paraphrases and the *Metrical History of Christianity* also reflected Taylor's increasing self-restriction as he sought to avoid the artistic pride of earlier poems in the First Series and pitfalls stemming from "the freedom of too much choice" (140). The poetry now shifted from inspiration to an obligation embodied in poems like Meditation 2.7, which was "primarily a rhymed addendum to the sermon" (149). Although Taylor occasionally managed, especially when treating the ceremonial types, "to impose a poetic rather than exegetical vision upon the material" (151), Davis cited Meditation 2.27 to illustrate the flat results in poems ordered not by personal experience but by "the external details of the Hebrew ritual" (154). Meditation 2.28, by contrast, was one of Taylor's better typological poems because it did not depend excessively on the sermon and thus provided an effective "bridge from sermon to the Lord's Supper" (159). Still, as Davis noted, it was the humble minister who predominated here, not the ambitious poet of the early First Series.

It was during the *Christographia* sequence, Davis argued, that Taylor entered the final stage in his poetic development. Having passed from his initial desire to fly "on the wings of his song to Christ's presence" to a "reluctant acknowledgment of his inevitable lisp" (165), he revealed in Meditation 2.43 his full resignation to the fact that the limits of language doomed his attempts to render praise worthy of Christ. Countering Norman Grabo's view of the interconnectedness of the poems and sermons in the *Christographia* sequence (1988:53), Davis argued that the poems in fact became less dependent on sermonic frameworks. At this point, too, the Song of Songs began to reclaim Taylor's attention as a meditative antidote to a series of distressing events: a general and personal decline in ministerial authority; disciplinary and civil disputes in Westfield; the deaths of friends and of his son James, the latter prompting "the only direct personal reference in all of the Meditations" (170); the poet's failing health; and — not surprisingly — the growing influence of Stoddard, whose views Taylor attacked once more in the Meditations on the Supper (Meds. 2.102-110). During this period the poet abandoned the ambitious *Metrical History* and the *Harmony of the Gospels* in order to pursue an inner "sanctuary of poetic harmony" that stressed future fulfillment rather than "the discord of the present" (175), a shift reflected in the increasingly formulaic references to sin and the calmer tone illustrated by Meditation 80. For Davis, Taylor's growing interiority and his return to the allegorical Song gave him a poetic freedom denied by the types, a freedom especially evident in Meditations 2.62 and 2.84. The futurity inherent in the Canticles allegory helped ease the pressures of writing effective praise and provided refuge from disturbing events in his daily life, which "rarely, if at all, intrude upon the ordered calm" of his assurance as a Bride of Christ preparing for death and the consummation of the spiritual marriage (190). After focusing on the Bridegroom (Meds. 2.115-128) and the Canticles garden (Meds. 2.129-132), Taylor concentrated on the Bride in an effort to assimilate her voice (Meds. 2.148-153). Taylor probably intended this last group, Davis suggested, to be his final unit; the poet likely felt ready "to put away even the images of the Song and to apprehend not through a representation of the real, but the Real" itself (197). Offering a valuable corrective to critics who overstated Taylor's selflessness, Davis presented a poet who was no shrinking violet, especially in light of his initial artistic ambitions. In its persuasive integration of Taylor's outer and inner lives, no other discussion conveyed so clear a sense of the unique personality behind the poetry.

While Scheick and Davis forced a timely reconsideration of Taylor's artistry, neither critic promoted a neo-formalist isolation of the poems, whether as verbal icons or as tissues of autonomous discourse. Although Scheick stressed cruxes in Puritan language and Davis stressed cruxes in Taylor's life, both grounded their readings in the poet's mental world and his deliberate reshaping of the materials of that world into art. This aesthetically sensitive approach to cultural and historical frameworks characterized contextual studies of the early 1990s. Critics were increasingly concerned with demonstrating how multiple contexts — scientific, biblical, literary, cultural, and psychological — affected Taylor's self-conception as a poet and the artistic results of his efforts. New work on Taylor's scientific models came from Catherine Rainwater, who followed her discussion of Taylor and the new astronomy (1984) with an examination of the pastor-physician's accommodation to the shift from Galenist medicine and a medieval vitalist cosmology to a more empirical and mechanical model of disease (1991). Taylor, ambivalent but not hostile toward these developments, struggled to integrate the new medicine with the "mystical underpinnings of hermetical theory" (52). Rainwater argued that in his attempt to synthesize disparate medical models, Taylor developed a "typological frame of reference" that joined Paracelsian medicine with Augustinian theology in the "unified vision of a poet who is also a healer and a minister" (55). In so doing, he gained confidence in interpreting a scientifically "revised Book of Nature" in terms of "a system circumscribed by a constant Book of God" (57). In Meditation 2.61, for example, Taylor blended the hermetical caduceus, Moses's brazen serpent, Aaron's staff, the Cross, and the seventeenth-century "Doctors Shop" into a vision of "heavenly alchemy" (65). And in Meditation 1.7 he conflated the *Logos* with his medical vision by defining the Christic Word and his own words as parallel stimulants of spiritual healing. Randall A. Clack identified an "alchemical cycle" in Meditations 1.6-9, in which Taylor "assumes the role of alchemist and then transfers the role onto God," the "Celestial Alchemist" who alone can effect the transmutation of sinner into saint (1992:7, 9).

The biblical side of Taylor's Word/world cosmology was explored by Rosemary Fithian Guruswamy and Jeffrey Hammond in studies of the poet's indebtedness to the verse of the Old Testament. Guruswamy, whose earlier study of the Meditations and the Psalms clarified the biblical precedents of Taylor's poetic process and voice (1985), connected the poet with a broad tradition in which the Psalmist provided a model not only for celebrants of redeemed experience but for defenders of New England's sacramental and providential mission (1990). As Guruswamy pointed out, David was frequently cited during the Lord's Supper controversy as a prototypical saint whose "relation" of faith in Psalm 66 foreshadowed the public relation that Taylor and the Mathers thought necessary for admission (301). Extending his earlier discussion of the eschatological significance of the Song of Songs for the late Meditations (1982/83), Hammond connected Taylor's gradual shift in the Second Series from typological to allegorical themes with his growing fascination with otherworldly themes (1990b). This shift suggested a compromise in the debate, with Mignon and Keller on one side and Davis on the other, over whether the Meditations were essentially static or whether they reflected varying aims and techniques. For Hammond, the Meditations reflected the poet's unchanging pursuit of greater meditative intimacy with Christ as well as his dynamic search for different biblical vehicles for enhancing such intimacy. Suggesting that Taylor's progress toward the Song, actually a return to more affective meditative modes of the First Series, was prompted by the beauty of the Canticles Bridegroom in the *Christographia* sermons, Hammond argued that as Taylor's concerns became more otherworldly, the Canticles Bride increasingly emerged as the eschatological identity for which he yearned, not as a literary persona but "as the fullest God-written prophecy of his essential self" (78).

Literary sources and contexts for the poetry emerged in work by Hammond, Percy Adams, and Lincoln Konkle. Adams, taking a fresh look at sound patterns in the verse, argued that Taylor's love of the sounds of words and word combinations resulted in "phonic echoes" that aligned him with poets like Dryden, Pope, and Gay rather than with Herbert (1991:12). Citing Taylor's skillful use of alliteration, consonance, and assonance, Adams agreed with Gene Russell (1971) that Taylor's rhymes seemed consistent with his probable pronunciation and that his use of phonic echoes actually made his off-rhymes less "incorrect" than they seemed (18). Taylor's sound effects, Adams argued, were fully functional elements that served to emphasize his themes, reinforce his rhetoric, and generally enhance the "sound-sense" unity of the poetry (26). Konkle, proposing a literary source for *Gods Determinations*, related the poem to late Renaissance masques as models for Taylor's attempt to give dramatic form to cosmic themes of creation, salvation, and the resolution of spiritual doubts (1990). Hammond invoked the conventions of genre as a means of connecting Taylor with New England popular literary culture in his study of that most typical of "Puritan" poems, the funeral elegy (1991). Citing a Puritan modal personality dichotomized by sin and grace, Hammond argued that New England funeral elegies, including Taylor's, urged survivors to translate· their mourning into a renewed identification with the redemptive paradigm. Arguing that Taylor was a more versatile poet than commonly thought, as adept in public and stylized forms as in private meditation, Hammond suggested a closer link between the Meditations and the "public" verse than usually recognized. Citing the presence of identical spiritual patterns in both sets of poems, he maintained that Taylor's public poetry was far richer and more complex than its general neglect by critics suggested.

Indeed, as the 1990s began, three-fourths of Taylor's verse remained virtually untouched by scholars, despite the thirty years since Donald Stanford published the *Metrical History* and the ten years since Thomas and Virginia Davis published the *Minor Poetry*. Raymond A. Craig's two-volume concordance to the Davis edition promised to stimulate more work on the minor poems, especially investigations into Taylor's diction and allusive range as he addressed specific social situations and a variety of external readers (1992). The concordance, which contained cross-references to orthographic variants and separate treatments of homographs, included an index of such high-frequency words as articles and pronouns as well as a word frequency index.

Cultural and psychological approaches to Taylor and his contemporaries centered on conceptions of identity embodied in Puritan poetry. A species of literary anthropology influenced chiefly by Clifford Geertz and Victor Turner connected Taylor's speaker with subjective codes mandated by his theology. This approach, which sought traces of cultural self-definition in Taylor's meditative voice, took Puritan constructions of personal identity and salvific experience as starting points for reading the poetry. A second approach to Taylor's selfhood, more explicitly psychoanalytic, interrogated these conscious formulations as a means of exposing deeper dynamics of identity, especially gender, that were embedded in the verse. While the anthropological critic took Puritan informants at their word as a means of effecting a historical reconstruction of inner experience, the psychoanalytic critic saw such pronouncements as masks concealing another level of experience that transcended the bounds of seventeenth-century New England. Identifying a representative, extrapersonal dimension in Taylor's voice, practitioners of both methods agreed that the Meditations could not be read simply as an expression of Wordsworth's "man speaking to men." Indeed, both approaches questioned the traditional view of the poetry as unique and unmediated autobiographical expression, thereby reinforcing the view of Taylor as a representative and not an exceptional Puritan.

Anthropological assumptions of a culturally-shaped self informed Hammond's challenge to two commonplaces in the criticism: that the Meditations were readerless and thus devoid of an identifiable rhetorical situation, and that they were literally confessional or autobiographical in the sense normally attributed to the post-romantic lyric (1990a). Arguing that much of the scholarship unwittingly translated Taylor's poetic aims into modern terms, Hammond maintained that the Meditations revealed less about Taylor's private personality than about how the poet wanted to be seen by his implied "reader": the Christ in his mind, as defined by Puritan Christology. For Hammond, Taylor presumed that Christ had clear "reading" expectations that profoundly shaped his meditating speaker as he strove to project a self consistent with theological assumption. Because abject humility was necessary for assurance, Taylor's apparent self-doubt actually reflected his optimistic assimilation of an identity capable of adopting Christ's perspective on his fallen self and flawed art. Although Hammond agreed with Karl Keller (1985) that Taylor was "acting" a part in the verse, he denied that Taylor's act was in any way deliberate, arguing instead that the poet unconsciously absorbed parameters of selfhood inseparable from Puritan definitions of the saved soul. What Taylor most desired, Hammond concluded, was to suppress his "carnal" individuality "in order to build up/edify that *other* self who could dare to be found acceptable in Christ's sight" (15). Michael Schuldiner applied similar Puritan definitions of redeemed experience to *Gods Determinations* (1991). Arguing that Puritans could attain a more certain assurance than often assumed, Schuldiner pointed out that Taylor's era saw a flowering of "experiential religion" as New England returned to Calvin's emphasis on the illumination of the Spirit (13). *Gods Determinations*, which addressed the stages leading to Calvin's Christian freedom, was Taylor's response to the "hope-fear dilemma" of aspiring saints and a dramatization of Puritan case divinity based on William Ames's *De conscientia* (Amsterdam: 1630), David Dickson's *Therapeutica Sacra* (London: 1656), and the poet's own pastoral experience (112). Unlike Solomon Stoddard, who offered the Lord's Supper as a means to conversion, Taylor adhered to the 1662 Half-Way Synod by extending the counsel of the assured saint or minister, a salve reflected in the Soul-Saint dialogues. As the *Treatise Concerning the Lord's Supper* made clear, Taylor did not consider the mere presence of the hope-fear dilemma to be sufficient for admission to the Supper. Rather, he insisted that the dilemma first be "in some measure resolved" by prayer and by advice from the experienced believer or minister (115), who interpreted Soul's fears in light of right reason. Such counsel, Schuldiner argued, instilled the "probable knowledge" that restored a balance of hope and fear. Once fear was held in check by redemptive hope, the Supper could become a legitimate vehicle for stirring "the affections to produce assurance of salvation" (122). Maintaining that the Stoddard/Taylor conflict reflected a disagreement over the role played by the understanding in the *ordo salutis*, Schuldiner challenged the usual distinction between the "liberal" Stoddard and the "conservative" Taylor. While Stoddard was conservative in judging the signs of spiritual growth but liberal in his view of the sacrament, Taylor balanced his exclusionary view of the Supper with "a more liberal attitude toward what constitutes saving faith," an attitude that accorded well with the range of emotions articulated in the Meditations (137).

These studies were ethnographic in the sense that they accepted Puritan definitions of salvific experience at face value. Other studies of Taylor's subjectivity interrogated these definitions in order to reveal psychological dynamics that such theological models may have served to suppress as much as to invoke. Walter Hughes, for example, argued that homoerotic implications of the spiritual marriage with Christ were implicit in Puritan poetry, including Taylor's (1990). Identifying a gendered construction of "desire" in the merging of spiritual and erotic themes enacted by Bradstreet, Wigglesworth, and Taylor, Hughes maintained that Taylor practiced "a poetics of panic" stemming from the "prospect of divine sodomy" implicit in his spiritual goals (118). Taylor's solution to homoerotic anxiety, Hughes argued, lay in exploiting the rich potential of language to diffuse and transcend this panic: his many roles and varied images in the Meditations enabled him to achieve "a kaleidoscopic polysexual ecstasy" by which he managed to escape the tortured relation to God represented in Wigglesworth's polarities of effeminacy and sadomasochism (120). Another argument for gender turmoil and its resolution in Taylor came from Ivy Schweitzer, who related Taylor's anxiety to a "poetics of tension" much like Herbert's (1991a:238). But while Herbert's "sacrificial model" was the Crucifixion (238), Taylor found his in the Incarnation and "the semiological system of sacramental worship" (239). Exploiting the Bible and Christ as twin bridges between the human and the divine, Taylor found in the semiology of the sacrament "a dialectical model for selfhood by which he could be present but absent in the related processes of writing and regeneration" (240). Schweitzer followed Michael Clark (1985a) in finding a dialectic of union as well as separation in the Supper and in Christ. Because "flesh was the medium God used to send himself down to earth," Taylor justified placing himself above the angels in "The Experience" (247). Arguing that male saints were humbled in a process of spiritual feminization or castration, Schweitzer examined Meditation 1.6 in terms of "Taylor's characteristic self-effacement and his simultaneous insertion of himself as transformed object into the figurative scheme of the poem" (250).

Anthropological and psychoanalytic approaches to Puritan selfhood soon received book-length treatments. Hammond, expanding earlier essays on the speaker/reader dynamic in Bradstreet, Wigglesworth, and Taylor (1990a), attempted to reconstruct a poetic based on Puritan definitions of redemptive experience and the literary codes by which poetry could serve as a catalyst for this experience (1993). Basing this aesthetic on theology, on artistic and exegetical traditions deriving from the Bible, and on the psychology of the saved soul, Hammond centered the Puritan experience of poetry on a paradigm of identity that featured the struggle of sin and grace within the individual believer. Countering a longstanding tendency to set Taylor apart from the artistic conventions of his time and place, Hammond argued that Puritan poems, including Taylor's, offered bridges to the Bible as the ultimate Text from which all true art derived — an overarching "metatext" toward which the Puritan text consistently pointed. Taylor's poetry, like Bradstreet's and Wigglesworth's, similarly encouraged the writer's and reader's assimilation of a "metaself," at once sinful and saintly, whose struggle with sin produced a more vivid hope of redemption. In public poems like *Gods Determinations* and the *Metrical History of Christianity*, Hammond argued, Taylor exploited a Wigglesworth-like rhetoric of persuasion in order to root the redemptive struggle in the reader's experience. Poetry dealing with external events, such as the love poems to his wife, his laments for deceased saints, and his contemplations of nature, projected a variety of voices — naturalist, elegist, spouse, and parent — unified by the broader paradigm of the sinful/saintly believer. Like Bradstreet, Taylor used poetry to fit earthly events into overriding patterns of conviction and consolation by which his own spiritual progress — and that of his readers — could be furthered. Hammond maintained that even the readerless Meditations invoked the Puritan speaking/reading dynamic as a means of intensifying Taylor's experience of the faith. In his private verse, the poet wrote for an "audience" of two: the Christ in his imagination, a Christ whose reading expectations mirrored demands that the faith made on all sincere believers; and the poet himself, for whom the texts revealed the extent of his conformity to the paradigmatic metaself of the true believer. "Reading" himself through poetry by assessing how Christ was "reading" him, Taylor documented his ongoing ritual search for inner patterns suggestive of salvation. His conscious artistic choices were thus based on a largely unconscious assimilation of a saved identity that was insistently neobiblical. By writing, he could transcend, however briefly, the sinful self and its worldly perspective and achieve a sense of gracious duality that matched the Theanthropic Christ whom he petitioned. Building on his earlier work on Taylor and the Song of Songs (1982/83, 1990b), Hammond maintained that in the later Meditations the poet's concentration on his hoped-for identity as the Canticles Bride prompted him very nearly to repudiate earthly selfhood altogether. Like Bradstreet in "As Weary Pilgrim," he wrote poetry as a means of losing one self in order to find another: the Word emerged not only as his salvific message and Christic reader but the ultimate pattern for his own textual identity.

While Hammond applied Puritan definitions of self-experience to a reader-response treatment of Taylor's poetry, Schweitzer questioned the manifest content of such definitions by arguing that Taylor's Puritan struggle revealed latent gender turmoil stemming from the human-divine relationship central to his identity as poet and believer (1991b). Schweitzer's provocative study of Taylor, Bradstreet, Roger Williams, and the Puritan elegy focused on patterns of "redeemed subjectivity" by which male believers underwent a "gynesis" — an appropriation of traits gendered as "feminine" — necessary for becoming humbled and selfless brides of Christ (32). This experience, Schweitzer argued, amounted to a psychic castration that accompanied conviction in sin. Only after assimilating a constructed feminine identity could the male saint achieve a masculinity reconstituted in terms of sonship in relation to God. For Schweitzer, this spiritual emasculation — a process performable only by male believers — reinforced the religious and social privilege assumed by the patriarchy of early New England. A political result of this patterning of self, she argued, was that the efficacy of actual women was canceled out: "earthly and fleshly femaleness" (27) was effaced from the saintly pattern as the reintegrated redeemed identity was gendered male. In her treatment of Puritan poetry as an expression of this inner dynamic, Schweitzer argued that the elegy, represented by John Fiske's poem on John Cotton, led mourners through a psychic castration necessary to their reconstitution as pious sons of the deceased. Williams interrogated this sense of spiritual lineage by juxtaposing Puritan and Native American perceptions and identities; he projected the marginalized voice of an "insider cast out" (186) as a means of critiquing Puritan selfhood. The inverse of this dynamic was enacted by Bradstreet, an outsider reshaped in conformity with cultural expectation. Redeemed subjectivity problematized her identity as a woman: torn between acquiescence and rebellion, she was fashioned by the Puritan patriarchy into a cultural construction as the idealized woman, an antidote to actual, threatening women like

Anne Hutchinson. This powerful patriarchy, represented by Bradstreet's family, Puritan leaders who simultaneously praised and patronized her, and later proponents of male-centered ideologies, coerced the poet into assuming a "patriarchal voice" (167) whose only source of power lay in her role as a mother who nurtured a system that denied her own deepest needs. Taylor, a male participant in psychic patterns mandated by his religion and culture, escaped such difficulties. Arguing that the turmoil recorded in the Meditations reflected the gender ambivalence demanded of all male believers, Schweitzer maintained that Taylor desired salvation as a "woman" in relation to the Christic Bridegroom (81). Nor did the poet shy away from the homoerotic implications of the spiritual marriage that he sought: indeed, they initiated the struggle by which he could enact the gynesis mandated by his faith and thereby refashion himself into a feminine other to Christ and to his own fallen self. Through the Bride, Schweitzer argued, Taylor "speaks as other than his earthly self, as the redeemed subject, uttering his desire for union with the divine in a role traditionally designated as feminine and scripturally sanctioned" (110). As a result of this dynamic, Taylor was able to achieve spiritual reconstruction through "male bonding" (116) as Christ's "second and sidekick" (119), and was thus made capable of joining Christ in enacting the divine (male) gaze upon the Bride and on himself as a transformed saint. Especially in the late Meditations on Canticles, the "I" of the poetry "slips imperceptibly back and forth between observer and participant" as a reflection of Taylor's liminal state (125).

Hammond and Schweitzer presented an interesting contrast that centered on whether past texts are to be seen as articulations of a closed historical system or as expressions of psychological patterns that transcend place and time. Hammond followed Rowe in arguing that the Puritan poem was best seen in terms of its otherness. He did not invoke poetic traits valued by modern critics — the conflicted speaker, the verbal play, the processual structures, even the linguistic and metaphorical sophistication — to support Taylor's universal or transhistorical appeal, but to demonstrate the poet's participation in alien experiential and aesthetic structures deriving from Scripture and scriptural exegesis. But in his desire to historicize Taylor's art within Puritan literary culture, Hammond said little about the quality of that art or its political or psychological relevance for modern readers. Perhaps inevitably, his cultural reading downplayed Taylor's originality as a poet. If Taylor was merely exploiting codes widespread in Puritan literary culture, on what basis could such originality be explained or defended? At root, Hammond reconfirmed Roy Harvey Pearce's statement of forty years earlier: "Reading Taylor's poetry, we read his Puritanism" (1950:46). But while Pearce argued that theological compulsion harmed the verse, Hammond suggested that such claims made sense only by positing the universality of post-romantic aesthetic criteria. Content with affirming that Taylor's poetry was admirably functional within Puritan culture, he sidestepped the problem of assessing its artistic appeal for modern readers by claiming that such evaluation was impossible without committing some degree of aesthetic anachronism. No such neutrality marred Schweitzer's study, which asserted a more usable past by focusing on structures of gender as relevant today as in the seventeenth century. For Schweitzer, the New England patriarchy that shaped Bradstreet's subjectivity extended into the 1950s of John Berryman. Also valuable, as is the case with many psychoanalytic studies, was her attempt to get beneath explicit patterns of Puritan self-representation in order to recover unconscious motives and desires. A male poet whose lifelong goal was to achieve an identity as Christ's bride was long overdue for a detailed analysis in terms of gender, perhaps owing to a reluctance among conservative scholars to discuss religious experience in such terms. Although such models of inner turmoil had figured in constructions of the Puritan psyche by Philip Greven (1977) and David Leverenz (1980), only Hughes and Karl Keller had developed the homoerotic implications of Taylor's themes. In "The Reflexion," Keller observed, Taylor was initially "feeble (therefore feminine) but after the divine rape he takes on a more active, masculine role, in imitation of Christ the Lover" (1970b:401). But in stressing transhistorical psychological models, Schweitzer risked simply translating Taylor's artistic and spiritual concerns from Puritan into Freudian terms, a potential problem whenever contemporary and ostensibly universal psychoanalytic models are applied to older texts. Schweitzer may have begged the question of the past's otherness by assigning a "feminine" label to the saint's passivity. Moreover, she may have judged Taylor and his culture too harshly for the masculinist structures that Puritans absorbed and promoted. Although she acknowledged the roots of such self-representation in Paul and Augustine, the patterns she described could be seen as biblical and Christian, and not exclusively Puritan, New English, American, or perhaps even "male."

As the diversity of this recent work suggests, Taylor studies are almost as rich with possibility today as in 1937, when Thomas Johnson presented the poet to the literary world. In some ways, Taylor remains one of the most studied but least understood figures in American literature. His odd blend of personal immediacy and historical distance illustrates the very issues that are currently reinvigorating the theory and practice of literary history. Teachers of early American literature know that despite its complex surface and remote themes, his poetry can excite readers coming to it for the first time. Yet few "good" poets from the past are so firmly rooted *in* that past — and the harder we look, the harder it is to explain why he continues to move us. As a poet who provokes difficult questions regarding the intersection of historical understanding and aesthetic value, Edward Taylor provides a case study second to none. Addressing these issues will require as many different scholarly and critical perspectives as can be brought to the task. There is certainly room for more of the historical research and close reading that literary scholars have traditionally pursued. But newer tools of semiotics, gender criticism, psychological criticism, cultural criticism, and even deconstruction can also shed light on this most linguistically and psychologically complex of Puritan poets. Whatever directions students of Taylor take in the future, it seems certain that their work will reflect a healthy awareness of the fact that the decision to answer one question always entails a choice *not* to answer others. Indeed, the literary historian cannot function without making a theorist's choices and assumptions, whether knowingly or not. In all this, consensus may not be the most realistic or even desirable goal. Like one of his alleged poetic successors, Edward Taylor contains multitudes, and the question of his value in a poststructuralist age may simply reduce to his ability to sustain multiple readings. He has always stood up well to the many approaches that scholars and critics have embraced in the past fifty years, and the odds seem good that he will continue to do so. Yet despite a half-century of commentary, most Taylorians would admit, if pressed, that something elusive remains in the poetry. For all the twists and turns in the scholarly story, Taylor's ongoing message to those who seek to read him better seems the same that he once issued to death itself: "I still am where I was." Whether or not the next phrase in the poem also applies to his critics is up to us.

Bibliography

1. Works by Edward Taylor

The Poetical Works of Edward Taylor. Ed. Thomas H. Johnson. New York: Rockland Editions, 1939. Reprint, Princeton: Princeton Univ. Press, 1943, 1966.
The Poems of Edward Taylor. Ed. Donald E. Stanford. New Haven: Yale Univ. Press, 1960.
Edward Taylor's Christographia. Ed. Norman S. Grabo. New Haven: Yale Univ. Press, 1962.
A Transcript of Edward Taylor's Metrical History of Christianity. Ed. Donald E. Stanford. Cleveland: Micro Photo, 1962.
The Diary of Edward Taylor. Ed. Francis Murphy. Springfield, Mass.: Connecticut Valley Historical Museum, 1964.
Edward Taylor's Treatise Concerning the Lord's Supper. Ed. Norman S. Grabo. East Lansing: Michigan State Univ. Press, 1966.
Edward Taylor's "Church Records" and Related Sermons. Ed. Thomas M. Davis and Virginia L. Davis. Boston: Twayne, 1981. Vol. 1 of *The Unpublished Writings of Edward Taylor.*
Edward Taylor vs. Solomon Stoddard: The Nature of the Lord's Supper. Ed. Thomas M. Davis and Virginia L. Davis. Boston: Twayne, 1981. Vol. 2 of *The Unpublished Writings of Edward Taylor.*
Edward Taylor's Minor Poetry. Ed. Thomas M. Davis and Virginia L. Davis. Boston: Twayne, 1981. Vol. 3 of *The Unpublished Writings of Edward Taylor.*
Edward Taylor's Harmony of the Gospels. 4 vols. Ed. Thomas M. Davis and Virginia L. Davis, with Betty L. Parks. Delmar, N.Y.: Scholars' Facsimiles & Reprints, 1983.
Upon the Types of the Old Testament. 2 vols. Ed. Charles W. Mignon. Lincoln: Univ. of Nebraska Press, 1989.

2. Critical Works

Abel, Darrel. 1963. "Edward Taylor." *American Literature: I. Colonial and Early National Writing.* Woodbury, N.Y.: Barron's Educational Series. 86-91.
Adams, Percy G. 1991. "Edward Taylor's Love Affair with Sounding Language." *Order in Variety: Essays and Poems in Honor of Donald E. Stanford.* Ed. R. W. Crump. Newark: Univ. of Delaware Press. 12-31.
Akiyama, Ken. 1963. "Edward Taylor's Poetry, An Introduction." *Studies in Humanities* (Doshisha Univ.) 64: 27-44.
———. 1968. "The Poetry and Typology of Edward Taylor." *The Rising Generation* 114: 507-09.

Aldridge, A. Owen. 1982. *Early American Literature: A Comparatist Approach.* Princeton: Princeton Univ. Press.

Alexis, Gerhard T. 1966. "Taylor's 'Meditation 8.'" *Explicator* 24 (9): Item 77.

———. 1969/70. "A Keen Nose for Taylor's Syntax." *Early American Literature* 4 (3): 97-101.

Allen, Judson Boyce. 1970. "Edward Taylor's Catholic Wasp: Exegetical Convention in 'Upon a Spider Catching a Fly.'" *English Language Notes* 7: 257-60.

Altick, Richard D. 1950. *The Scholar Adventurers.* N.Y.: Macmillan.

Arner, Robert D. 1969. "Edward Taylor's Gaming Imagery: 'Meditation 1.40.'" *Early American Literature* 4 (1): 38-40.

———. 1973a. "Folk Metaphors in Edward Taylor's 'Meditation 1.40.'" *Seventeenth-Century News* 31: 6-9.

———. 1973b. "Notes on the Structure of Edward Taylor's *Gods Determinations.*" *Studies in the Humanities* 3: 27-29.

———. 1973c. "Proverbs in Edward Taylor's *Gods Determinations.*" *Southern Folklore Quarterly* 37: 1-13.

Bach, Bert C. 1966. "Self-Depreciation in Edward Taylor's Sacramental Meditations." *Cithara* 6 (1): 49-58.

Bales, Kent, and William J. Aull. 1970. "Touching Taylor Overly: A Note on 'Meditation Six.'" *Early American Literature* 5 (2): 57-59.

Ball, Kenneth. 1969/70. "Rhetoric in Edward Taylor's *Preparatory Meditations.*" *Early American Literature* 4 (3): 79-88.

Ballinger, Martha. 1965. "The Metaphysical Echo." *English Studies in Africa* 8: 71-80.

Barbour, Dennis H. 1981/82. "*Gods Determinations* and the Hexameral Tradition." *Early American Literature* 16: 213-25.

Barbour, James W. 1975. "The Prose Context of Edward Taylor's Anti-Stoddard Meditations." *Early American Literature* 10: 144-57.

Baym, Nina, et al., eds. 1989. *The Norton Anthology of American Literature.* 2 vols. Third edition. New York: W. W. Norton. Vol. 1.

Benét, William Rose, and Norman Holmes Pearson, eds. 1938. *Oxford Anthology of American Literature.* 2 vols. New York: Oxford Univ. Press. Vol. 1.

Benton, Robert M. 1967. "Edward Taylor's Use of His Text." *American Literature* 39: 31-41.

Bercovitch, Sacvan. 1970. "Introduction," Special Issue on Typology. *Early American Literature* 5 (1): 5-10.

———. 1975. *The Puritan Origins of the American Self.* New Haven: Yale Univ. Press.

Black, Mindele. 1956. "Edward Taylor: Heavens Sugar Cake." *New England Quarterly* 29: 159-81.

Blake, Howard. 1940. "Seventeenth-Century Yankee." *Poetry* 56: 165-69.

Blake, Kathleen. 1971. "Edward Taylor's Protestant Poetic: Nontransubstantiating Metaphor." *American Literature* 43: 1-24.

Blau, Herbert. 1953. "Heaven's Sugar Cake: Theology and Imagery in the Poetry of Edward Taylor." *New England Quarterly* 26: 337-60.

Boll, Robert N., and Thomas M. Davis. 1971. "Saint Augustine and Edward Taylor's Meditation 138(2)." *English Language Notes* 8: 183-85.

Bottorff, William K. 1968. "Edward Taylor, an Explication: 'Another Meditation at the Same Time.'" *Early American Literature* 3: 17-21.

Bray, James. 1974. "John Fiske: Puritan Precursor of Edward Taylor." *Early American Literature* 9: 27-38.

Breitkreuz, Hartmut. 1971. "Motif and Literary Genesis." *English Language Notes* 8: 267-69.

Brown, Wallace Cable. 1944. "Edward Taylor: An American 'Metaphysical.'" *American Literature* 16: 186-97.

Brumm, Ursula. 1968. "The 'Tree of Life' in Edward Taylor's Meditations." *Early American Literature* 3: 72-87.

———. 1970. *American Thought and Religious Typology*. German orig. 1963. Trans. John Hoaglund. New Brunswick: Rutgers Univ. Press.

———. 1972. "Edward Taylor and the Poetic Use of Religious Imagery." *Typology and Early American Literature*. Ed. Sacvan Bercovitch. Amherst: Univ. of Massachusetts Press. 191-206.

———. 1973. *Puritanismus und Literatur in Amerika*. Darmstadt: Wissenschaftliche Buchgesellschaft.

———. 1982. "'Tuning' the Song of Praise: Observations on the Use of Numbers in Edward Taylor's *Preparatory Meditations*." *Early American Literature* 17: 103-18.

———. 1983. "The Art of Puritan Meditation in New England." *Studies in New England Puritanism*. Ed. Winfried Herget. Frankfurt: Lang. 139-67.

———. 1985. "Meditative Poetry in New England." *Puritan Poets*. Ed. Peter White. 318-36.

———. 1987. "Edward Taylor: 'Meditation 1,34.'" *Amerikanische Lyrik: Perspektiven und Interpretationen*. Ed. Rudolf Haas. Berlin: Schmidt. 143-54.

Bush, Sargent, Jr. 1969/70. "Paradox, Puritanism, and Taylor's *Gods Determinations*." *Early American Literature* 4 (3): 48-66.

Cairns, William B., ed. 1910. *Selections from Early American Writers*. New York: Macmillan.

Caldwell, Patricia. 1983. *The Puritan Conversion Narrative: The Beginnings of American Expression*. Cambridge: Cambridge Univ. Press.

Callow, James T. 1969/70. "Edward Taylor Obeys Saint Paul." *Early American Literature* 4 (3): 89-96.

Carlisle, E. F. 1968. "The Puritan Structure of Edward Taylor's Poetry." *American Quarterly* 20: 147-63.

Chmaj, Betty E. 1964. "The Metaphors of Resurrection." *Universitas* 2: 91-109.

Clack, Randall A. 1992. "The Transmutation of Soul: The Opus Alchymicum Celestial and Edward Taylor's 'Meditation 1.8.'" *Seventeenth-Century News* 50: 6-10.

Clare, Sister M. Theresa. 1960. "Taylor's 'Meditation Sixty-Two." *Explicator* 19 (3): Item 16.

Clark, Michael. 1978/79. "'The Crucified Phrase': Sign and Desire in Puritan Semiology." *Early American Literature* 13: 278-93.

———. 1985a. "The Honeyed Knot of Puritan Aesthetics." *Puritan Poets*. Ed. Peter White. 67-83.

———. 1985b. "The Subject of the Text in Early American Literature." *Early American Literature* 20: 120-30.

Clendenning, John. 1964. "Piety and Imagery in Edward Taylor's 'The Reflexion.'" *American Quarterly* 16: 203-10.

Cohen, Charles Lloyd. 1986. *God's Caress: The Psychology of Puritan Religious Experience*. New York: Oxford Univ. Press.

Colacurcio, Michael J. 1967. "*Gods Determinations Touching Half-Way Membership*: Occasion and Audience in Edward Taylor." *American Literature* 39: 298-314.

———. 1978. "Does American Literature Have a History?" *Early American Literature* 13: 110-32.

Combellack, C. R. B. 1970. "Taylor's 'Upon Wedlock, and Death of Children.'" *Explicator* 29 (2): Item 12.

Craig, Raymond A. 1992. *A Concordance to the Minor Poetry of Edward Taylor (1642?-1729): American Colonial Poet*. 2 vols. Lewiston, N. Y.: Edwin Mellen Press.

Curtis, Jared R. 1964. "Edward Taylor and Emily Dickinson: Voices and Visions." *Susquehanna University Studies* 7: 159-67.

Daly, Robert. 1977. "Puritan Poetics: The World, the Flesh, and God." *Early American Literature* 12: 136-62.

———. 1978. *God's Altar: The World and the Flesh in Puritan Poetry*. Berkeley: Univ. of California Press.

———. 1990. "Recognizing Early American Literature." *Early American Literature* 25: 187-99.

Damico, Anthony. 1982/83. "The Conceit of Dyeing in Edward Taylor's *Preparatory Meditations*, Second Series, Number One." *Early American Literature* 17: 227-38.

Damon, S. Foster. 1939. Review of Johnson, *Poetical Works*. *New England Quarterly* 12: 777-80.

Davie, Donald. 1976. "Edward Taylor and Isaac Watts." *The Yale Review* 65: 498-514.

Davis, Thomas M. 1969/70. "Edward Taylor and the Traditions of Puritan Typology." *Early American Literature* 4 (3): 27-47.

———. 1970. "The Exegetical Traditions of Puritan Typology." *Early American Literature* 5 (1): 11-50.

———. 1970/71. "Edward Taylor's 'Occasional Meditations.'" *Early American Literature* 5 (3): 17-29.

———. 1972. "Edward Taylor's 'Valedictory' Poems." *Early American Literature* 7: 38-63.

———. 1974. "Solomon Stoddard's Sermon on the Lord's Supper as a Converting Ordinance." *Resources for American Literary Study* 4: 205-24.

———. 1976/77. "Edward Taylor's Elegies on the Mathers." *Early American Literature* 11: 231-44.

———. 1978a. "Edward Taylor to Samuel Sewall, Nov. 17, 1704." *Early American Literature* 13: 107-9.

———. 1978b. "Scatology Restored." *American Notes and Queries Supplement*, Vol. 1: *Studies in English and American Literature*. Ed. John L. Cutler and Lawrence S. Thompson. Troy, N. Y.: Whitston. 233-34.

———. 1981a. "Introduction." *Edward Taylor's "Church Records" and Related Sermons*. Vol. 1 of *The Unpublished Writings of Edward Taylor*. Ed. Thomas M. Davis and Virginia L. Davis. Boston: Twayne. xi-xl.

———. 1981b. "Introduction." *Edward Taylor vs. Solomon Stoddard: The Nature of the Lord's Supper*. Vol. 2 of *The Unpublished Writings of Edward Taylor*. Ed. Thomas M. Davis and Virginia L. Davis. Boston: Twayne. 1-57.

———. 1981c. "Introduction." *Edward Taylor's Minor Poetry*. Vol. 3 of *The Unpublished Writings of Edward Taylor*. Ed. Thomas M. Davis and Virginia L. Davis. Boston: Twayne. xi-xxii.

———. 1983. "Introduction." *Edward Taylor's Harmony of the Gospels*. Ed. Thomas M. Davis and Virginia L. Davis, with Betty L. Parks. 4 vols. Delmar, N. Y.: Scholars' Facsimiles & Reprints. 1:i-lvii.

———. 1986. "Edward Taylor's Elegy on Deacon David Dewey." *Proceedings of the American Antiquarian Society* 96 (Part 1): 75-84.

———. 1990. "Editing Edward Taylor." *Studies in Puritan American Spirituality* 1: 19-27.

———. 1992. *A Reading of Edward Taylor*. Newark: Univ. of Delaware Press.

Davis, Thomas M., and Virginia L. Davis. 1971/72. "Edward Taylor's Library: Another Note." *Early American Literature* 6: 271-73.

———. 1972. "Edward Taylor on the Day of Judgment." *American Literature* 43: 525-47.

———. 1977. "Edward Taylor's Metrical Paraphrases of the Psalms." *American Literature* 48: 455-70.

Davis, Thomas M., and Jeff Jeske. 1976. "Solomon Stoddard's 'Arguments' Concerning Admission to the Lord's Supper." *Papers of the American Antiquarian Society* 86: 75-112.

Delbanco, Andrew. 1989. *The Puritan Ordeal*. Cambridge: Harvard Univ. Press.

Del Fattore, Joan. 1983/84. "John Webster's *Metallographia*: A Source for Alchemical Imagery in the *Preparatory Meditations*." *Early American Literature* 18: 233-41.

DeNuccio, Jerome D. 1988. "Taylor's *Preparatory Meditation* 1.22." *Explicator* 46 (2): 9-11.

———. 1989. "Linguistic Dilemma in Edward Taylor's 'Meditation 1.22.'" *English Language Notes* 26 (3): 19-24.

De Prospo, R. C. 1989. "The Latest Early American Literature." *Early American Literature* 24: 248-56.

———. 1992. "Marginalizing Early American Literature." *New Literary History* 23: 233-65.

Doepke, Dale. 1970/71. "A Suggestion for Reading Edward Taylor's 'The Preface.'" *Early American Literature* 5 (3): 80-82.

Eberwein, Jane Donahue. 1978. "Edward Taylor." *Early American Poetry*. Ed. Jane Donahue Eberwein. Madison: Univ. of Wisconsin Press. 62-72.

Elliott, Emory, ed. 1991. *American Literature*. 2 vols. Englewood Cliffs, N.J.: Prentice Hall. Vol. 1.

Emerson, Everett. 1969/70. "A Note from the Editor," Special Issue on Edward Taylor. *Early American Literature* 4 (3): 3.

———. 1977. *Puritanism in America, 1620-1750*. Boston: Twayne.

Feidelson, Charles, Jr. 1953. *Symbolism and American Literature*. Chicago: Univ. of Chicago Press.

Fender, Stephen. 1964. "Edward Taylor and 'The Application of Redemption.'" *Modern Language Review* 59: 331-34.

———. 1992. *Sea Changes: British Emigration and American Literature*. Cambridge: Cambridge Univ. Press.

Fish, Stanley. 1980. *Is There a Text in This Class? The Authority of Interpretive Communities*. Cambridge: Harvard Univ. Press.

Foerster, Norman, ed. 1947. *American Poetry and Prose*. 2 vols. Third edition. Boston: Houghton Mifflin. Vol. 1.

Forstater, Arthur, and Thomas M. Davis. 1976. "Edward Taylor's 'A Fig for Thee Oh! Death.'" *Discoveries and Considerations: Essays on Early American Literature and Aesthetics Presented to Harold Jantz*. Ed. Calvin Israel. Albany: State Univ. of New York Press. 67-81.

Garrison, Joseph M., Jr. 1968. "The 'Worship-Mould': A Note on Edward Taylor's *Preparatory Meditations*." *Early American Literature* 3: 127-31.

———. 1970. "Teaching Early American Literature: Some Suggestions." *College English* 31: 487-97.

Gatta, John, Jr. 1975. "The Comic Design of *Gods Determinations touching his Elect*." *Early American Literature* 10: 121-43.

———. 1979. "Edward Taylor and Thomas Hooker: Two Physicians of the Poore Doubting Soul." *Notre Dame English Journal* 12: 1-12.

———. 1982. "Little Lower than God: The Super-Angelic Anthropology of Edward Taylor." *Harvard Theological Review* 75: 361-68.

———. 1989. *Gracious Laughter: The Meditative Wit of Edward Taylor*. Columbia: Univ. of Missouri Press.

Gefvert, Constance J. 1971. "Introduction." *Edward Taylor: An Annotated Bibliography, 1668-1970*. Kent, Ohio: Kent State Univ. Press. xiii-xxxiii.

Gelpi, Albert. 1975. *The Tenth Muse: The Psyche of the American Poet*. Cambridge: Harvard Univ. Press.

Giovannini, G. 1948. "Taylor's 'The Glory of and Grace in the Church Set Out.'" *Explicator* 6 (4): Item 26.

Goodman, William B. 1954. "Edward Taylor Writes His Love." *New England Quarterly* 27: 510-15.

Grabo, Norman S. 1960a. "Catholic Tradition, Puritan Literature, and Edward Taylor." *Papers of the Michigan Academy of Science, Arts, and Letters* 45: 395-402.

———. 1960b. "Edward Taylor on the Lord's Supper." *Boston Public Library Quarterly* 12 (Jan.): 22-36.

———. 1960c. "The Poet to the Pope: Edward Taylor to Solomon Stoddard." *American Literature* 32: 197-201.

———. 1960d. "Taylor's 'Sacramental Meditation Six.'" *Explicator* 18 (7): Item 40.

———. 1961a. *Edward Taylor*. New York: Twayne.

———. 1961b. Review of Stanford, *Poems*. *William and Mary Quarterly* 18: 140-42.

———. 1962a. "'The Appeale Tried': Another Edward Taylor Manuscript." *American Literature* 34: 394-400.

———. 1962b. "Introduction." *Edward Taylor's Christographia*. Ed. Norman S. Grabo. New Haven: Yale Univ. Press. xi-xliv.

———. 1962c. "The Veiled Vision: The Role of Aesthetics in Early American Intellectual History." *William and Mary Quarterly* 19: 493-510. Reprint, *The American Puritan Imagination: Essays in Revaluation*. Ed. Sacvan Bercovitch. London: Cambridge Univ. Press, 1974. 19-33.

———. 1964. "Edward Taylor's Spiritual Huswifery." *PMLA* 79: 554-60.

———. 1966. "Introduction." *Edward Taylor's Treatise Concerning the Lord's Supper*. Ed. Norman S. Grabo. East Lansing: Michigan State Univ. Press. ix-li.

———. 1969. "Puritan Devotion and American Literary History." *Themes and Directions in American Literature: Essays in Honor of Leon Howard*. Ed. Ray B. Browne and Donald Pizer. West Lafayette, Indiana: Purdue Univ. Studies. 6-21.

———. 1970. "*Gods Determinations*: Touching Taylor's Critics." *Seventeenth-Century News* 28: 22-24.

———. 1971. "Edward Taylor." *Fifteen American Authors before 1900: Bibliographic Essays on Research and Criticism*. Ed. Robert A. Rees and Earl N. Harbert. Madison: Univ. of Wisconsin Press. 333-56.

———. 1978. "Colonial American Theology: Holiness and the Lyric Impulse." *Essays in Honor of Russell B. Nye*. Ed. Joseph Waldmeir. East Lansing: Michigan State Univ. Press. 74-91.

———. 1987. "Ideology and the Early American Frontier." *Early American Literature* 22: 274-90.

———. 1988. *Edward Taylor: Revised Edition*. Boston: Twayne.

———. 1990. "Editing Taylor's 'Christographia' and 'Treatise Concerning the Lord's Supper.'" *Studies in Puritan American Spirituality* 1: 13-18.

Grabo, Norman S., and Jana Wainright. 1984. "Edward Taylor." *Fifteen American Authors before 1900: Bibliographic Essays on Research and Criticism*. Ed. Earl N. Harbert and Robert A. Rees. Madison: Univ. of Wisconsin Press. 439-67.

Grant, Douglas. 1961. "Poet in a Wilderness." *Times Literary Supplement* 60 (3 Feb.): 72.

Greven, Philip. 1977. *The Protestant Temperament: Patterns of Child-Rearing, Religious Experience, and the Self in Early America*. New York: Knopf.

Griffin, Edward M. 1968/69. "The Structure and Language of Taylor's 'Meditation 2.112.'" *Early American Literature* 3: 205-8.

Griffith, Clark. 1966. "Edward Taylor and the Momentum of Metaphor." *ELH* 33: 448-60.

Grube, Karen Gordon. 1978/79. "The 'Secret Sweet Mysterie' of Numbers in Edward Taylor's Meditation 80, Second Series." *Early American Literature* 13: 231-37.

Gura, Philip. 1988. "The Study of Colonial American Literature, 1966-1987: A Vade Mecum." *William and Mary Quarterly* 45: 305-41.

[Guruswamy,] Rosemary Fithian. 1985. "'Words of My Mouth, Meditations of My Heart': Edward Taylor's *Preparatory Meditations* and the Book of Psalms." *Early American Literature* 20: 89-119.

———. 1990. "The Sweet Defender of New England." *New England Quarterly* 63: 294-302.

Haims, Lynn. 1979. "The Face of God: Puritan Iconography in Early American Poetry, Sermons, and Tombstone Carving." *Early American Literature* 14: 15-47.

———. 1985. "Puritan Iconography: The Art of Edward Taylor's *Gods Determinations*." *Puritan Poets*. Ed. Peter White. 84-98.

Hall, David D. 1983. "On Native Ground: From the History of Printing to the History of the Book." *Proceedings of the American Antiquarian Society* 93: 313-36.

———. 1989. *Worlds of Wonder, Days of Judgment: Popular Religious Belief in Early New England*. New York: Knopf.

Hall, Dean, and Thomas M. Davis. 1975. "The Two Versions of Edward Taylor's Foundation Day Sermon." *Resources for American Literary Study* 5: 199-216.

Hambrick-Stowe, Charles E. 1982. *The Practice of Piety: Puritan Devotional Disciplines in Seventeenth-Century New England*. Chapel Hill: Univ. of North Carolina Press.

———. 1988. "Introduction." *Early New England Meditative Poetry: Anne Bradstreet and Edward Taylor*. Ed. Charles E. Hambrick-Stowe. New York: Paulist Press. 7-62.

Hammond, Jeffrey A. 1982. "Reading Taylor Exegetically: The *Preparatory Meditations* and the Commentary Tradition." *Texas Studies in Literature and Language* 24: 347-71.

———. 1982/83. "A Puritan *Ars Moriendi*: Edward Taylor's Late Meditations on the Song of Songs." *Early American Literature* 17: 191-214.

———. 1987. "Where Are We Going, Where Have We Been?: Puritan Poetics Reconsidered." *Early American Literature* 22: 114-32.

———. 1990a. "Who Is Edward Taylor?: Voice and Reader in the *Preparatory Meditations*." *American Poetry* 7 (3): 2-19.

———. 1990b. "Approaching the Garden: Edward Taylor's Progress toward the Song of Songs." *Studies in Puritan American Spirituality* 1: 65-87.

———. 1991. "The Puritan Elegiac Ritual: From Sinful Silence to Apostolic Voice." *Studies in Puritan American Spirituality* 2: 77-106.

———. 1993. *Sinful Self, Saintly Self: The Puritan Experience of Poetry*. Athens: Univ. of Georgia Press.

Hammond, Jeff, and Thomas M. Davis. 1973. "Edward Taylor: A Note on Visual Imagery." *Early American Literature* 8: 126-31.

Hart, James D. 1941. *The Oxford Companion to American Literature*. New York: Oxford Univ. Press.

Hedberg, Johannes. 1960. "Meditations Linguistic and Literary on Meditation Twenty-Nine by Edward Taylor." *Moderna Språk* 54: 253-70.

Higby, John. 1972. "Taylor's 'Huswifery.'" *Explicator* 30 (7): Item 60.

Hodges, Robert R. 1959. "Edward Taylor's 'Artificiall Man.'" *American Literature* 31: 76-77.

Holifield, E. Brooks. 1974. *The Covenant Sealed: The Development of Puritan Sacramental Theology in Old and New England, 1570-1720*. New Haven: Yale Univ. Press.

Howard, Alan B. 1972. "The World as Emblem: Language and Vision in the Poetry of Edward Taylor." *American Literature* 44: 359-84.

Hughes, Walter. 1990. "'Meat Out of the Eater': Panic and Desire in American Puritan Poetry." *Engendering Men: The Question of Male Feminist Criticism*. Ed. Joseph A. Boone and Michael Cadden. New York: Routledge. 102-21.

Hutchison, Percy. 1940. "Edward Taylor, Early American Poet of Mysticism." *New York Times Book Review*. Jan. 28: 3.

Isani, Mukhtar Ali. 1971. "The Pouring of the Sixth Vial: A Letter in a Taylor-Sewall Debate." *Proceedings of the Massachusetts Historical Society* 83: 123-29.

———. 1972. "Edward Taylor and the 'Turks.'" *Early American Literature* 7: 120-23.

———. 1975. "Edward Taylor and Ovid's *Art of Love*: The Text of a Newly-Discovered Manuscript." *Early American Literature* 10: 67-74.

Israel, Calvin. 1966. "Edward Taylor's *Barleybreaks*." *American Notes and Queries* 4: 147-48.

Jacobs, Hayes B. 1960. "Stop Picking on Edward Taylor." *Harpers* 220 (May): 71-72.

Jacobson, Sibyl C. 1973. "Image Patterns in Edward Taylor: Prayer and Proof." *Concerning Poetry* 6 (1): 59-67.

Jantz, Harold S. 1944. *The First Century of New England Verse*. Reprint, New York: Russell and Russell, 1962.

———. 1976. "American Baroque: Three Representative Poets." *Discoveries and Considerations: Essays on Early American Literature and Aesthetics Presented to Harold Jantz*. Ed. Calvin Israel. Albany: State Univ. of New York Press. 3-23.

———. 1985. "Baroque Free Verse in New England and Pennsylvania." *Puritan Poets*. Ed. Peter White. 258-73.

Johnson, Parker H. 1980. "Poetry and Praise in Edward Taylor's *Preparatory Meditations*." *American Literature* 52: 84-96.

Johnson, Thomas H. 1937. "Edward Taylor: A Puritan 'Sacred Poet.'" *New England Quarterly* 10: 290-322.

———. 1938. "Poetry." *The Puritans*. Ed. Perry Miller and Thomas H. Johnson. Reprint, New York: Harper and Row, 1963. 545-52.

———. 1939a. "Edward Taylor." *The Poetical Works of Edward Taylor.* Ed. Thomas H. Johnson. New York: Rockland Editions. 11-28.

———. 1939b. "The Discovery of Edward Taylor's Poetry." *Colophon,* New Graphic Series, 1 (2): 101-4.

———. 1941. "A Seventeenth-Century Printing of Some Verses of Edward Taylor." *New England Quarterly* 14: 139-41.

———. 1942. "The Topical Verses of Edward Taylor." *Publications of the Colonial Society of Massachusetts* 34: 513-54.

———. 1943. "Some Edward Taylor Gleanings." *New England Quarterly* 16: 280-96.

———. 1944. "Edward Taylor." *Dictionary of American Biography:* Vol. 21: Supplement I. Ed. Harris E. Starr. New York: Charles Scribner's Sons. 681-82.

———. 1960. "Colonial Voice Reheard in Verse" [review of Stanford, *Poems*]. *Saturday Review* (Aug. 6: 24).

———. 1966. "Foreword to the Paperback Edition." *The Poetical Works of Edward Taylor.* Ed. Thomas H. Johnson. Princeton: Princeton Univ. Press. 8.

Johnston, Thomas E., Jr. 1968. "A Note on the Voices of Anne Bradstreet, Edward Taylor, Roger Williams, and Philip Pain." *Early American Literature* 3: 125-26.

———. 1968/69. "Edward Taylor: An American Emblematist." *Early American Literature* 3: 186-98.

Jones, Howard Mumford, et al., eds. 1952. *Major American Writers.* 2 vols. Third edition. New York: Harcourt, Brace and Company. Vol. 1.

Jones, Jesse C. 1974. "A Note on the Number of Edward Taylor's *Preparatory Meditations.*" *Early American Literature* 9: 81-82.

Jordan, Raymond J. 1962. "Taylor's 'The Ebb and Flow.'" *Explicator* 20 (8): Item 67.

Junkins, Donald. 1965. "Edward Taylor's Revisions." *American Literature* 37: 135-52.

———. 1968. "'Should Stars Wooe Lobster Claws?': A Study of Edward Taylor's Poetic Practice and Theory." *Early American Literature* 3: 88-117.

———. 1969/70. "Edward Taylor's Creative Process." *Early American Literature* 4 (3): 67-78.

Kaiser, Leo M., and Donald E. Stanford. 1965. "The Latin Poems of 'Edward Taylor.'" *Yale University Library Gazette* 40: 75-81.

Kehler, Joel R. 1975. "Physiology and Metaphor in Edward Taylor's 'Meditation. Can. 1.3.'" *Early American Literature* 9: 315-20.

Keller, Karl. 1969/70. "The Example of Edward Taylor." *Early American Literature* 4 (3): 5-26.

———. 1970a. "'The World Slickt Up in Types': Edward Taylor as a Version of Emerson." *Early American Literature* 5 (1): 124-40.

———. 1970b. "The Rev. Mr. Edward Taylor's Bawdry." *New England Quarterly* 43: 382-406.

———. 1973. "The Words of Edward Taylor." *A Concordance to the Poems of Edward Taylor.* Ed. Gene Russell. Washington: Microcard Editions. xv-xix.

———. 1975a. *The Example of Edward Taylor.* Amherst: Univ. of Massachusetts Press.

———. 1975b. "A Modern Version of Edward Taylor." *Early American Literature* 9: 321-24.

———. 1978. "Edward Taylor and the Mathers." *Moderna Språk* 72: 119-35.

———. 1979. *The Only Kangaroo among the Beauty: Emily Dickinson and America*. Baltimore: Johns Hopkins Univ. Press.

———. 1985. "Edward Taylor, The Acting Poet." *Puritan Poets*. Ed. Peter White. 185-97.

Kibbey, Ann. 1986. *The Interpretation of Material Shapes in Puritanism: A Study of Rhetoric, Prejudice, and Violence*. Cambridge: Cambridge Univ. Press.

King, John Owen, III. 1983. *The Iron of Melancholy: Structures of Spiritual Conversion in America from the Puritan Conscience to Victorian Neurosis*. Middletown, Connecticut: Wesleyan Univ. Press.

Koelling, Deborah Spangler. 1982. "Taylor on Taylor: A Family Memoir of Edward Taylor." *Resources for American Literary Study* 12: 29-42.

Konkle, Lincoln. 1990. "Puritan Epic Theater: A Brechtian Reading of Edward Taylor's *Gods Determinations*." *Communications from the International Brecht Society* 19 (2): 58-71.

Krishnamurthi, M. G. 1969. "Edward Taylor: A Note on the American Literary Tradition." *Indian Essays in American Literature: Papers in Honor of Robert E. Spiller*. Ed. Sujit Mukherjee and D. V. K. Raghavacharyulu. Bombay: Popular Prakashan. 27-39.

Kropf, Carl R. 1983. "The Nationalistic Criticism of Early American Literature." *Early American Literature* 18: 17-30.

Lalli, Biancamaria Tedeschini. 1956. "Edward Taylor." *Studi Americani* 2: 9-43.

Lang, Erdmute. 1967. "Meditation 42 von Edward Taylor." *Jahrbuch für Amerikastudien* 12: 92-108.

Laurentia, Sister M. 1949. "Taylor's 'Meditation 42.'" *Explicator* 8 (3): Item 19.

Leighton, Ann. 1970. *Early American Gardens: For Meate or Medicine*. Boston: Houghton Mifflin.

Lenhart, Charmenz S. 1956. *Musical Influences on American Poetry*. Athens: Univ. of Georgia Press.

Leverenz, David. 1980. *The Language of Puritan Feeling: An Exploration in Literature, Psychology, and Social History*. New Brunswick: Rutgers Univ. Press.

Lewalski, Barbara Kiefer. 1979. *Protestant Poetics and the Seventeenth-Century Religious Lyric*. Princeton: Princeton Univ. Press.

Lind, Sidney E. 1948. "Edward Taylor: A Revaluation." *New England Quarterly* 21: 518-30.

Link, Franz H. 1971. "Edward Taylors Dichtung als Lobpreis Gottes." *Jahrbuch für Amerikastudien* 16: 77-101.

Lockwood, John H. 1922. *Westfield and Its Historic Influences*. Springfield, Mass.: privately printed.

Lowance, Mason I., Jr. 1980. *The Language of Canaan: Metaphor and Symbol in New England from the Puritans to the Transcendentalists*. Cambridge: Harvard Univ. Press.

―――. 1985. "Religion in Puritan Poetry: The Doctrine of Accommodation." *Puritan Poets.* Ed. Peter White. 33-46.
Ludwig, Allan I. 1966. *Graven Images: New England Stonecarving and its Symbols, 1650-1815.* Middletown, Connecticut: Wesleyan Univ. Press.
Lutz, Cora E. 1982. "Ezra Stiles and the Bones of the Giant of Claverack." *Yale University Library Gazette* 57 (1-2): 18-25.
Lynen, John F. 1969. *The Design of the Present: Essays on Time and Form in American Literature.* New Haven: Yale Univ. Press.
MacGregor, Alan Leander. 1988. "Edward Taylor and the Impertinent Metaphor." *American Literature* 60: 337-58.
Manierre, William R., II. 1962. "Verbal Patterns in the Poetry of Edward Taylor." *College English* 23: 296-99.
Martin, Carter. 1985. "A Fantastic Pairing: Edward Taylor and Donald Barthelme." *The Scope of the Fantastic: Theory, Technique, Major Authors.* Ed. Robert A. Collins and Howard D. Pearce. Westport, Connecticut: Greenwood. 183-90.
Martin, Donald L. 1978. "Edward Taylor's *Garzia Horti.*" *American Notes and Queries Supplement.* Vol. 1: *Studies in English and American Literature.* Ed. John L. Cutler and Lawrence S. Thompson. Troy, N. Y.: Whitston. 235-37.
Martz, Louis L. 1954. *The Poetry of Meditation: A Study of English Religious Literature in the Seventeenth Century.* New Haven: Yale Univ. Press.
―――. 1960. "Foreword." *The Poems of Edward Taylor.* Ed. Donald E. Stanford. xiii-xxxvii.
Matthiessen, F. O. 1928. "Michael Wigglesworth, A Puritan Artist." *New England Quarterly* 1: 491-504.
―――. 1950. "Introduction." *The Oxford Book of American Verse.* Ed. F. O. Matthiessen. New York: Oxford Univ. Press. ix-xxxiii.
Maynard, Reid. 1972. "The Poetry of Edward Taylor: A Puritan Apologia." *Caliban* 8: 3-17.
McMichael, George, ed. 1989. *Anthology of American Literature.* 2 vols. Fourth edition. New York: Macmillan. Vol. 1.
McNamara, Anne Marie. 1958. "Taylor's 'Sacramental Meditation Six.'" *Explicator* 17 (1): Item 3.
McWilliams, John. 1983. "Writing Literary History: The Limits of Nationalism." *Resources for American Literary Study* 13: 127-33.
Medlicott, Alexander, Jr. 1962. "Notes on Edward Taylor from the Diaries of Stephen Williams." *American Literature* 34: 270-74.
Meserole, Harrison T. 1968. "Edward Taylor." *Seventeenth-Century American Poetry.* Ed. Harrison T. Meserole. Reprint, University Park: Pennsylvania State Univ. Press, 1985. 119-23.
―――. 1973. "Edward Taylor's Sources." *Directions in Literary Criticism: Contemporary Approaches to Literature.* Ed. Stanley Weintraub and Philip Young. University Park: Pennsylvania State Univ. Press. 121-26.

———. 1976. "New Voices from Seventeenth-Century America." *Discoveries and Considerations: Essays on Early American Literature and Aesthetics Presented to Harold Jantz.* Ed. Calvin Israel. Albany: State Univ. of New York Press. 24-45.

———. 1989. "'By Chaucer's Boots': Some Medieval Strains in Colonial American Literature." *Medievalism in American Culture.* Ed. Bernard Rosenthal and Paul E. Szarmach. Binghamton: SUNY Binghamton Center for Medieval and Early Renaissance Studies. 113-28.

Mignon, Charles W. 1965. "Some Notes on the History of the Edward Taylor Manuscripts." *Yale University Library Gazette* 39: 168-73.

———. 1966a. "Diction in Edward Taylor's *Preparatory Meditations.*" *American Speech* 41: 243-53.

———. 1966b. "Another Taylor Manuscript at Yale." *Yale University Library Gazette* 41: 72-73.

———. 1968. "Edward Taylor's *Preparatory Meditations*: A Decorum of Imperfection." *PMLA* 83: 1423-28.

———. 1969/70. "A Principle of Order in Edward Taylor's *Preparatory Meditations.*" *Early American Literature* 4 (3): 110-16.

———. 1977/78. "The Nebraska Edward Taylor Manuscript: 'Upon the Types of the Old Testament.'" *Early American Literature* 12: 296-301.

———. 1980. "Christ the Glory of All Types: The Initial Sermon from Edward Taylor's 'Upon the Types of the Old Testament.'" *William and Mary Quarterly* 37: 286-301.

———. 1989. "Introduction." *Upon the Types of the Old Testament.* Ed. Charles W. Mignon. 2 vols. Lincoln: Univ. of Nebraska Press. 1:xix-lxxvii.

———. 1990. "Taylor's *Upon the Types*: The Making of the Nebraska Edition." *Studies in Puritan American Spirituality* 1: 28-33.

Miller, Perry. 1939. *The New England Mind: The Seventeenth Century.* Reprint, Boston: Beacon Press, 1961.

———. 1940. "From Edwards to Emerson." *New England Quarterly* 13: 589-617. Reprint, Perry Miller, *Errand into the Wilderness.* New York: Harper & Row, 1964. 184-203.

———. 1953. *The New England Mind: From Colony to Province.* Reprint, Boston: Beacon Press, 1961.

———, ed. 1956. *The American Puritans: Their Prose and Poetry.* New York: Doubleday.

Monteiro, George. 1969. "Taylor's 'Meditation Eight.'" *Explicator* 27 (6): Item 45.

Morgan, Edmund S. 1963. *Visible Saints: The History of a Puritan Idea.* Reprint, Ithaca: Cornell Univ. Press, 1965.

Morison, Samuel Eliot. 1956. *The Intellectual Life of Colonial New England.* Ithaca: Cornell Univ. Press.

Murdock, Kenneth B. 1927. "Introduction." *Handkerchiefs from Paul.* Ed. Kenneth B. Murdock. Cambridge: Harvard Univ. Press. xv-lxxiii.

———. 1948. "Writers of New England." *Literary History of the United States.* Ed. Robert E. Spiller et al. New York: Macmillan. 54-70.

———. 1949. *Literature and Theology in Colonial New England.* Cambridge: Harvard Univ. Press.

———. 1951. "The Colonial and Revolutionary Period." *The Literature of the American People: An Historical and Cultural Survey.* Ed. Arthur Hobson Quinn. New York: Appleton-Century-Crofts. 1-171.

Murphy, Francis. 1959. "An Edward Taylor Manuscript Book." *American Literature* 31: 188-89.

———. 1962. "Edward Taylor's Attitude Toward Publication: A Question Concerning Authority." *American Literature* 34: 393-94.

———. 1964. "Introduction." *The Diary of Edward Taylor.* Ed. Francis Murphy. Springfield, Mass.: Connecticut Valley Historical Museum. 7-22.

———. 1971. "A Letter on Edward Taylor's Bible." *Early American Literature* 6: 91.

Neufeld, Morris A. 1951. "A Meditation upon the Glory of God." *Yale University Library Gazette* 25: 110-111.

Nicolaisen, Peter. 1966. *Die Bildlichkeit in der Dichtung Edward Taylors.* Neumünster: Karl Wachholtz Verlag.

North, Michael. 1979. "Edward Taylor's Metaphors of Promise." *American Literature* 51: 1-16.

Ong, Walter J., S.J. 1958. *Ramus: Method and the Decay of Dialogue.* Cambridge: Harvard Univ. Press.

Oreovicz, Cheryl Z. 1976. "Edward Taylor and the Alchemy of Grace." *Seventeenth-Century News* 34: 33-36.

———. 1985. "Investigating 'The *America* of Nature': Alchemy in Early American Poetry." *Puritan Poets.* Ed. Peter White. 99-110.

Parker, David L. 1976/77. "Edward Taylor's Preparationism: A New Perspective on the Taylor-Stoddard Controversy." *Early American Literature* 11: 259-78.

Patterson, J. Daniel. 1984. "Taylor's 'Preparatory Meditation 2.1.'" *Explicator* 43 (1): 22-23.

———. 1985. "A Reconsideration of Edward Taylor's 'The Preface,' Lines 9-12." *Early American Literature* 20: 64-66.

———. 1987. "*Gods Determinations*: The Occasion, The Audience, and Taylor's Hope for New England." *Early American Literature* 22: 63-81.

———. 1989a. "Notes on Emending Edward Taylor's *Gods Determinations.*" *American Notes and Queries* 2: 13-15.

———. 1989b. "Edward Taylor's 'Christ's Reply,' Stanza Eight." *American Notes and Queries* 2: 132-33.

Pearce, Roy Harvey. 1950. "Edward Taylor: The Poet as Puritan." *New England Quarterly* 23: 31-46.

———. 1961. *The Continuity of American Poetry.* Princeton: Princeton Univ. Press.

Pellegrini, Anna Maria. 1980. "Edward Taylor fra teologia e poesia." *Studi di letteratura inglese e americana.* Milan: Univ. Cattolica. 107-26.

Penner, Allen R. 1967. "Edward Taylor's Meditation One." *American Literature* 39: 193-99.

Pérez Gallego, Cándido. 1966. "'Sweet' en Edward Taylor." *Filología Moderna* 6: 273-92.

Perkins, George, et al., eds. 1985. *The American Tradition in Literature*. 2 vols. Sixth edition. New York: Random House. Vol. 1.

Pettit, Norman. 1966. *The Heart Prepared: Grace and Conversion in Puritan Spiritual Life*. New Haven: Yale Univ. Press.

———. 1975. "The Puritan Legacy." *New England Quarterly* 48: 283-94.

Pinsker, Sanford. 1975. "Carnal Love/Excremental Skies: A Reading of Edward Taylor's 'Upon the Sweeping Flood.'" *Concerning Poetry* 8 (1): 53-54.

Plumstead, A. W. 1963. "Puritanism and Nineteenth-Century American Literature." *Queen's Quarterly* 70: 209-22.

Prosser, Evan. 1967. "Edward Taylor's Poetry." *New England Quarterly* 40: 375-98.

Rainwater, Catherine. 1984. "Edward Taylor's Reluctant Revolution: The New Astronomy in the *Preparatory Meditations*." *American Poetry* 1 (2): 4-17.

———. 1991. "'This Brazen Serpent is a Doctors Shop': Edward Taylor's Medical Vision." *Studies in Puritan American Spirituality* 2: 51-75.

Rainwater, Catherine, and William J. Scheick. 1980. "Seventeenth-Century American Poetry: A Reference Guide Updated." *Resources for American Literary Study* 10: 121-45.

Reed, Michael D. 1974. "Edward Taylor's Poetry: Puritan Structure and Form." *American Literature* 46: 304-12.

Reinsdorf, Walter. 1970. "Edward Taylor's Baroque Expression." *Greyfriar* 11: 31-36.

Reiter, Robert. 1970. "Poetry and Typology: Edward Taylor's *Preparatory Meditations*, Second Series, Numbers 1-30." *Early American Literature* 5 (1): 111-23.

Rowe, Karen E. 1968. "A Biblical Illumination of Taylorian Art." *American Literature* 40: 370-74.

———. 1974. "Sacred or Profane?: Edward Taylor's Meditations on Canticles." *Modern Philology* 72: 123-38.

———. 1985. "Prophetic Visions: Typology and Colonial American Poetry." *Puritan Poets*. Ed. Peter White. 47-66.

———. 1986. *Saint and Singer: Edward Taylor's Typology and the Poetics of Meditation*. Cambridge: Cambridge Univ. Press.

———. 1990. "Edward Taylor." *Heath Anthology of American Literature*. Ed. Paul Lauter et al. 2 vols. Lexington, Mass.: D. C. Heath. 1:342-46.

Ruland, Richard, and Malcolm Bradbury. 1991. *From Puritanism to Postmodernism: A History of American Literature*. New York: Viking.

Russell, Gene. 1969. "Taylor's 'Upon Wedlock, and Death of Children.'" *Explicator* 27 (9): Item 71.

———. 1971. "Dialectal and Phonetic Features of Edward Taylor's Rhymes: A Brief Study Based upon a Computer Concordance of His Poems." *American Literature* 43: 165-80.

———. 1973. "The Computer and the Poet: Contemporary Notes on Archaic Language." *A Concordance to the Poems of Edward Taylor*. Ed. Gene Russell. Washington: Microcard Editions. xx-xxiv.

Salska, Agnieszka. 1984. "Puritan Poetry: Its Public and Private Strain." *Early American Literature* 19: 107-21.

Sargent, Ritamarie. 1984. "Poetry and the Puritan Faith: The Elegies of Anne Bradstreet and Edward Taylor." *A Salzburg Miscellany: English and American Studies 1964-1984*. Ed. Wilfried Haslauer. Salzburg: Institut für Anglistik & Amerikanistik, Universität Salzburg. 1:149-60.

Scheick, William J. 1970. "A Viper's Nest, the Featherbed of Faith: Edward Taylor on the Will." *Early American Literature* 5 (2): 45-56.

———. 1971a. "Nonsense from a Lisping Child: Edward Taylor on the Word as Piety." *Texas Studies in Literature and Language* 13: 39-53.

———. 1971b. "Tending the Lord in All Admiring Style: Edward Taylor's *Preparatory Meditations*." *Language and Style* 4: 163-87.

———. 1972. "Man's Wildred State and the Curious Needlework of Providence: The Self in Edward Taylor's *Preparatory Meditations*." *Tennessee Studies in Literature* 17: 129-37.

———. 1974a. *The Will and the Word: The Poetry of Edward Taylor*. Athens: Univ. of Georgia Press.

———. 1974b. Review of Russell, *A Concordance to the Poems of Edward Taylor*. *Resources for American Literary Study* 4: 230-31.

———. 1975. "Typology and Allegory: A Comparative Study of George Herbert and Edward Taylor." *Essays in Literature* 2: 76-86.

———. 1976. "'That Blazing Star in Joshua': Edward Taylor's 'Meditation 2.10' and Increase Mather's *Kometographia*." *Seventeenth-Century News* 34: 36-37.

———. 1977. "'The Inward Tacles and the Outward Traces': Edward Taylor's Elusive Transitions." *Early American Literature* 12: 163-76.

———. 1979. "The Jawbones Schema of Edward Taylor's *Gods Determinations*." *Puritan Influences in American Literature*. Ed. Emory Elliott. Urbana: Univ. of Illinois Press. 38-54.

———. 1983a. "Edward Taylor's Herbalism in *Preparatory Meditations*." *American Poetry* 1 (1): 64-71.

———. 1983b. "Edward Taylor's Optics." *American Literature* 55: 234-40.

———. 1983c. "Edward Taylor." *American Writers before 1800: A Biographical and Critical Dictionary*. 3 vols. Ed. James A. Levernier and Douglas R. Wilmes. Westport, Connecticut: Greenwood Press. 1:1411-13.

———. 1985. "Tombless Virtue and Hidden Text: New England Puritan Funeral Elegies." *Puritan Poets*. Ed. Peter White. 286-302.

———. 1988a. "Order and Disorder in Taylor's Poetry: Meditation 1.8." *American Poetry* 5 (2): 2-11.

———. 1988b. "The Poetry of Colonial America." *Columbia Literary History of the United States*. Ed. Emory Elliott. New York: Columbia Univ. Press. 83-97.

——. 1990. "Unfolding the Serpent in Taylor's 'Meditation 1.19.'" *Studies in Puritan American Spirituality* 1: 34-64.
——. 1992. *Design in Puritan American Literature*. Lexington: Univ. Press of Kentucky, 1992.
Scheick, William J., and JoElla Doggett. 1977. *Seventeenth-Century American Poetry: A Reference Guide*. Boston: G. K. Hall.
Schuldiner, Michael. 1978. "Edward Taylor's 'Problematic' Imagery." *Early American Literature* 13: 92-101.
——. 1986. "The Christian Hero and the Classical Journey in Edward Taylor's 'Preparatory Meditations. First Series.'" *Huntington Library Quarterly* 49: 113-32.
——. 1991. *Gifts and Works: Spiritual Life and Political Controversy in Seventeenth-Century Massachusetts*. Macon, Georgia: Mercer Univ. Press.
Schulze, Fritz W. 1969. "Strophe, Vers, und Reim in Edward Taylors 'Meditations.'" *Literatur und Sprache der Vereinigten Staaten: Aufsätze zu Ehren von Hans Galinsky*. Ed. Hans Helmcke, Klaus Lubbers, and Renate Schmidt-von Bardeleben. Heidelberg: Winter Verlag. 11-33.
Schweitzer, Ivy. 1991a. "Semiotics of the Sacrament in Edward Taylor's *Preparatory Meditations*." *Praise Disjoined: Changing Patterns of Salvation in 17th-Century English Literature*. Ed. William P. Shaw. New York: Peter Lang. 237-57.
——. 1991b. *The Work of Self-Representation: Lyric Poetry in Colonial New England*. Chapel Hill: Univ. of North Carolina Press.
Sebouhian, George. 1981/82. "Conversion Morphology and the Structure of *Gods Determinations*." *Early American Literature* 16: 226-40.
Secor, Robert. 1968. "Taylor's 'Upon a Spider Catching a Fly.'" *Explicator* 26 (5): Item 42.
Seelye, John. 1977. *Prophetic Waters: The River in Early American Life and Literature*. New York: Oxford Univ. Press.
Sharma, Mohan Lal. 1970. "Of Spinning, Weaving, and Mystical Poetry: The Fine Yarn of Taylor, Indian Yogis, and Persian Sufis." *Mahfil* 6 (2-3): 51-61.
Shawcross, John T. 1988. "Some Colonial American Poetry and George Herbert." *Early American Literature* 23: 28-51.
Shea, Daniel B., Jr. 1968. *Spiritual Autobiography in Early America*. Princeton: Princeton Univ. Press.
Shepherd, Emmy. 1962. "Edward Taylor's Injunction Against Publication." *American Literature* 33: 512-13.
Shields, David S. 1990. "The Object of the Text in Early American Literature." *Early American Literature* 25: 307-15.
Shields, John C. 1984. "Jerome in Colonial New England: Edward Taylor's Attitude Toward Classical Paganism." *Studies in Philology* 81: 161-84.
Sibley, John L. 1881. *Biographical Sketches of Graduates of Harvard University*. 3 vols. Cambridge: C. W. Sever. 2: 397-412, 534-36.
Siebel, Kathy, and Thomas M. Davis. 1969/70. "Edward Taylor and the Cleansing of *Aqua Vitae*." *Early American Literature* 4 (3): 102-9.

Silverman, Kenneth. 1968. "Edward Taylor." *Colonial American Poetry*. Ed. Kenneth Silverman. New York: Hafner. 173-79.

Simison, Barbara Damon. 1954. "Poems by Edward Taylor." *Yale University Library Gazette* 28: 93-102, 161-70; 29: 25-34, 71-80.

Simmons, Jes. 1983. "Taylor's 'Upon Wedlock, and Death of Children.'" *Explicator* 42 (1): 17-18.

Simonetti, Francis A. 1973. "Prosody as a Unifying Element in 'Huswifery.'" *Ball State University Forum* 14 (4): 30-31.

Slethaug, Gordon E. 1973. "Edward Taylor's Copy of Thomas Taylor's *Types*: A New Taylor Document." *Early American Literature* 8: 132-39.

Sluder, Lawrence Lan. 1973. "God in the Background: Edward Taylor as Naturalist." *Early American Literature* 7: 265-71.

Smith, A. J. 1962. Review of Stanford, *Poems*. *Review of English Studies* 8: 80-83.

Sowd, David. 1975. "Edward Taylor's Answer to a 'Popish Pamphlet.'" *Early American Literature* 9: 307-14.

Spengemann, William C. 1983. "Discovering the Literature of British America." *Early American Literature* 18: 3-16.

———. 1989. *A Mirror for Americanists: Reflections on the Idea of American Literature*. Hanover, N. H.: University Press of New England.

Spiller, Robert, and Harold Blodgett, eds. 1949. *The Roots of National Culture: American Literature to 1830*. New York: Macmillan.

Stanford, Donald E. 1955. "Edward Taylor and the Lord's Supper." *American Literature* 27: 172-78.

———. 1956. "Sacramental Meditations by Edward Taylor." *Yale University Library Gazette* 31: 61-75.

———. 1957. "Nineteen Unpublished Poems by Edward Taylor." *American Literature* 29: 18-46.

———. 1959. "The Giant Bones of Claverack, New York, 1705." *New York History* 40 (Jan.): 47-61.

———. 1960a. "Introduction." *The Poems of Edward Taylor*. Ed. Donald E. Stanford. New Haven: Yale Univ. Press. xxxix-lxii.

———. 1960b. "The Puritan Poet As Preacher — An Edward Taylor Sermon." *Studies in American Literature*. Ed. Waldo McNeir and Leo B. Levy. Baton Rouge: Louisiana State Univ. Press. 1-10.

———. 1960c. "The Earliest Poems of Edward Taylor." *American Literature* 32: 136-51.

———. 1961a. "The Parentage of Edward Taylor." *American Literature* 33: 215-21.

———. 1961b. "Edward Taylor's Metrical History of Christianity." *American Literature* 33: 279-95.

———. 1962. Review of Grabo, *Edward Taylor*. *American Literature* 34: 412.

———. 1964. "Edward Taylor's 'Spiritual Relation.'" *American Literature* 35: 467-75.

———. 1965. *Edward Taylor*. Minneapolis: Univ. of Minnesota Press.

———. 1971a. "Edward Taylor Versus the 'Young Cockerill' Benjamin Ruggles: A Hitherto Unpublished Episode from the Annals of Early New England Church History." *New England Quarterly* 44: 459-68.
———. 1971b. "Two Notes on Edward Taylor." *Early American Literature* 6: 89-90.
———. 1972. "Edward Taylor." *Major Writers of Early American Literature*. Ed. Everett Emerson. Madison: Univ. of Wisconsin Press. 59-91.
———. 1973. "Edward Taylor and the 'Hermophrodite' Poems of John Cleveland." *Early American Literature* 8: 59-61.
———. 1976. "The Imagination of Death in the Poetry of Philip Pain, Edward Taylor, and George Herbert." *Studies in the Literary Imagination* 9 (2): 53-67.
———. 1984. "Edward Taylor." *Dictionary of Literary Biography*. Vol. 24: *American Colonial Writers, 1606-1734*. Ed. Emory Elliott. Detroit: Gale Research Company. 310-21.
———. 1990. "*The Poems of Edward Taylor*: The Making of the Yale Edition." *Studies in Puritan American Spirituality* 1: 3-12.
Stauffer, Donald Barlow. 1974. *A Short History of American Poetry*. New York: E. P. Dutton.
Stein, Roger B. 1972. "Seascape and the American Imagination: The Puritan Seventeenth Century." *Early American Literature* 7: 17-27.
Stewart, Randall. 1946. "Puritan Literature and the Flowering of New England." *William and Mary Quarterly*, 3d series, 3: 319-42.
Tashjian, Dickran, and Ann Tashjian. 1974. *Memorials for Children of Change: The Art of Early New England Stonecarving*. Middletown, Connecticut: Wesleyan Univ. Press.
Taylor, Henry Wyllys. 1857. "Edward Taylor." *Annals of the American Pulpit*. 2 vols. Ed. William B. Sprague. New York: Robert Carter and Brothers. 1:177-81.
Terry, John Taylor. 1892. *Rev. Edward Taylor*. New York: DeVinne Press.
Thomas, Jean L. 1965. "Drama and Doctrine in *Gods Determinations*." *American Literature* 36: 452-62.
Thorpe, Peter. 1966. "Edward Taylor as Poet." *New England Quarterly* 39: 356-72.
[Tichi,] Cecilia Halbert. 1966. "Tree of Life Imagery in the Poetry of Edward Taylor." *American Literature* 38: 22-34.
Turco, Lewis Putnam. 1986. *Visions and Revisions of American Poetry*. Fayetteville: Univ. of Arkansas Press.
Tyler, Moses Coit. 1878. *A History of American Literature, 1607-1765*. Reprint, Ithaca: Cornell Univ. Press, 1949.
Waggoner, Hyatt H. 1964. "Puritan Poetry." *Criticism* 6: 291-312.
———. 1968. *American Poets: From the Puritans to the Present*. Boston: Houghton Mifflin.
Walker, Jeffrey. 1985. "Anagrams and Acrostics; Puritan Poetic Wit." *Puritan Poets*. Ed. Peter White. 247-57.
Warren, Austin. 1941. "Edward Taylor's Poetry: Colonial Baroque." *Kenyon Review* 3: 355-71.

———. 1960. "Meditations of a Poet" [review of Stanford, *Poems*]. *New York Times Book Review* 65 (July 24): 5, 18.

———. 1962. "Edward Taylor." *Major Writers of America*. 2 vols. Ed. Perry Miller. New York: Harcourt, Brace, & World. 1:51-62.

Watkins, Owen C. 1972. *The Puritan Experience*. London: Routledge and Kegan Paul.

Watters, David H. 1981. *"With Bodilie Eyes": Eschatological Themes in Puritan Literature and Gravestone Art*. Ann Arbor: UMI Research Press.

Weathers, Willie T. 1946. "Edward Taylor, Hellenistic Puritan." *American Literature* 18: 18-26.

———. 1954. "Edward Taylor and the Cambridge Platonists." *American Literature* 26: 1-31.

Weiss, Klaus. 1984. *Grundlegung einer puritanischen Mimesislehre: Eine literatur- und geistesgeschichtliche Studie der Schriften Edward Taylors und anderer puritanischer Autoren*. Paderborn: Ferdinand Schöningh.

Werge, Thomas. 1968/69. "The Tree of Life in Edward Taylor's Poetry: The Sources of a Puritan Image." *Early American Literature* 3: 199-204.

White, Peter. 1978. "An Analysis of Edward Taylor's 'Preparatory Meditation 2.1.'" *Concerning Poetry* 11 (2): 19-23.

———. 1985. "Introduction." *Puritan Poets and Poetics: Seventeenth-Century American Poetry in Theory and Practice*. Ed. Peter White. University Park: Pennsylvania State Univ. Press. 1-6.

Williams, Oscar, ed. 1948. *A Little Treasury of American Poetry*. New York: Charles Scribner's Sons.

Williams, Stanley T. 1951. *The Beginnings of American Poetry (1620-1855)*. Uppsala: Almqvist and Wiksells.

Winslow, Ola Elizabeth. 1962. Review of Grabo, *Edward Taylor*. *William and Mary Quarterly* 19: 611-12.

Witherspoon, Alexander M., and Frank J. Warnke, eds. 1963. *Seventeenth-Century Prose and Poetry*. Second edition. New York: Harcourt, Brace, & World.

Woodward, Robert H. 1963. "Automata in Hawthorne's 'Artist of the Beautiful' and Taylor's 'Meditation 56.'" *Emerson Society Quarterly* 31 (2): 63-66.

Wright, Nathalia. 1946. "The Morality Tradition in the Poetry of Edward Taylor." *American Literature* 18: 1-17.

Wright, Thomas Goddard. 1920. *Literary Culture in Early New England 1620-1730*. Reprint, New York: Russell and Russell, 1966.

Ziff, Larzer. 1973. *Puritanism in America: New Culture in a New World*. New York: Viking.

———. 1986. "Literary Culture in Colonial America." *The New History of Literature, VIII: American Literature to 1900*. Ed. Marcus Cunliffe. London: Sphere Books. 23-52.

Zilboorg, Caroline. 1978. "Taylor's Meditation Thirty-Eight (First Series)." *Explicator* 37 (1): 3.

Index

Abel, Darrel, 53
Adams, Percy G., 134
Akiyama, Ken, 43
Albertus Magnus, 15, 49
Aldridge, A. Owen, 100, 101
Alexis, Gerhard T., 43, 55, 56, 61
Allen, Judson Boyce, 69
Altick, Richard D., 3
Ames, William, 27, 101, 136
Aquinas, Thomas, 15
Arner, Robert D., 44, 49, 64, 65, 85
Augustine, 50, 51, 64, 70, 74, 78, 97, 98, 103, 141
Aull, William J., 74

Bach, Bert C., 41
Bales, Kent, 74
Ball, Kenneth, 55, 56, 61
Ballinger, Martha, 47
Barbour, Dennis H., 104, 105
Barbour, James W., 62
Barthelme, Donald, 121
Barthes, Roland, 118
Baxter, Richard, 10, 20, 25, 35, 39, 51, 90, 112, 116
Baym, Nina, 125
Benét, William Rose, 8
Benton, Robert M., 39, 56
Bercovitch, Sacvan, 55, 58, 60, 61, 83, 112
Berryman, John, 141
Beuteln, Tobias, 64
Black, Mindele, 17, 18, 20, 58
Blackmur, R. P., 40, 41
Blake, Howard, 8
Blake, Kathleen, 71, 76, 91
Blau, Herbert, 18
Blodgett, Harold, 8
Boll, Robert N., 70
Bottorff, William K., 43
Bradbury, Malcolm, 125, 126
Bradford, William, 9
Bradstreet, Anne, 1, 2, 6, 9, 11, 20, 37, 38, 47, 90, 91, 96, 100, 114, 119, 128, 137-41
Bray, James, 89

Breitkreuz, Hartmut, 69
Brown, Wallace Cable, 11, 12, 15
Browne, Sir Thomas, 49
Brumm, Ursula, 47, 50-53, 58, 60, 70, 87, 92, 103-05, 114
Bunyan, John, 28, 49
Bush, Sargent, Jr., 56, 57, 61, 75, 85, 86, 106

Cairns, William B., 2
Calamy, Edmund, 114
Caldwell, Patricia, 112
Callow, James T., 57
Calvin, John, 19, 24, 50, 58, 61, 63, 74, 78, 118, 136
Carlisle, E. F., 39-41
Chauncy, Charles, 5, 29, 119
Chmaj, Betty E., 47
Clack, Randall A., 133
Clare, Sister M. Theresa, 48
Clark, Michael, 91, 110, 111, 118, 126, 137
Clendenning, John, 42, 50
Cleveland, John, 66
Cohen, Charles Lloyd, 112, 117
Colacurcio, Michael J., 45, 84, 85, 113, 121
Combellack, C. R. B., 73
Copernicus, 102
Cotton, Charles, 44
Cotton, John, 86, 139
Cowley, Abraham, 28
Craig, Raymond A., 135
Crashaw, Richard, 3, 4, 11, 18, 68
Cruz, Sor Juana Inés de la, 100
Cudworth, Ralph, 14
Curtis, Jared R., 47
Cyprian, 64

Daly, Robert, 55, 89-91, 106, 110, 119, 120, 126, 127
Damico, Anthony, 103
Damon, S. Foster, 7, 8
David, 71, 98, 105, 129, 133
Davie, Donald, 67
Davies, Sir John, 4

Davis, Thomas M., xi, 57-64, 67, 68, 70, 72, 73, 75, 94-99, 104, 105, 107, 124, 127-33, 135
Davis, Virginia L., xi, 63, 64, 94-96, 135
Delbanco, Andrew, 112, 113
Del Fattore, Joan, 103
DeNuccio, Jerome D., 112, 118
De Prospo, R. C., 122, 126
Dewey, David, 1, 97
Dickinson, Emily, 7, 12, 17, 34, 47, 81, 87, 88, 125
Dickson, David, 136
Doepke, Dale, 74
Doggett, JoElla, xi
Donne, John, 3-6, 8, 12, 16, 18, 25, 37, 68, 71, 96, 101
Doolittle, Thomas, 27
Downame, John, 101
Dryden, John, 44, 67, 134
Du Bartas, Guillaume, 12, 28, 104
Dummer, Jeremiah, 62
Dunster, David, 89

Eberwein, Jane Donahue, 92
Edwards, Jonathan, 9, 31, 47, 81, 86, 120
Eliot, T. S., 3, 6, 12, 25, 47
Elliott, Emory, 125
Emerson, Everett, 55, 88
Emerson, Ralph Waldo, 47, 48, 59-61, 81, 120

Feidelson, Charles, Jr., 45
Fender, Stephen, 37, 44, 126
Fish, Stanley, 2, 3
Fiske, John, 68, 89, 139
Fitch, James, 95
Flaccius, Matthias, 29
Fletcher, Giles and Phineas, 13
Foerster, Norman, 8
Forstater, Arthur, 63
Foucault, Michel, 111
Foxe, John, 29
Franklin, Benjamin, 9
Freneau, Philip, 12, 109

Galen, 65, 133
Garrison, Joseph M., Jr., 44, 92
Gatta, John, Jr., 85, 86, 116, 117, 121, 127

Gay, John, 134
Geertz, Clifford, 135
Gefvert, Constance J., xi, 5, 53, 55
Gelpi, Albert, 67, 87, 88, 92, 104
Giovannini, G., 14
Golding, Arthur, 67
Góngora, Luis de, 100
Goodman, William B., 12
Grabo, Norman S., xi, 13, 15, 19-21, 22, 23, 25-40, 43, 44, 46, 49, 51-53, 55-57, 59, 61, 68, 73, 75, 77, 79, 84-86, 88, 90-92, 100, 109, 112, 114-17, 122, 124, 131
Grant, Douglas, 26, 46
Greenblatt, Stephen, 121
Greven, Philip, 112, 141
Griffin, Edward M., 43
Griffith, Clark, 43, 44, 75, 111
Grube, Karen Gordon, 66
Guild, William, 59
Gura, Philip, 122
[Guruswamy,] Rosemary Fithian, 105, 108, 118, 133

Haims, Lynn, 69, 106
Hall, David D., 112, 122
Hall, Dean, 63
Hambrick-Stowe, Charles E., 112-15
Hammond, Jeffrey A., 68, 105-08, 118, 122, 133-36, 138-41
Hart, James D., 8
Harvey, Christopher, 71
Hawthorne, Nathaniel, 81
Hedberg, Johannes, 26, 43, 50, 74
Heidegger, Martin, 111, 126
Herbert, George, 3-6, 8, 16-18, 24, 28, 37, 38, 41, 48, 49, 51, 67, 71, 72, 87, 101, 134, 137
Higby, John, 73
Hodges, Robert R., 15, 49
Holifield, E. Brooks, 62
Homer, 14
Hooker, Samuel, 23, 62, 119
Hooker, Thomas, 25, 37, 44, 57, 75, 86, 114
Hopkins, Gerard Manley, 25, 34
Howard, Alan, 68, 70, 72, 127
Hughes, Walter, 137, 141

Index

Hull, John, 5
Hutchinson, Anne, 140
Hutchison, Percy, 36

Ignatius of Loyola, 25, 35
Isani, Mukhtar Ali, 62, 66, 67
Israel, Calvin, 49

Jacobs, Hayes, 26
Jacobson, Sibyl C., 74
Jantz, Harold S., 3, 10, 12, 18, 36, 68, 89, 100, 101, 119
Jerome, 101
Jeske, Jeff, 63
Johnson, Edward, 28, 68, 89
Johnson, Parker H., 117
Johnson, Samuel, 12
Johnson, Thomas H., xi, 1-9, 11, 15, 16, 18, 20-24, 27, 29, 36, 46, 49, 141
Johnston, Thomas E., Jr., 49, 51, 68
Jones, Howard Mumford, 9
Jones, Jesse C., 76, 77
Jordan, Raymond J., 42
Junkins, Donald, 39, 40, 42, 55-57, 61, 75
Justin Martyr, 64

Kaiser, Leo M., 29
Keach, Benjamin, 59, 98
Kehler, Joel R., 65, 71
Keller, Karl, xi, 55, 56, 58-61, 64, 68, 70, 79-85, 87, 88, 90-92, 100, 104, 109, 110, 112, 114, 116-19, 121, 126, 128, 133, 136, 141
Kibbey, Ann, 112
King, John Owen, III, 112
Koelling, Deborah Spangler, 98
Konkle, Lincoln, 134
Krishnamurthi, M. G., 46
Kropf, Carl R., 122

Lacan, Jaques, 111
Lalli, Biancamaria Tedeschini, 12, 13
Lang, Erdmute, 43, 75
Laurentia, Sister M., 15
Lee, Samuel, 28
Leighton, Ann, 65
Lenhart, Charmenz S., 9
Leverenz, David, 112, 141

Lewalski, Barbara Kiefer, 55, 68, 71-73, 76, 87, 92, 104, 105, 107, 118, 127
Lightfoot, John, 97
Lind, Sydney E., 11, 14-16, 26, 45, 49
Link, Franz H., 75
Lockwood, John H., 2
Lowance, Mason I., Jr., 104, 107-08, 121
Ludwig, Allan I., 49, 68, 69
Luther, Martin, 58, 74
Lutz, Cora E., 103
Lynen, John F., 45-47

MacGregor, Alan Leander, 111, 126
Manierre, William R., II, 44
Marino, Giambattista, 100
Martin, Carter, 121
Martin, Donald L., 65
Martz, Louis L., 13, 23-26, 30, 33, 34, 37, 38, 40, 46, 48, 73, 75, 84, 101, 114
Marvell, Andrew, 13, 50
Mather, Cotton, 1, 6, 19-21, 24, 31, 35, 36, 47, 64, 81, 86, 97
Mather, Increase, 1, 5, 19-21, 30, 31, 33, 35, 47, 63, 64, 65, 116
Mather, Richard, 63
Mather, Samuel, 58, 59, 98, 104
Matthiessen, F. O., 2, 3, 8
Maynard, Reid, 61
McMichael, George, 125
McNamara, Anne Marie, 15
McWilliams, John, 109, 122, 123
Medlicott, Alexander, Jr., 27
Melville, Herman, 81
Meserole, Harrison T., 53, 64, 89, 100
Mignon, Charles W., xi, 30, 41, 44, 55-57, 61, 64, 72, 74, 75, 79, 95, 98, 99, 107, 117, 124, 128, 133
Miller, Perry, 2, 6, 8, 9, 11, 13, 29, 36, 47, 52
Milton, John, 13, 66, 94, 96
Monteiro, George, 43
More, Henry, 14
Morgan, Edmund S., 38, 112
Morison, Samuel Eliot, 3, 9

Index

Müller, Johann, 100
Murdock, Kenneth B., 2, 3, 10, 11, 31
Murphy, Francis, xi, 28, 30, 35, 52, 69

Neufeld, Morris A., 20
Nicholas of Lyra, 69
Nicolaisen, Peter, 50-53, 55
North, Michael, 76, 111

Oates, Joyce Carol, 88
Odo of Chriton, 70
Ong, Walter J., S.J., 9
Oreovicz, Cheryl Z., 65, 103
Origen, 28, 58, 64, 97, 98
Orta, Garcia de, 65
Ovid, 66, 67

Pain, Philip, 33, 37, 67
Paracelsus, 133
Parker, David L., 86, 113
Parks, Betty L., 95
Parrington, Vernon Louis, 3, 7
Patterson, J. Daniel, 113, 119
Paul, 57, 58, 71, 99, 141
Pearce, Roy Harvey, 16-18, 33, 40, 42, 45, 49, 56, 57, 75, 84, 141
Pearse, Edward, 63
Pearson, Norman Holmes, 8, 23
Pellegrini, Anna Maria, 101, 102
Penner, Allen R., 43
Pérez Gallego, Cándido, 44
Perkins, George, 125
Perkins, William, 43
Pettit, Norman, 38, 83, 112
Philo, 58
Pinsker, Sanford, 73
Pliny the Elder, 103
Plumstead, A. W., 47
Poole, Matthew, 97, 98
Pope, Alexander, 7, 134
Pound, Ezra, 88
Prosser, Evan, 40

Quarles, Francis, 4, 13, 38, 49, 50, 68

Rainwater, Catherine, xi, 102, 103, 133
Reed, Michael D., 76

Reinsdorf, Walter, 13, 67, 68
Reiter, Robert, 58, 59, 61, 107
Ricouer, Paul, 111
Rowe, Karen E., 49, 50, 70, 105, 107-09, 115, 116, 118, 127, 140
Ruggles, Benjamin, 62
Ruland, Richard, 125, 126
Russell, Gene, 42, 74, 134

Sales, Francis de, 35
Salska, Agnieszka, 119, 120
Sandys, George, 67
Sargent, Ritamarie, 119
Saussure, Ferdinand de, 82
Scheick, William J., xi, 55, 65-67, 70, 74, 77-86, 88-92, 102, 106, 108-10, 115, 117-20, 125, 127, 128, 132
Schuldiner, Michael, 70, 71, 118, 119, 124, 136, 137
Schulze, Fritz W., 44
Schweitzer, Ivy, 137, 139-41
Scupoli, Lorenzo, 27, 28
Sebouhian, George, 113
Secor, Robert, 42
Seelye, John, 89
Sewall, Samuel, 5, 62
Sharma, Mohan Lal, 88
Shawcross, John T., 101
Shea, Daniel B., Jr., 29
Shepard, Thomas, 28, 31, 50
Shepherd, Emmy, 34
Shields, David S., 126, 127
Shields, John C., 100, 101
Sibbes, Richard, 75
Sibley, John L., 2
Sidney, Sir Philip, 49
Siebel, Kathy, 57, 58
Silverman, Kenneth, 53, 55
Simison, Barbara Damon, 20
Simmons, Jes, 102
Simonetti, Francis A., 73
Slethaug, Gordon E., 69
Sluder, Lawrence Lan, 65
Smart, Christopher, 100
Smith, A. J., 26
Sowd, David, 62
Spengemann, William C., 122
Spenser, Edmund, 13
Spiller, Robert, 8

Stanford, Donald E., xi, 7, 18-20, 22, 23, 26-30, 32, 34, 35, 37, 38, 44, 50, 62, 64, 66, 67, 73, 85, 86, 88, 101, 113, 117, 124, 135
Stauffer, Donald Barlow, 88
Stein, Roger B., 89
Stevens, Wallace, 17
Stewart, Randall, 47
Stiles, Ezra, 4, 23, 30, 104
Stoddard, Solomon, 1, 19, 20, 27, 29, 31, 32, 58, 62, 63, 86, 95-97, 108, 130-32, 136, 137
Suckling, Sir John, 49
Sylvester, Joshua, 13, 28

Tashjian, Ann, 68, 69
Tashjian, Dickran, 68, 69
Taylor, Edward: rediscovery of his poetry, 1-4; artistic assessments of, 1, 2, 4-8, 10-12, 16, 19, 23, 25-29, 34, 37, 40-46, 48, 49, 51, 66-68, 72, 82, 85, 100, 101, 108, 109, 115, 116, 125, 140, 141; and English poets, 1, 3-9, 11-13, 17, 18, 24-26, 28, 37, 38, 41, 44, 48-50, 66-68, 71, 87, 100, 101, 122, 123, 134, 137; and Puritan poets, 1-3, 5-7, 10, 20, 28, 37, 38, 47, 67, 68, 81, 89-91, 99-101, 119, 120, 134, 137-40; as proto-American poet, 3, 4, 7, 8, 12, 26, 34, 46-48, 52, 60, 61, 67, 68, 79, 81, 82, 86-88, 92, 100, 104, 110, 120-23, 125-27; and the New Criticism, 3, 6, 13, 22, 23, 31, 41, 53, 107, 132; use of metaphor, 4, 8, 11, 31, 33, 34, 43, 58, 66, 68, 75-77, 79, 89-91, 104, 107, 111; use of imagery, 4, 9-12, 14, 15, 17, 18, 25-27, 33-35, 38, 40-44, 46, 48-52, 56, 59, 63-66, 68-71, 73-76, 86, 88-90, 102, 103, 106, 109, 110, 120, 127, 128, 133; source studies of, 4, 13-15, 27-29, 34, 35, 37, 39, 42, 44, 45, 47-53, 57, 58, 63-71, 73, 74, 86, 100-09, 114, 116; and medieval traditions, 4, 13, 28, 37, 45, 50, 58, 69, 70; use of prosody, 4, 23, 33, 38, 42, 44, 47, 73, 74, 76, 82, 89, 90, 96, 103, 134; use of rhetoric, 4, 41, 44, 51, 55, 56, 58, 66, 105; as unorthodox Puritan, 5, 6, 8, 9, 11, 14, 17, 18, 22, 35, 52, 60, 69, 80, 84, 106; and New England orthodoxy, 5, 6, 9, 10, 15, 18-20, 24, 29, 32, 37-40, 53, 61, 62, 70, 72, 79, 80, 95, 96, 99; and the Lord's Supper, 5, 18-20, 27, 29, 31, 32, 40, 58, 61-63, 73, 80, 83, 95, 96, 99, 108, 113, 117, 129-31, 136, 137; use of typology, 5, 24, 27, 43, 47, 50-53, 55, 58-61, 64, 66, 67, 69-72, 81, 87, 88, 98, 99, 103, 104, 106-09, 117, 130-33; as public poet, 6, 45, 63, 64, 84, 85, 92, 97, 113, 115, 119, 134, 135; as artistic primitive, 7, 8, 25, 42, 45, 46, 61, 67, 73, 79, 82, 84; and classical traditions, 5, 6, 13, 14, 66, 67, 101, 119, 127; and Ramism, 9, 10, 16, 33, 45, 58, 89, 90; and Puritan spiritual experience, 13, 16, 18, 19, 23-26, 33-35, 38, 41, 56, 57, 77-79, 81, 83, 85, 86, 89-92, 107, 110, 112-20; and the Bible, 14, 15, 24, 26-28, 37, 39, 43, 45, 47, 49-53, 57-63, 65, 69-79, 87, 90, 92, 97-100, 103-110, 116, 117, 120, 125, 129, 132-34, 137, 138; psychological approaches to, 15, 31, 69, 77, 79, 92, 112-14, 137, 139-41; poetic practice of, 16, 17, 24, 25, 30-36, 38-41, 43-47, 51, 52, 56-61, 67, 68, 71-84, 87, 88, 90, 92, 102, 103, 106-17, 120, 127-32, 136-40; poetic speaker of, 16, 36, 40, 41, 44, 56, 57, 59, 77, 78, 80, 81, 83, 96, 105, 111-13, 116-20, 126, 129-31, 135-40; as minister and preacher, 19, 20, 27-32, 39, 63, 64, 80, 88, 92, 95, 96, 98, 99, 115; and mystical experience, 20, 22, 24, 32-38, 56, 57, 61, 71, 72, 75-79, 81, 88, 104, 113-18; and meditative traditions, 25, 26, 30, 31, 33-35, 38, 39, 41,

51, 57, 59, 71, 75-77, 112-14; poetic development of, 28, 29, 33, 49, 58, 59, 64, 72-74, 96, 97, 113, 118, 119, 129-34; and Renaissance science, 28, 48, 49, 64-66, 102, 103, 133; Christology of, 30, 40, 42, 43, 59, 77-79, 82, 90, 97, 98, 100, 105, 108, 110, 116, 120, 133, 136, 140; reader-response approaches to, 45, 65, 85, 105, 111, 113, 128, 135, 136, 138, 139; archetypal approaches to, 81, 87, 89; semiological approaches to, 91, 110-12, 126; deconstructive approaches to, 111, 112, 126; anthropological approaches to, 126, 127, 135-39. Works: topical and occasional poems, 4, 6-8, 2, 13, 23, 28, 30, 31, 40, 42, 50, 62, 65-67, 69, 73, 97, 103, 119, 125, 129, 135; *Gods Determinations*, 1, 4, 6, 8, 13-14, 16, 18, 23, 34, 36-37, 44-48, 51, 57, 61, 65, 66, 69, 74, 84-86, 92, 96, 101, 104-06, 111, 113, 115, 116, 119, 120, 127-29, 133, 134, 136, 138; *Preparatory Meditations* (general), 1, 4, 6-8, 15, 18, 20, 22-28, 33-36, 39-42, 46, 48-51, 56, 57, 61, 66, 68, 74-84, 86-92, 96, 100, 109-20, 125, 128, 136-40; First Series, 25, 43, 44, 49, 50, 56, 57, 63-65, 68, 70, 71, 73-76, 86, 87, 102, 103, 105, 109, 112, 118-20, 127-30, 133, 134, 137; "Prologue," 4, 23, 41, 111; "The Experience," 66, 72, 117, 125, 130, 137; "The Return," 66, 117; "The Reflexion," 12, 18, 41, 42, 50, 66, 75, 117, 125; Second Series, 15, 19, 24, 25, 39, 43, 44, 48-50, 52, 56-60, 62-66, 70-73, 89, 95, 98-109, 120, 121, 127, 130-34, 139; *Metrical History of Christianity*, 23, 29, 67, 85, 97, 131, 132, 135, 138; Job paraphrases, 63, 96, 97, 131; Psalm paraphrases, 63, 96, 125, 129; "Valediction," 63, 125; "A Fig for Thee, Oh! Death," 23, 63, 68, 125; *Diary*, 2, 28, 30, 126; "Profession of Faith," 32, 86, 95; "Spiritual Relation," 29, 86, 95; "Foundation Day" Sermon, 19, 20, 63, 95, 96, 129; "The Appeale Tried," 29, 95; *Treatise Concerning the Lord's Supper*, 30-32, 58, 72, 95, 96, 125, 136; *Upon the Types of the Old Testament*, 64, 95, 98, 99, 107, 131; *Christographia*, 17, 19, 22, 29, 30, 32, 35, 38, 43, 57, 58, 97, 104, 131, 134; *Harmony of the Gospels*, 95, 97, 132

Taylor, Elizabeth Fitch, 12, 23, 119, 130
Taylor, Henry Wyllys, 1, 2, 8, 35, 98
Taylor, James, 132
Taylor, Richard, 27
Taylor, Ruth Wyllys, 131
Taylor, Thomas, 69, 98
Taylor, William, 26
Terry, John Taylor, 2
Tertullian, 50, 64
Theocritus, 14
Theophylact, 97
Thomas, Jean L., 44, 45
Thorpe, Peter, 42
[Tichi,] Cecilia Halbert, 50
Traherne, Thomas, 3, 71
Turco, Lewis Putnam, 120
Turner, Victor, 135
Tuve, Rosemond, 79
Tyler, Moses Coit, 2, 11, 15
Tyndale, William, 58
Vaughan, Henry, 71

Waggoner, Hyatt H., 48, 86, 87
Wainright, Jana, xi
Walker, Jeffrey, 119
Warnke, Frank J., 9
Warren, Austin, 9, 11, 12, 23, 34, 38, 39, 46
Watkins, Owen C., 112
Watters, David H., 105, 106
Watts, Isaac, 46, 67
Weathers, Willie T., 13, 14, 18, 19, 29, 100
Webster, John, 65, 103
Weiss, Klaus, 120
Werge, Thomas, 50
White, Hayden, 121

White, Peter, 70, 119
Whitman, Walt, 17, 23, 47, 48, 87, 88, 104, 125
Whitney, Geoffrey, 68
Wigglesworth, Michael, 1, 2, 7, 20, 28, 30, 50, 57, 91, 96, 137, 138
Wilde, Oscar, 4
Wilkins, John, 49
Willard, Samuel, 20, 35, 57
Williams, Oscar, 8
Williams, Roger, 7, 37, 139
Williams, Stanley T., 11, 26, 45
Williams, Stephen, 27
Williams, William Carlos, 88
Wilson, Thomas, 55
Willoughby, Francis, 119

Winslow, Ola Elizabeth, 37
Winters, Yvor, 22
Wither, George, 49, 68
Witherspoon, Alexander M., 9
Wolcott, Roger, 1
Woodward, Robert H., 49
Wordsworth, William, 135
Wright, Nathalia, 13, 28, 45
Wright, Thomas Goddard, 2, 3
Wylie, Elinor, 47

Ziff, Larzer, 61, 115
Zilboorg, Caroline, 73

OHIO UNIVERSITY LIBRARY
Please return this book as soon as you have finished with it. In order to avoid a fine it must be returned by the latest date stamped below.

JA